LIMITS OF THE WELFARE STATE

For Shaun

Limits of the welfare state:

Critical views on post-war Sweden

edited by
JOHN FRY
University of Saskatchewan

SAXON HOUSE

Published by
Saxon House, Teakfield Limited,
Westmead, Farnborough, Hants., England

Reprinted 1980

British Library Cataloguing in Publication Data

Limits of the welfare state.
   1. Sweden - Social conditions - Addresses, essays, lectures
   2. Sweden - Politics and government- - 1905 -
      Addresses, essays, lectures
      309.1'485'05   HN573.5

ISBN 0 566 00235 3

Printed and bound by Ilfadrove Limited,
Barry, Glamorgan, S. Wales.

Contents

Acknowledgements

For kind permission to publish in English translation, the articles contained in this Reader the Editor wishes to thank both the authors themselves and the following Swedish journals. The chapter number under which the essays are arranged in this collection is placed in brackets after the author's name.

ZENIT for the essays by Lennart Berntson (2, 5, 10), Ingvar Johnsson (4), E. Tommy Nillson (4), Gunnar Olafsson (4), Jan Annerstedt (7), Göran Therborn (8), Stig Larsson (9), Kurt Sjöström (9), Gunnar Persson (10), Olle Jepsson (11, 12) and Gunnar Ågren (11, 12). The essay by Karl Anders Larsson (6) appeared in *Häften for Kritiska Studier* and the essay by Kenneth Kvist (3) and Gunnar Agren (3) appeared in *Socialistisk Debatt.*

For her support and assistance in the actual translation of the works I would like to express my deep appreciation to my wife, Britt Skarsten Fry. Also, I should like to thank Shaun, Somers and Stina for their indispensable co-operation at home while I worked on these translations. And finally, I am indebted to Collene Fuglerud and Brenda Roberts for their superb secretarial skills and uncanny ability to decipher my hieroglyphics.

J.A.F.

1 Introduction

In many respects Sweden has become something of a Mecca for left-liberal and social democratic politicians, trade unionists and academics in the west. The curious bit of politico-economic mythology which portrays Scandinavia in general and Sweden in particular as the sensible middle road between the evils of laissez-faire capitalism and totalitarian communism is especially widespread in North America. The ill-informed characterisation of Sweden as the model for socialism perpetuated by the same outside admirers has been re-enforced by the Swedish Labour Party's acceptance, indeed encouragement of such an image. This situation is in large part due to the fact that most available English language literature on this aspect of contemporary Sweden is either translations of the work of leading social democratic academics, the Myrdals, et al., or is written by non-Scandinavian speaking observers who are largely dependent either on these translations or on English language reports made available by government agencies.

'Limits of the Welfare State' represents an effort to counteract this mis-characterisation by presenting the English speaking audience with an overview of post war Swedish developments in the areas of economy, class relationships, politics and social policy as seen by Swedes who occupy positions to the left of social democracy. While the discussions in their concrete aspects deal with the Swedish situation, they nevertheless make clear the broader implications of their critical analyses for social democracy and the ideology of the welfare state in general. In short, they present an analysis of the specific limitations of the Swedish welfare state and the general limitations of such an approach in any national context.

In 1976, Rune Hägelund, a member of the board of the Swedish Employers' Federation (SAF), a former professor of economics, and current president and chairman of the board of two of Sweden's major companies made the following statement concerning Swedish 'socialism', 'Sweden is a funny country to call socialist. In France or Austria the government owns a much larger share of industry, and I would expect that in a socialist country personal income taxes would be low and company taxes high, whereas in Sweden it is the opposite. It has the world's highest personal income taxes and it's a tax haven for companies!' (Quoted in *Sweden Now*, no.2, 1976)

Had such a candid and succinct observation of Swedish 'socialism'

1

come from the left, it most certainly would have been received with much suspicion. As it is however, it appears somewhat at odds with golden middle road image projected by many western observers.

In addition to misinformation, it seems clear that two basic and related factors lie at the root of Sweden's widespread image abroad as a classless socialist society. The first is the acceptance of a liberal democratic theory of the state which perceives its function and intent as being a popularly mandated neutral arbitrator of conflicting demands from various interest groups in society for the available resources and rewards. Such an orientation does not reject, but doesn't even suspect the bourgeois class character of the state in such a society and its overall function of maintaining and expanding conditions favourable for an economy based on a capital/wage-labour relationship.

Indeed this position follows logically from the second factor, crucial to any misunderstanding of socio-political and economic processes, namely, the widely held view of society as being comprised of mutually interdependent and complementary groups. Such a position fails to perceive any fundamental structural conflicts between the various groups that constitute the liberal democratic, 'free enterprise' society. The recognition of 'stratification' is generally confined to the criteria of income, educational, cultural, etc. differentials. Thus a society such as Sweden which by means of tax transfers, etc. appears to be levelling out income and educational opportunities between the various income strata of wage and salary earners, seems well on the way to becoming a 'classless' society.

Such a fantasy is only possible if one ignores the criteria of owner-ship of the means of production as the *basic* criteria for the identification of objectively opposed classes. The fact that the gap in terms of ownership and the appropriation of surplus value continues to widen is not at all mentioned in the scholarly literature, as the conceptual poverty of the dominant theories of 'stratification' renders them conveniently incapable of even perceiving these funda-mental class divisions.

The comprehensive and generous delivery of an unprecedented barrage of social services is the most visible activity of the state, and thus it appears its primary business is ensuring the well being of its citizens. Indeed that is one objective and it would be inaccurate and unfair to deny its value and primacy in the minds of many socially conscious reformers. However just as it would be ludicrous to con-clude from the fact that a farmer heats his henhouse well, pipes in relaxing music, feeds the chickens a nourishing diet and makes sure the veterinarian visits at the first sign of illness among the hens, that

2

his primary interest is in the intrinsic happiness and fulfilment of his chickens and not in their productivity, so it is naive to view social services in Sweden and elsewhere as being delivered for the sole purpose of benefiting the less fortunate. Certainly that is the ideology. But in a country where the tax burden and so the financing of social services falls directly upon the wage and salary earner, such social services also entail a transfer of the cost of the reproduction of the labour force (including occupational and geographical mobility, training and re-training, 'repair', and support for the non-productive years, etc.) from the employers to the employees via the medium of the state. To a great extent, the primary objective of such social services is to perform the function of mopping-up operations in the wake of the adverse health and social consequences of the capitalist system of production.

Social welfare policies, no matter how extensive, do not alter the basic objective class distinctions in capitalist society, indeed they are in large measure introduced by a class oriented state apparatus precisely to re-enforce it. Thus, to the extent that the economy remains subject to the domestic and international contradictions of capital, the basis of such social care remains tenuous. The hold on social security is contingent upon the competitive strength of domestic capital and in worsened domestic and international economic conditions, the proximity to national bankruptcy and/or the retraction of such services is greater the more extensive the social policies. Sweden's current freeze on the introduction of new costly social expenditures is not a reflection of the absence of extensive social need, but rather is due to a worsening domestic economic situation under the impact of intensified international competition. Instead the government's focus has shifted to the relatively inexpensive and ideologically advantageous issue of 'industrial democracy' (within the general framework of capital/wage-labour economic relationships).

In September 1976, the labour party which had held power for forty-four years in Sweden was narrowly defeated at the polls by a coalition of the Centre, Liberal and Moderate parties under the leader-ship of Thorbjorn Faldin, leader of the largest of the three, the Centre party. As a result of a far reaching reform put into effect in 1971, the Swedish parliament was restructured into a unicameral institution comprising of 350 elected members. Further, this same reform ensured that as long as a single party received more than 4 per cent of the popular vote, it would be permitted to seat a number of represen-tatives in more or less direct proportion to its share of the popular vote.

3

In the September 1973 election this new arrangement had led to an even split of the popular vote between the Centre, Liberal and Moderate coalition and the loosely aligned Labour and Communist (VPK) parties. The result was the somewhat begrudgingly accepted continued rule of the Swedish Labour party under Olof Palme with a combined Labour/Communist representation of 175 seats (50 per cent) in the parliament. Though it was seldom resorted to because of either Liberal or Centre party support on most legislation, this was potentially a government by lottery.

Throughout its forty-four years in office the Swedish Labour party had frequently been dependent on the support of one or more of the other parties (especially the Liberals and Communists) to carry through its legislation in the parliament for they seldom held a clear majority of the seats themselves. Only in the 1940 (53.8 per cent) and 1968 (50.1 per cent) elections were they able to govern alone, otherwise they have averaged approximately 45 per cent of the electoral support.

Indeed the defeat of the labour party in 1976 represented only a marginal shift in the popular vote to the advantage of the 'bourgeois' [1] parties (particularly to the Centre and the more right wing, Moderate) and not a landslide public disenchantment with the 'socialist' parties. It appears that the issue of heavy state investment in nuclear power was the primary factor tipping the scales toward the apparently more cautious approach of the 'bourgeois' parties. In this connection it should be pointed out that apart from a rhetoric of caution, the position of the new coalition government on the issue of nuclear power has altered in no essential way from that taken by the previous government. The legal and financial commitments, as well as the past investments of the Labour government, along with the economic exigencies of such an energy source, as much as ensured a continued Swedish commitment to the comprehensive and rapid domestic expansion of nuclear power.

The transfer of state power from the Labour party to the 'bourgeois' coalition has been misleadingly characterised by some observers in the West as a retreat from social democracy and the welfare state. [2] Here a few points should be clarified. The equation of welfare states with social democratic governments has long been a widespread but overly simplistic correlation. As Larsson and Sjöström point out in their article in this reader, every party in a capitalist society has a commitment to some form of welfare state policies. Thus, if we were to equate social democratic or labour parties with welfare state pro-grammes and liberal, conservative, fascist, etc. with either anti- or absent welfare state measures, it becomes inexplicable why the now ruling 'bourgeois' coalition government in Sweden continues to support

4

and finance those welfare state measures introduced by the previous Labour party. Or in more extreme illustration, it becomes problematic as to why the government of Hitler was even more success- ful than the Roosevelt administration in re-employing the nation through social and economic policies and practices characteristically 'welfare state'. Indeed, in this respect we might well say of the Swedish Centre, Liberal and Moderate parties, that they are more social democratic and welfare state oriented than are most 'official' social democratic parties in other Western countries because of their undeniably more extensive commitment to welfare state policies. The point of course, is that it is incorrect to dichotomise labour/social democratic parties and liberal/conservative parties. The distinction appears rather to be one of the quantity of welfare state measures and not qualitative differences. In making international comparisons however, even this distinction is, as suggested above, frequently mis- leading.

This is not to suggest that significant differences in policies may not exist between the pre-1976 Labour government and the present Faldin coalition. In the area of agriculture for example the new government is attempting to revitalise Swedish agriculture, in part through the re- extension of subsidies and other forms of support to smaller agricultural enterprises which had been squeezed out of operation by the Labour government's heavy commitment to imports and larger agricultural enterprises. These developments are not too surprising considering the Centre party's strong support from petit bourgeois farmers (the new prime minister, Thorbjorn Faldin, being himself a farmer).

In the area of industrial policy, the term of the new government has witnessed no significant changes. There has been an official ideological reassurance of less socialisation but in practice little has altered. Indeed, widespread socialisation in Sweden has long been a dominant myth while only 10 per cent of manufacturing industry is state owned. Compared to other advanced capitalist countries, public ownership of the economy is significantly less in Sweden. In the shipbuilding industry however, there has been continued socialisation. But this has been characteristic of most socialisation in capitalist countries, that is, state investment in declining or stagnating branches of industry from which private capital was already retreating and not in the expansive and competitive sectors — these have been left discreetly in the hands of private capital. The large scale plans of the previous government to invest heavily in the construction of a state owned steel industry in Northern Sweden close to the country's huge iron ore deposits have been dramatically trimmed down. In face of the reality of intensified international competition, particularly from Japan, (in large measure already the cause of the failing Swedish shipbuilding industry) and declining world steel prices, first the Labour government and now the new coalition have steadily retreated from the grand plans outlined in the early seventies.

The central problem facing the current government is an issue that had already begun to cause concern to the previous regime — that of financing rapidly rising social service costs. The recession of 1975-76 proved more severe and the subsequent upswing weaker than the government had anticipated. Consequently its reserves, designed to cover any deficit during such an economic downswing proved inadequate, obliging the present government to turn increasingly to borrowing and deficit spending in order to cover rising state expenditures in this area. The continuing stagnation of large sectors of the Swedish economy have resulted in an official 6 per cent unemployment rate (1.5 per cent unemployed and 4.5 per cent engaged in state financed job retraining programmes). By international comparison the rate is moderate. However, as pointed out earlier, the more extensive the social reforms a state is committed to, the closer the proximity to bankruptcy (or deficit spending) during periods of sustained economic stagnation.

The more expensive of Sweden's social care and labour market policies — those responding to rising structural unemployment, early pension, job retraining and geographical relocation of the work force — are precisely those most immediately burdened by the worsening domestic economic situation. Inasmuch as the financing of such programmes falls exclusively upon the wage earning class, a rise in structural unemployment both increases the demand on such resources and decreases the revenues to finance them, doubly aggravating the new financial pressure on the relevant state agencies. If structural unemployment continues to rise, the security of the welfare state begins to fade in like proportion — an insurance against social need as long as society doesn't require it.

In this respect there has been, and this is not peculiar to Sweden, if not a dismantling of such welfare state programmes, at least an economically expedient redefinition of the individual eligibility requirements for such benefits. In this way it is hoped to ease the financial burden on the state due to a deteriorating domestic economic situation while retaining the framework and ideological advantages of the welfare state.

While largely committed to the same general economic, social, labour market, energy and defense policies of the previous government, the new coalition government in Sweden is faced with increasing

difficulty in financing the rising costs of the programmes involved —
particularly in the area of social and labour market policies. Thus, the
limited scope for new and costly reforms already experienced by the
Labour party has been inherited by the new coalition and further
aggravated by a worsening economic situation over which it has little
control.

The mid-sixties stand as a watershed period for the post war re-
emergence of intense economic competition between the major
capitalist centres. Sweden's heavy emphasis on specialised production
and a relatively advanced level of technology in its productive
machinery enabled it to maintain a reasonably stable economy. Even
that early however, the stagnant growth rate of jobs in industry was
becoming manifest and for the past decade it has been largely
expanded employment in the public sector which has accommodated
the growing labour force.

The continued rapid pace of technological innovation in industry,
necessitated in large part by the need to cut costs in face of intensified
international competition, and a below average rate of economic
growth have further decreased the number of additional jobs made
available in the private sector. Thus rapid structural changes in the
work place, increased occupational insecurity, rising structural
unemployment and regional imbalance continually place increased
pressure on the state to either absorb the unemployed into the public
sector or to train, retrain, relocate or compensate the affected work
force. The number requiring such support, to say nothing of those in
need of physical and mental health care and early pension as a direct
result of the speeded up work pace, deteriorating work milieu and too
frequent occupational and geographical displacement grows steadily —
as does the consequent financial demand on the state. As elsewhere in
the West, immigrant labour, females, the very young and the older
workers are those most immediately and adversely affected. Indeed,
the previous governments virtual freeze on extra-Scandinavian
immigration in the early seventies, in face of these emergent problems
has never become a political issue and has continued to be endorsed
and enforced with at least the same resolution by the present
coalition government.

The one area in which reforms have continued, though at a somewhat slower pace than under the previous government, is in the realm
job reform and 'industrial democracy'. In this period of state financial
restraints these politically and ideologically advantageous and
economically inexpensive innovations have become a primary focal
point of government activity. In this area too, present developments
largely represent a modified version of programmes initiated by the

previous Palme government.

The end of forty-four years of uninterrupted government by the Swedish Labour party is a significant development in itself. However, the assumption of power by the new Centre led 'bourgeois' coalition has thus far resulted in no major reversals or revisions of previous social, economic, labour market or defense policies. The government is of course still relatively young and to some extent the persistence of Swedish Labour party initiated policies may be due in large measure to its institutional and legal commitment to see certain existing pro- grammes through to their completion before embarking on new ones of their own. It is also most certainly due to the forty-four year entrenchment of a Labour party oriented bureaucracy in other non- elected sectors of the state apparatus. Indeed, in this respect the Labour party itself in its fledgling years in office was confronted by the same constraints due to a strongly 'bourgeois' oriented state bureaucracy. Another factor is certainly the entrenchment in Swedish political culture of numerous welfare state attitudes. Many social and labour market programmes which in other countries are only partially and with reservation accepted by the general public have come to be perceived by broad sections of the Swedish population as, quite simply, their basic rights. In short, there has been a significant reification of the basic welfare state philosophy and practice among Swedes. Thus, among both the 'bourgeois' politicians and their electorate, the political culture of the welfare state has penetrated deep. They are in important respects, as intimated earlier, more basic supporters of the welfare state than are numerous formally espoused welfare state advocates in other Western countries.

It can reasonably be expected that whichever bloc holds power after the 1979 elections, it will be the financial constraints arising from a further worsened economic situation and not party philosophy which will determine the scope for new and continued welfare state pro- grammes.

The articles in this book are presented for the first time in English. Each deals with a central aspect of the Swedish welfare state. Together, their common theoretical point of departure presents a comprehensive view of the character, trends and difficulties in contemporary Sweden and in welfare states in general.

John A. Fry, 1978

Notes

[1] In Sweden the Centre, Liberal and Moderate parties are popularly referred to in the Press and everyday discussions as the 'Bourgeois' parties, while the Swedish Labour party and its allies on the left are referred to as 'Socialist' parties.

[2] See, for example, the US based *Time* magazine's distinction between the 'mixed economy' of current Sweden and the 'Social Democracy' of Norway and Denmark. *Time*, March 1978.

2 The State and Parliamentarianism in Sweden

Lennart Berntson

The radicalisation within the West European working class and the student world has actualised anew the question of the state and parliamentarism's role in a revolutionary strategy. This article will not discuss different theories of the state, but rather the function it fills in Sweden today. That is to say, I attempt to demonstrate how the state and parliamentarism are used by the ruling class to maintain its position in Swedish society, and also to draw several conclusions concerning how a revolutionary movement must relate to these institutions.

The concept state/state apparatus which is used below embraces the following five sectors: (1) The armed forces — military and police, (2) The civil administration — departments and civil service, (3) The judiciary — courts, the parliamentary Commissioner for the Judiciary and Civil administration, the parliamentary Commissioner for Military Affairs, (4) Government and parliament — the political organs in the state apparatus, (5) the complex of social — and business — political organisations which are often called welfare institutions. [1]

The term parliamentarism shall refer to the following phenomena: (1) those rules — majority rules — in accordance with which positions in executive organs, committees, directorships, authorities, etc. are assigned, (2) the process by which political decisions are presently made — initiatives, motions, investigations, consideration, committee deliberation, etc.

To understand the present role of the state we must consider it to some extent in historical perspective. Against this background we can then ask: How was the presence of a ruling class reconciled with representative parliamentary forms? What are the tasks of the state in creating political stability? How are these carried out? In relation to the state, is the parliament a dominant institution?

The bourgeois state is the principle mainstay in every capitalist system of production. It is both the precondition and the power centre of capitalism. Above all, two aspects of the capitalist state should be brought out, namely its repressive and its economic functions. Economically, the state must support and promote conditions favourable for the private accumulation of capital. Repressively, it has the task by means of the police and the military, of defending the bourgeois social system against revolutionary criticism and opposition. Two things should be emphasised here. The character of the state apparatus, that is whether it is feudal, bourgeois or socialist, is not determined by its personnel composition, but rather by its affect on the character of the production relations and the growth pattern of the productive forces. While this aspect of the state is relatively transparent, the repressive side is somewhat more obscured and mystified. It becomes clearly manifest only in a polarised or revolutionary situation in which the very existence of the dominant class is at stake. In Western Europe however, such situations are relatively rare. Thus under more 'normal' conditions these repressive tasks and efforts are carried out by public prosecutors, courts and police. However, the universal, lofty and impartial character of legislation hinders direct observations and perception of the oppressive measures and intervention against opposition movements.

The development of the State in Sweden

In Sweden the transformation from predominantly mercantile to capitalist relations of production occurred during the first decades of the nineteenth century. Initial industrial expansion was preceded by the 1789 and 1809 political break-throughs of the peasantry and aspiring bureaucrat strata. The state then developed into an institution in which two social groupings, the nobility and the bourgeois commoners merged to become a relatively socially and ideologically homogeneous class of public officials. The state received its own ideology in Bostrom's philosophy and developed a specific cultural and social pattern of behaviour which came to characterise the administration, the university, culture and politics. To a great extent the bureaucracy became self-recruiting and came to occupy a central political role, initially in the 'standsriksdag' (upper class parliament) and later in the first house of the (then) two house parliament. In the 1870s more than 40 per cent of the representatives to the first house [2] were by profession leading bureaucrats within the state administration, while the second house was dominated by the wealthy farmers from the farmers' party. [3]

Regardless of the weak political representation of the expanding bourgeoisie, the state was nevertheless bourgeois in both economic and repressive aspects. Specifically, the measures taken under the bureaucracy's business policy promoted the development of a capitalist mode of production. Mercantile regulations were abolished,

11

the mobility of the labour force was increased, business freedom and free trade was brought into force and inheritance regulations and commercial law were liberalised. [4]

When the working class organised politically and in unions around the turn of the century, a series of state interventions were taken with the intent of hindering and limiting the movements development. Protection for strikebreakers was strengthened through the Akarps law, organising strikes was made more difficult, the right to unionise was attacked, strikes were forbidden during the term of a contract, and in 1909 the Lindmanska government attempted to introduce anti-union strike legislation. Union leaders and labour politicians were imprisoned. The state apparatus repressed the efforts of the working class and strengthened the positions of the industrial bourgeoisie by means of police, legislation and the military. [5]

As mentioned earlier, state power in Sweden, politically dominated by a special civil servant strata had taken on a central role in the development of capitalism. Long prior to the realisation of parliamentarism and the construction of the political parties, the bourgeois economic and political function of the state was clearly defined and determined in relation to the established capitalist relations of production. The Canadian political scientist, C.B. Macpherson makes this clear: 'In our Western society, the democratic franchise was only instituted after the liberal society and the liberal state were firmly established.' [6]

The gradual realisation of parliamentarism during the period 1917-21 was related to a broadening of the franchise and the emergence of political parties. This involved change in a few important respects, in part because there was a democratisation of the regulations for appointing the government, municipal administrations, committees, etc., and in part as an incapsulation of the political parties in the deliberative and administrative work of the state apparatus. The introduction of parliamentarism and the public franchise in no way however, altered the basic function and character of the state. The circle of parties and persons allowed to participate in the formal decision making process was broadened. Nevertheless, the economic and political framework of the state continued to be structured by the capitalist relations of production and the bourgeoisies social hegemony in civil society. Both these factors had been shaped and determined by the beginning of the preceding century.

An example can best illustrate how this social hegemony in the civil society limited social democracies possibilities and ambitions even after the establishment of political democracy. In 1909, Västmanlands county council was dominated by large estate owners, public officials and industrialists who were replaced with a left majority of small farmers, craftsmen and labourers. Regardless of this left majority, the public officials of the right wing were allowed to control the executive and administrative bodies. In short it was assumed that they both possessed greater legal technical knowledge and had better contacts with the county government board. By virtue of their cultural legitimacy and social superiority, public officials and company owners could continue to govern politically in spite of their numerical inferiority. The left only took over these institutions after being first schooled in the legal system which gave sanction to the society against which they struggled. The bourgeois political function of the county council in relation to capitalism continued as earlier. [7]

The first social democratic government in 1920 was burdened with a series of imposed conditions from the side of the monarchy, the right wing parties and large companies. Accepted by the social democrats, these demands were designed to block each and every step towards a radical restructuring of society. The right wing and the monarchy made the following demands on the fledgling social democratic government: (1) no republic, (2) no disarmament, (3) 'law and order' must be maintained, (4) the Swedish Labour Party (SAP) must not be influenced by 'outsiders' — that is to say, by the party's programme. [8] For reasons of cold realism, the recognition of a social democratic government was recommended by even the liberals: 'Step by step social democracy has matured into the practical work of the state, and it would be "madness" to *a priori* condemn it as incompetent to govern. On the contrary, the social democrats must have their chance just as the rest of us. The road to increased political maturity is through a feeling of responsibility and the responsibility of forming the government is the best means to confront general and vague programme points with the realities of limited possibilities. It is not only educational for the party, but it is wholesome and necessary for the whole country.' [9]

The fifteen years following 1920 were characterised by high unemployment and thereby occasioned sharpened opposition at the grass roots. The crisis of the thirties demanded increased state intervention. The ever growing social character of the relations of production called for co-ordination and planning at the social level. The obvious instrument to effect this was thus the state apparatus. It was social democracy and not the bourgeois parties which put into effect the necessary broadening of the economic role of the state, primarily within social and business policies. The political opposition of the bourgeoisie first to parliamentarism and then to the new economic function of the state, must be seen against the background of the important role fulfilled by the state apparatus in every capitalist system. Both the universal franchise and the new economic policy entailed unexplored risks. This was accentuated in that they were introduced — against the political opposition of the bourgeoisie — by the labour movement. For social democracy in its turn, the broadening economic tasks of the state pushed forward by the party, meant the beginning of the common identification of welfare, state intervention and social democracy, which since then has placed its mystifying mark on Swedish political life. The political stability which characterised the post war period, was established partially through the 'Saltsjobads' agreement by means of which so-called Labour peace was definitely instituted, and partially through the incorporation of the various special interest groups into a system of norms and rules for conflict resolutions and co-operation with the state apparatus and business. We shall have more to say of these developments below.

During the last forty years the activities of the state, particularly within the economy, have increased substantially. The rules regulating appointments to the formally responsible posts have been democratised through parliamentarism and universal suffrage. Regardless of this, the state's economic character — to support and promote the development of capitalism — remained the same even though this development as we have seen, demanded an enlargement of the public sector. In the same manner, the repressive functions of the state remained unaltered. Inasmuch as the state is both a 'welfare instrument' and a repressive force, observations of the latter function particularly, are obscured when it is mystified behind such phrases as 'law and order', 'general security', etc. Only in a couple of instances, 1917/18 and during the thirties, when antagonisms increased, has military intervention finally been taken on behalf of the security of the ruling class.

The ruling class in Sweden

Many recoil at the mere assertion that in Sweden — 'The Peoples' Home' — there exists a ruling class: the financial aid industrial bourgeoisie. It rules above all on the basis of its exclusive control over society's production resources. About 100 large companies account for more than one half of industrial production, approximately 60 of these are owned by 15 families, which are in turn clustered around 3 [10] large banks. This group of owners and directors are close to being correctly identified as the nucleus of the ruling class, which in turn can be distinguished as the nucleus of what is usually called the upper class, the powers that be, Social Group I, etc. More or less directly related to and integrated with the financial/industrial bourgeoisie there exists a series of strata such as public officials, directors, military leaders, prestigeous doctors, teachers, lawyers, consultants, and more. Together these groups constitute no united and monolithic bloc, nor are they sharply discernable from lower social strata. On the contrary, there exists within this group antagonisms and conflicts, and the dividing line with other strata is often difficult to define. Nevertheless, on the basis of an institutional network of families, relations, personal contacts, marriages, schools, clubs, companies and organisations, together they form a relatively homogeneous, coherent and specific social class, superior to all other classes in society. The general stability among this class is based upon a deep rooted cultural and social hegemony in civil society.

As we have seen, the largest companies and banks occupy a completely dominant position in the Swedish economy. Economic development, growth of the GNP and social planning must consequently be development, growth and planning along lines which coincide with the interests of these companies. By means of the central role played by this group by virtue of its control over the means of production, it can be readily stated that it constitutes a ruling class. The means for exercising this power is no longer primarily through the instrumentality of the military or police, but rather by policy effected through the state apparatus and mass media. The exertion of power does not rest primarily on force but rather upon consent which in turn is affected by means of the social hegemony and cultural legitimacy of the ruling class.

The composition of the upper class is not the same today as it was in the 1860s. It then consisted of the monarchy, large landowners, tradesmen, manufacturers, and public officials. Today it is comprised of industry and bank owners, company heads, together with the top strata within the state, political parties and organisations. Then as now, the Swedish industrial bourgeoisie is weakly represented politically. During the period of industrialisation, public officials dominated the political apparatus. Today this role is carried out by the top strata within social democracy, with the important difference that the previous strata of public officials were more directly connected — socially and ideologically — to the industrial bourgeoisie than is the case with the social democratic leaders. The definite transition from public official dominance to increased representation by social democracy came about in two phases. First in connection with the introduction of parliamentarism 1917-21. Further during the thirties in connection with the new economic role of the state which in its turn was connected to the beginning of the social reform policy put through by SAP. Consequently three things coincide here which should be studied more closely. Specifically, social democracy's political breakthrough, the expansion of state economic power and the introduction of social policy.

The leading political group in Sweden consists primarily of two separate, but unequal strata, in part the ruling class and in part the upper levels within SAP and the Swedish Confederation of Trade Unions (LO). The first group is directly related to the production system and has definite class interests, while the other has no specific class interests possible to relate to the economic system, but is instead dependent upon its parliamentary influence in state and municipal administration. However as I tried to point out earlier these administrations fulfil a bourgeois function in relation to the system of production — that is to say it supports and promotes the growth and stability of capitalism. It follows from this that the frame of reference for social democratic labour movement action is shaped by the scope and action possibilities of the state apparatus, which is in turn determined by the prevailing system of production. The social and trade policy once specific to the social democrats in Sweden, but now accepted by all other parties, supports both the economic growth of Swedish capitalism and political stability while at the same time it provides the party with an adequate parliamentary basis. Consequently the leading strata within social democracy bases its position of power upon ensuring both the hegemony of ruling class interests and working class corporative interests.

The political function of the State

How then do the ruling class and the upper strata of the labour movement now co-operate within the framework of representative or bourgeois democracy? What function does parliamentarism fulfil? The bourgeois state is not or can never be an instrument for a radical transformation of the social structure. Rather, its primary function is to create, within the framework of the given conflicting interests between different groups, the necessary stability for the systems economic growth. Stability however, rests upon an asymmetrical state of equilibrium between the overall interests of the bourgeoisie and the special interests of wage earners. Through negotiations attempts are made to overcome conflicts between these opposing interests. Or as it has also been expressed:

All those latent conflicts which are rooted at the base level
are transferred upwards to the bureaucratic-corporative
level and compromised away. But a bureaucratic agreement of course does not entail any real solution but only
a temporary cooling-out of objective conflicts. [11]

Consequently, parliamentarism has not only involved an application
of majority rule with regard to the selection of the parliament and
government, but also the introduction of administrative and
corporative praxis in political questions. In precisely the same way
that the free collective bargaining rights of the trade unions were
circumscribed by different laws and agreements, within the political
system there also exists a series of formal and informal rules,
regulations and unwritten laws which limit and determine the
ambitions and possible options of the reformist labour movement.
Today the foremost exponent of these rules — 'the democratic rules
of the game' — is the social democratic party itself. The dual position
of the reformist upper strata, between the demands from its social
base (the working class) and the political limitations to which they
have for decades been subjected through integration in the 'practical
work of the state', makes it more vulnerable than the bourgeois parties.
Specifically, in every major political question social democracy must
hold back possible demands for total solutions arising from within the
working class which might collide with the bourgeoisie's hegemoneous
interests, in precisely the same manner that LO in this year's wage
negotiations must restrain wage demands with consideration to the
ruling classes' demand for a 'reasonable' rate of profit.

capital + labour conflict

It is against the background of these asymmetrical and opposed
interests that one must view the state's efforts to compromise the
viewpoints and demands of the various sectors. The state no longer
attempts to 'regulate, control or even oppose associations (trade
unions) but rather to exploit them'. [12] On the other hand,
organisations can obtain a certain degree of influence within the
established framework for the exertion of political power.

The difference between hegemoneous and corporative interests is
clear from the disparate character of different political questions. The
hegemoneous interest of the ruling class has its counterpart in a series
of political issues which are never or extremely seldom touched upon
publicly and are only very formally referred to parliament for
ultimate decision. To this group belong the issues of the international
movement of capital, the import and export of profits, regulations for
stock exchange, capital investments, depreciation, energy tax, export
subsidies, investment funds, localisation grants, defense orders, co-
operative industry, defense, state power, the Investment Bank and

ASEA-ATOM. These issues affect in a direct and concrete manner, industry's and companies' conditions of existence and thereby the economy in its entirety. However, precisely because of their overall character, this group of issues can be elevated to general questions and in certain cases be given the stamp of secrecy assuming the character of technical problems. In line with the broader agreement concerning the depoliticisation of this type of issue there exists an increase in the number of administrative questions. Business representatives claim also that 'the administration has acquired increased importance due to the fact that many issues have acquired an increasingly more technically complicated character, which has in turn given us increased influence at the technical, non-political level.' [13] Wage earners' right of determination over these issues is completely absent. Instead their corporative interests are reflected in the following type of political issues: employment, housing, schools, illness care, pensions, rent, and family allowances. These, but few others, are defined as wage earner issues. Thus wage earners are unable to lay claim to issues concerning the whole but only to a part of it. Workers cannot make demands regarding the control of the company's total outlay, but only to a portion of its wages.

It is in the domain between the corporative interest of the wage earners and the hegemoneous interest of the ruling class that the state fulfils the function of adjuster, facilitater, compromiser and horse trader. The treatment in the 1967 parliament of investment guarantees represents an example of this. The social democrats who had earlier persistently opposed such proposals, now accepted the right wing parties' demand for investment guarantees on the condition that the right wing support the government's rejection of demands for further increase in foreign aid. Here the particular demands of the bourgeoisie were accepted on the sly, in preference to a demand which affected a broader public. The most significant political function of the bourgeois state is to provide the necessary stability or 'common values' for economic development and growth. The state's most well utilised and proven instruments for fulfilling this requirement consist of the committee apparatus, government wage negotiations, the parliamentary committee system, and informal deliberations.

The committee apparatus exists at two levels. Organisationally it is constituted of committees, experts, departments, the civil service, delegations and informed contacts. Timewise, it spans from the primary initiative and committee directive to departmental treatment and parliamentary decision. Before any decision is made every issue must proceed through a well integrated parliamentary process based upon organised relations between the different parties and interest groups. Within that process it is difficult to distinguish in part the committee from the decision making phase, and in part the parliamentary from the extra-parliamentary work. In practice these are intimately related to one another and can only be formally separated. Rather than have issues brought up in open political struggle, objective class interests and conflicts are elevated to the level of negotiations and compromise decisions emerge on the basis of procured empirical material. A Swedish political scientist says of such procedures:

> An essential task of all committees is to achieve compromises between considerations of different viewpoints by means of confidential deliberations. If committees are to be able to fulfil that function, all publicity concerning the negotiations and results be excluded until the presentation of the final report. Politicians or interest representatives can as a rule suggest and accept compromises only if they are certain that their comments remain within a small circle of initiated people. [14]

The government wage negotiations which are carried out with SACO, TCO (the Swedish Central Organisation of Salaried Employees), SR (Swedish Radio) and LO's civil servants organisation, provide another important method of binding organisations together and exploiting them for manipulative purposes. Negotiations are used as pressure instruments in both directions. In part the state can press organisations for concessions in social and political questions under the threat of denials of extra wage increases, in part interest groups utilise negotiations for example to attain increased influence on committees and in other agencies. Special note should be given to the pressure which the social democratic government can bring to bear on the LO in wage negotiations under the guise of loyalty. As for agriculture, since the thirties the state has regularly carried out negotiations with farmers' organisations which fulfil a function parallel to wage negotiations.

Primarily by means of the continual negotiations and compromises in parliamentary committees, the political parties are bound together within the scope of the given set of 'democratic game rules'. The fact that there is always an immense number of issues being processed in committees, parliamentary commissions and specially appointed committees, ensures an integrating effect on the co-operation between the parliamentary parties involved. Compromises are aimed at quantitative displacements. 'That which we receive in one issue, you shall receive in return in another'. The political parties are bound together in a fine net of negotiations, commitments, pledges, understandings, promises, contacts, loyalties and mutual dependence. It was this network of negotiations and compromises that the upper strata of the social democratic labour movement developed at the beginning of the nineteen hundreds, through co-operation with the liberals and others. Once this had occurred, the possibility for any thorough going social transformation was excluded. Social democratic actions had to be limited to gradual social reforms while the SAP gave the economic tasks of the bourgeois state an increasingly state capitalist form.

Finally, there takes place within the framework of the day to day work of the state and its relationship to other parties and organisations, a series of 'informal contacts', deliberations and negotiations. Inasmuch as many administrative laws have the character of frame of reference legislation, their practical application takes on increased significance. The praxis which is thus instituted, is not determined by democratic or even representatively elected assemblies, but rather by corporative appointed bodies. In these bodies there occur a mutual adjustment of conflicting interests between the state and organisations and between the organisations themselves.

By means of the relative smallness and concentration in Stockholm of the top politico-bureaucratic strata, there is created an understood accord which facilitates contacts. The de-politicisation of an increasing number of issues within this strata has had the result that 'contacts are intensified and to a great extent have become much more informal'. [15]

Co-operation between the industrial bourgeoisie and the leading strata of SAP and LO began in earnest during the latter part of the thirties with the assumption of government power by SAP and the Saltsjobads agreement between SAF (the Swedish Employers Federation) and LO. Trade Union organisations were finally established, though under the constant threat of anti-union legislation in a system of rules and unwritten laws concerning how labour market conflicts should be resolved. Through the use of the state's committee apparatus and positions in the administration, organisations were tied closer to the state and could in this manner be more easily used as instruments for social control. The statistics concerning representatives on committees shows a striking increase at the end of the thirties. [16] Further, organisations won 'a real foothold in the administration during the forties, and since then the expansion has continued at an undiminished pace. During the fifties alone twenty new agencies were established.' [17] With social democracy as the central force, the corporative co-operation between organisations, the state and industry began in earnest, a move which to a certain degree explains the political stability of Swedish society.

For more than one hundred years the bourgeois function of the state apparatus has been determined by the capitalist relations of production. Neither the establishment of parliamentarism and universal suffrage, nor the economic improvements which commenced during the post-war period have altered this fact. Today, however, the higher level of development of late capitalism demands greater political stability and co-ordination of economic activity. It is against this background and within the framework of the political objectives of the state that one should view the use of the committee apparatus, wage negotiations, the system commissions and informal contacts for the purpose of adjusting and mediating the demands of different parties and interest groups.

The central objection from the ranks of both the bourgeois and reformist parties to the conception of the state as an instrument of the ruling class, is the claim that it is the group in the parliament which has a popularly elected majority behind it which in the final analysis has the deciding judgement on political questions. In short, it is claimed that in relation to the rest of the state apparatus, parliament occupies a dominant position.

But let us look more closely at parliament. Just as is the case with the US presidency, not simply anyone can become a member of parliament in Sweden. In the first place, it is not the electorate who select their member of parliament. They are chosen within the respective parties after a multi-year testing of their trustworthiness and competence. Further, parties select in the first instance candidates who already sit as members of parliament. In 1933, 60 per cent of the members of the second house [18] had sat in parliament more than sixteen years, and 52 per cent of the first house. The corresponding figures in 1961 were 72 per cent and 48 per cent respectively. Furthermore, the candidates had to have been active at the municipal level. More than 70 per cent of all members of parliament have municipal experience. Finally, members must belong to some interest organisation, preferably also to a religious or temperance organisation. In 1963 approximately 90 per cent of the members of the National parliament were associated with one or another of the larger interest organisations in Sweden. For this reason one can say that parliament today is as much a fortress for organisations as it is for parties. [19] This is especially true of wage earner organisations. To an increasingly high degree these informal requirements set a distinct stamp on the social background of members. A full 90 per cent of them are government advisors, public officials, company owners, civil servants, farmers and lawyers.

The most striking development is the number of workers in the parliament. If we look at the most directly recruited house (that is, the second house), we find the following development: 1906 — 5 members, 1912 — 19 members, 1922 — 28 members, 1933 — 37 members, and 1961 — 10 members. Apart from several years during the thirties, the percentage of members of parliament who were workers has not reached more than approximately 5 per cent. In contrast to this there has been a great increase in the number of lawyers, accounting for nearly 30 per cent of the total members of parliament. [20] The consequences of these observations cannot be other than that recruitment to parliamentary posts is very strongly controlled by the already established power strata within parties and organisations. Recruitment within the apparatus is guarded from above. Thus, in its composition the parliament does not differentiate itself from other sectors of the state apparatus.

However, it is not only the social composition of the parliament which is controlled from above but also, since the beginning of the thirties, power within the state apparatus has been transferred from the parliament by means of committees to the government and the ministries. Apart from parliament's role as an information and debate centre, its most important function today is to act as a gauge of the power relationship between the political parties. On the basis of this balance, study commissions and committees are established, compromises are forced through and the government's line is pushed into effect on specific issues. The parliament consequently, is not a dominant institution, but rather along with the entire state apparatus, an integrated and subserviant balance mechanism which regulates the relative position of the parties.

Political conclusions

The objective conflicts in today's Sweden lay frozen under an iceberg of negotiation channels, compromises, mutual understanding and corporative ideology. These processes must be broken down so that contradictions can once again be transferred to open political struggle. It must be the task of a revolutionary movement to activate and polarise these conflicts which are currently solved by means of compromise at the upper levels. Such an activation implies an immediate confrontation with the state apparatus at its police, judicial and political levels. Within the student and Vietnam movement this confrontation has not often occurred at the first two levels. However, to the degree that the dissolution is successful, it will lead to a confrontation even with the political representatives of the state apparatus. First the police and the courts then the politicians and finally the military. It is in approximately this order that the different sectors of the state apparatus are brought to bear on a revolutionary movement.

Without doubt the foremost guarantor today of the corporative negotiation system is the top strata within SAP and LO. Attempts to break down this corporativism leads to conflicts with SAP and its demand for 'objectivity' and respect for the 'democratic rules of conduct'. Depending upon different factors, social democracy will opt for a line which either seeks to isolate or to integrate the revolutionary critique. On the Vietnam issue, they succeeded with the latter strategy, while on the student issue they attempted the former. The latter approach elevates the problem to the contexts of extra- and internal-parliamentary negotiations. The weakness of the debate carried out until now is that it has concentrated on the issue of for or against participation in elections. In the contemporary situation however, electorial participation is not the most important link in the state's use of parliamentarism. Most important, that which must be brought to the foreground, is the issue concerning the forms and methods of making political decisions. The corporative negotiation system must be rejected totally. Today, a revolutionary movement can never be permitted to: (1) delegate decisions and power within the organisation to a top strata in the central committees, party directorship, executive committees, parliamentary groups, etc. (2) allow representatives in these groups to take part in the various commissions, committees, parliamentary committees, etc. set up by the state apparatus — that is to say, never concentrate power within the organisation so as to permit the top strata to become involved in or accept the established corporative form of political decision making. Politically it is upon these forms of negotiation and the integration of all opposition critique, that co-operation between the ruling class and social democracy rests. Today these forms have a significantly more integrating effect on the revolutionary opposition than does electoral participation. This is due to the shifting of the centre of gravity within the parliamentary process, away from the electoral process and the parliament, to the framework of negotiations within commissions, wage negotiations, committees and informal contacts. Electoral participation not only can but should be accepted provided that: (1) there is no established power strata within the party or movement, (2) participation is used for the purpose of activating the objective conflicts and contradictions in society, (3) it is combined with a clearly formulated objective reflecting the intention of going no further into the corporative parliamentary process than to the level of the popularly elected assembly.

Only when these requirements have been fulfilled to an acceptable degree can one hope that a revolutionary and democratic movement can develop into something other than one among many well tutored apparatuses.

Notes

[1]   Perry Anderson, 'Statenoch Monopolkapitalismen', *Zenit NR.1/68*, p.101.

[2]   Sweden now has a one house parliament, see note 18.

[3]   Sten Carlsson, *Bonde, Pràst och ambetsman*, p.94.
Skold Halvarsson, Riksdagens sociala sammansättning under hundra ar i *Samhalle och Riksdag*, part 1.

[4]   Eli Heckscher, *Svenskt arbete och liv*. The section dealing with liberal business policy, pp 275-9.

[5]   Jorgen Westerstahl, *Fackforenings Rorelsen*, pp 237-340.

[6]   C.B. Macpherson, *Den Mangty dig a demokratin*, p.14.

[7]   Göran B. Nilsson, *Kring demokratins genombrött. Uppsatsen om demokratisk genombrött med forhinder*, pp 116-35.

[8]   Gunnar Gerdner, *Det Svenska regerings Problemet 1917-1921*, pp 230-2.

[9]   Ibid, p.210.

[10] With the 1972 merger of the Skandinaviska Bank and Stockholms Enskilda Bank to form the Skandinavisk Enskilda Banks, this number has been reduced to 2.

[11] *Zenit MR.4/68*, p.39.

[12] Gunnar Heckscher, *Staten och Organisztioner*, p.255.

[13] Nils Elvander, *Intresse organisationerna*, p.278.

[14] Hans Meijer, *Kommitteepolitik och Kommitteearbete*, p.256.

[15] Elvander, op.cit., p.225.

[16] Meijer, op.cit., pp 98-9.

[17] Elvander, op.cit., p.224.

[18] Shortly after the publication of this article, Swedish parliament was changed to a one house system. This change however has not altered the nature and function of parliament described here, but rather has streamlined its operations.

[19] Meijer, op.cit., p.84.

[20] Information taken from Skold, Halvarsson, see note 3.

This article orginally appeared in Swedish in the Independent Socialist political journal *Zenit* in the early seventies.

3 Social Democracy in the Seventies

Kenneth Kvist and Gunnar Ågren

There exist two misunderstandings concerning Swedish social democracy. The first is that SAP (Swedish Labour Party) can still be viewed as a reformist movement — that is to say, a movement which aims to reach socialism through a series of successive reforms. Clearly, one meets many social democrats who are convinced reformists. There are also formulations in SAP's programme which can be viewed as reformist. However, after more than forty years of government power, it can be stated that SAP's practical policies have not only conserved but even reinforced capitalism. The power of large finance is now greater than ever. Co-operation between the government and big finance has gone further in Sweden than in most other capitalist countries. Social planning is organised according to the wishes of big finance. Localisation — labour market — finance — and tax policy is biased in favour of the capitalist class and primarily of its upper strata.

The other misconception deals with SAP's organisational structure. There are those who view the party as an integrated force. This perspective usually leads in principal to two incorrect ways of perceiving social democracy. One is to view the party as a 'homogeneous' progressive force with which one can deal. The other is to treat social democracy as a reactionary mass.

In reality Swedish social democracy is a deeply splintered and multi-faceted movement. It can be sub-divided into at least five different strata and currents.

1 The bulk of party membership is made up of 'collectively-associated' and generally passive members. The overwhelming majority of these vote social democrat, but that is over and above the membership group which is chosen via the union, (their only tie with the party).

2 A relatively large group of party members is made of those 'loyal to the death' who have been stamped by the poor Sweden of the thirties, the 'People's Home' romantic, together with the anti-communist frenzy of the fifties. This group has a fear of radical politics but at the same time a deep rooted animosity towards the bourgeois parties.

Suspicion of intellectual workers is also widespread, a fact which results in certain antagonisms within SAP. These social democrats self-sacrificingly support 'the movement', and many radicals both within and without SAP have butted their heads bloody against them. One of SAP's problems is gaining new recruits to this group.

3   A stratum of employed party functionaries, bureaucrats in the government administration, municipal advisors, party appointed representatives in the trade union and tenants' movement, etc. sign themselves up for party membership. This strata is now growing rapidly and is not of insignificant size. They are dependent upon the party apparatus for their livelihood. Within this strata is the party's leadership who act as couriers to and supervisors of the membership. Increasingly, recruitment to these positions is shifting from the politically active to the career civil servant. So far, recruitment to this strata has presented no great problems for SAP even if at times the party must scrape the bottom of its resources for loyal younger members.

4   The fourth group consists of the party's established left. To this group may be assigned a large section of the party's intellectual cadre, such as for example, the organisation Socialistisk Debatt, (Social democratic working group against the EEC (SAME)), together with diverse low income and global conscious groups. These groups often have a correct critique of capitalism and social democracy but in order to legitimise themselves they are often responsible for aggressive attacks against the revolutionary workers movement. Ideologically, this left group is not united. Bourgeois idealism is blended with fragments of a Marxist social perspective. The aims of the members of this group are also divided. There are those who want to create a career for themselves as a left wing within the leadership. There are also those who have expectations of changing social democracy to a socialist party. When reality corrects that belief, they are often drawn to the left.

5   Fifthly, there exists an outspoken left-oriented opposition made up for example, of workers who are connected to a more powerful economic struggle and who have socialist expectations. One can also include here a section of the youth union cadres. Of these, the party has particular difficulty in retaining those who take part in the anti-

imperialist struggle. Within this group there are spokesmen for co-operation between social democrats and communists. United action in day to day struggles is easy to achieve with these social democrats.

These streams and groups are by no means solidly organised factions and their existence does not hinder the nearly total control of the leadership over the organisation. However their presence forces into the open a splintering of social democracy's appearance.

II

Social democracy has succeeded in maintaining a dominant position within the working class ever since the party breakup in 1917. Since 1930 they have occupied a unique position among Swedish political parties. Numerous interrelated factors have contributed to their situation.

Swedish capitalism has had a favourable economic development. This was particularly the case during the post war period up to the mid-sixties. During this period large segments of the Swedish working class experienced improved economic standards. This has provided a fertile soil for class co-operation policies and social democratic illusions. To be sure, these economic improvements have been acquired at the price of increased work intensity and a worsened work milieu. However these effects have only come to the fore in later years.

In this economic development the SAP leadership understood well that they should support capitalism's most advanced and promising forces: large finance. At an early stage they have developed state monopoly capitalism by means of direct supportive measures, tax reliefs, assistance in capital formation, direct economic co-operation and gifts from the state to big capital. Through conferences, Torsdagsclubb (Thursday's club) and Harpsunds democracy. the groundwork was laid for a co-operation based on trust with capital's leading figures. They have often taken care of the long range interests of big finances in a better manner than did the bourgeois parties. However, the radical language in which the social democratic policy is couched has the consequence that a number of capitalists give open economic support to the bourgeois parties.

Unlike the situation in numerous other European countries, Swedish social democracy has not had to fight against particularly strong bourgeois opponents. On the contrary, the bourgeois parties in Sweden have been characterised by uncertainty, vacillation and an

27

incapacity to formulate collective demands. To a great extent this is probably related to the absence of a united class base for the Swedish bourgeois parties. The petite bourgeoisie has been comparatively weakly developed in Sweden.

The leadership of SAP has succeeded in developing a strong, centralised power apparatus both within the party and the trade union movement. Since the party has moved into a more solid governing position, there has been a subsiding of its critique of the class legislation (the collective bargaining law and the law concerning labour courts) which the right wing government had pressed through in 1928. Instead, under the pretext of facilitating the carrying out of a 'united wage policy', they have pressed through a centralisation of the trade union movement. This in turn has been tied to a policy of class co-operation through the Saltsjobads agreement and a series of other co-operation agreements with SAF. Under the ideological protection of the myth of the 'People's Home' they have tried to disarm the working class.

SAP has also benefited from the internal problems of the communist party. The revolutionary opposition within the labour movement was particularly hard hit by the party split in 1929. At that time the communist party lost pretty much all union influence. That occurred in a period when the objective conditions for a breakthrough of a communist policy must have been quite favourable. Instead however, the radical opposition was seriously weakened for many years afterwards.

Two ideological factors have aided SAP. They have successfully spread a confused conception of the role of the state. In 1902, Branting wrote: [1] 'To the degree that an organised labour party, with the help of the general franchise enters the modern state (and municipality), it will be stripped of its oppressive and harrassing character, while its power to in large measure give protection and assistance to the socially weak will move into the foreground.'

This conception has since characterised the party's theory of the state, or more correctly put, its lack of such an approach renders it incapable of conceptualising the state as an organ for maintaining the power position of the ruling class. Thus, when the state and monopoly capitalism developed their policy of co-operation, SAP succeeded in portraying the trend as a step in the reformist strategy towards socialism. Reforms and measures taken to strengthen the capitalist system have thereby been successfully presented as progressive developments in the interest of the working class. Often the leadership of the Swedish Labour Party was itself fully convinced of the truthfulness of the delusions it spread.

28

The second ideological factor employed by the SAP leadership has been a ruthless anti-communist agitation. During the second world war this approach was exploited in order to place the communist party in a semi-illegal position: with the help of the bourgeois propaganda apparatus, they have succeeded since the end of the forties in blowing new life into anti-communism. The leadership of the Swedish Labour Party declared that every work place was to be a battle ground in the struggle against communism. Fantastic spy stories and flaming rubrics concerning mysteriously disappeared aircraft have been played up in the media. By means of such campaigns they have to a great extent succeeded in isolating the radical worker from his workmates and dampened the influence of the most aggressive workers. A policy of class co-operation was thereby able to develop during the fifties without the majority of workers being able to see any alternative.

III

Today the Swedish Labour Party is in a crisis. Not however in the sense of an explosive crisis. In the short run, the party has the ability to mobilise members and sympathisers which should not be under-estimated. We need only reflect on the 1968 election campaign.

In the long run however the SAP leadership will have an increasingly difficult time keeping its domain intact and maintaining its dominant position within the labour movement. The following are the primary causes of this crisis.

Ever since the thirties SAP has attempted to deal with capitalism's economic crisis with the same techniques, namely, public relief work and gifts to capital (tax reliefs, tax free investment funds, and now even grants for inventory development, as well as grants for so-called milieu protection measures, etc.). There has been a growth and development of state monopoly capitalism. A growing public sector, rising unproductive outlays, and above all, expenditures on military arma-ments have been used as long term economic stabilisers for capitalism.

These public expenditures have succeeded in creating certain jobs and increased demand, above all in the area of heavy industry. They have thereby been able to shift and periodically moderate tendencies towards crises of over-production. However, they have also brought with them increasing taxes for the working population and price increases due to the fact that these non-productive expenditures have not been matched by any production which can be demanded by the monies pumped into them.

Thus the increase in the economic role of the state cannot

indefinitely, and now hardly at all, be of assistance in concealing capitalism's growing internal contradictions. These developments are definitely beginning to outstrip SAP's economic policy and the party lacks the ability to alter its course. It has become too deeply rooted in a general policy of class co-operation.

The increases in real wages achieved during the greater part of the post war period have been acquired at the cost of a violently increased work pace and a worsened work milieu. An example of this can be found in the introduction of the efficiency improvement system during the fifties. Initially it was marked only by a stimulation of the wage drift. The reckoning came several years later: nervous illnesses, ulcers, insomnia and long term sick leave.

In many cases the dislocation of the population which occurred in the tracks of monopolisation and rationalisation resulted in wage advantages, but at the same time in exhorbitant rents, deteriorating living milieu, uprootedness and social isolation. Social democracy has been irresolute in the face of this problematic. On the one hand they have viewed it as the necessary price for a progress expedient technological development which in an abstract manner has been disassociated from its class context. On the other hand they have tended to view the consequences of capitalism exclusively as service and care problems, which are dealt with by strengthened social measures in a spirit of developmental optimism. In this way they have developed a service and care apparatus which serves the interests of monopoly capital.

Today the situation has been reached where the human exhaustion — the surplus and waste of capitalism — can no longer be concealed by an 'active labour market policy' and improved social service resources. The people on sick leave, on early pensions, receiving social assistance, in labour care queues, misusing drugs, have now reached such enormous numbers that it is clear the problem cannot be solved by the social service apparatus. It has also now become so costly that the government has for example signalled an expenditure stop for hospital care at precisely the moment that health conditions are deteriorating.

Social democracy has occupied a unique position in capitalist society. While they have pursued a policy which has strengthened capitalism they have at the same time had a mass base in the working class. This popular tie has had its counterpart in certain reform demands in SAP's policies. The rising bureaucratisation and centralisation within the party and trade union movement which have been necessary conditions for continued class co-operation, has at the same time worsened the relationship between the leadership and the base. The SAP leadership and the LO bureaucracy have lost their sensitivity to popular moods and demands issuing from the struggle in the work place. This fact was expressed clearly during the strike wave of 1969/70. Another manifestation of the same phenomenon is the fact that they have remained aloof from the 'solidarity movement' which has developed during later years. Only now that the movement has gained broad support have they made an attempt to take over its leadership.

Ideological disarmament has been another necessary condition for the policy of class co-operation. Occasionally the social democrats have tried to present themselves as the bearer of a socialist philosophical heritage, even though it is a utopian form of 'socialism'. However the study groups and activities which they sponsor are geared to serve the interests of bourgeois political economy. Issues of exploitation, the class character of the state, and the intrinsic crises of capitalism are not considered. Thus, a leading party spokesman is able to state that 'what is good for business is good for the people'. A party in which this can occur is hard pressed to pass itself off as socialist.

For simple tactical reasons also it has been seen to be advantageous to present SAP as a reform minded popular party rather than a labour party. This has not taken place without opposition. Neither has the development been pushed as far programatically as it has been for example in West German social democracy. It has also brought with it problems for the party. To be sure, the accentuation of SAP as a bourgeois reform party entails advantages from the viewpoint of the class co-operation policy and in the party's efforts to win over the so-called marginal voters. At the same time however, such an approach gives rise to a situation in which a large traditionally social democratic strata can view the centre party, for example, as an equivalent alternative to the Swedish Labour Party.

In addition to this, the social democrats classic method of struggle against radical opposition within the working class — anti-communist agitation — has lost its effectiveness. This is in the first instance related to the altered international power conditions. Furthermore, US imperialism is presently exposed in all its brutality and can no longer be portrayed as a bulwark for freedom. The international organisations have grossly compromised themselves through their close co-operation with the CIA and other American interests. Today, the 'Socialistic International' is a parodic discussion club to which few apportion any political significance, least of all as a socialist organ.

Nevertheless, leading social democrats make desperate attempts to resurrect the communist bogy man. In their search for 'left-orientation' and socialism they join company with reactionaries such as Tage Adolfsson and Rune Moberg.

This crisis in social democracy creates special problems for the party leadership. On the one hand they lack the will, strength and resources to break with the policy of class co-operation which has existed until now. On the other hand, they must at least in rhetoric appease the radical demands made by grass roots party members. In short they must continue a policy in accordance with the conditions of big finance while at the same time projecting the illusion of seeking radical objectives.

The SAP leadership's method of solving this problem is actually brilliant in its effrontary and simplicity. They sit on two stools at the same time. The 1972 SAP convention exemplifies this. Two major reports were presented − one bone to each camp. The business policy report outlines the actual policy and contains a long list of concrete political demands which practically speaking are all, in the interest of big finance. The equality report was written to appease the party's left and contains a series of radical impulses but is completely lacking in concrete proposals.

IV

One of the two main documents presented to the 1972 Swedish Labour Party conference was the equality report. This was written by a joint study group from SAP and LO. The chairwoman of the group was Alva Myrdal and it also included a number of people from the established party left. The most prominent feature of the report is a certain rhetorical radicalism and a cautious self criticism, an uncertainty concerning the character of capitalist society and the means with which it should be attacked, together with a total absence of concrete political proposals.

There are sections in the equality report which contain both radicalism and a quite devastating critique of the consequences of the trusteeship policy. For example:

> Welfare is built by the people at work. Society's possibilities for increasing welfare is dependent upon as many as possible contributing their productive effort. If more people are employed the total production is increased. The society which does not protect and take care of the will and ability to work squanders resources and deprives itself of possibilities to improve people's conditions.

Somewhat later in the report it is stated:

Unemployment repeatedly increases over and over from recession to recession and a portion of that unemployment remains even during boom years.

In several short years from 1968 to 1971, the proportion of older unmarried men employed has decreased from three-quarters to approximately two-thirds.

One wonders why the social democrats became so angry with Jorn Swensson during the parliamentary debate on unemployment! Perhaps the irritation is due to their irresolution concerning the explanation of the development:

Huge human costs have followed in the tracks of rapid economic transformation, which the instruments of the distribution policy have not been directed towards over-coming; migration from rural areas, unemployment in these localities and stress and overloading in the expanding areas, isolation in the countryside, the accelerated production pace's exhaustion of human beings, etc. These offer an insight into the milieu and resource destruction which the heavy emphasis upon only 'economic' profit has established.

It has long been normal to utilise 'economic' measurement, such as the increase in total production or — seen from an individual viewpoint — real wage increases, as a measurement of standard development.

One can notice how a profitability ideology is presented in contrast to an implied 'human' ideology. Had it come into currency prior to Marx, this viewpoint would have been progressive. What is interesting about the profit conception is not its maliciousness but rather that it manifests a power relationship. As long as capitalism exists the search for profits will determine the essential aspects of society's develop-ment. A moralising of this fact is transformed into a mere platitude if one does not attack capitalism. And this the social democrats do not.

For the same reason the defense against the left takes somewhat the character of a parody, even though they resort to the devious practice of caricaturing their opponents and blending together both 'left' and 'right'.

The objective has been to cast suspicion upon the integrity of the stirring of the labour movement. The technology being to make the movement responsible for even those ideas it has always fought against but which have nevertheless persisted because they are aspects of every society having capitalist relations of production.

The aversion to giving large powers to the democratic organs, the government and parliament has for long characterised both right and left opposition — ever since the struggle for the franchise. From both conservative and revolutionary camps, it has been preferred that power over business life lie outside democratic control.

Who has preferred that power lay outside democratic control? The illusions concerning the role of the state comes across very clearly in the equality report:

In a society which claims solidarity as a basic principle, is demanded organised co-operation and strengthened influence in society in order to strengthen the position of the weak and in order that a redistribution of the unevenly distributed resources and opportunities can occur.

This 'strong society' which is spoken of is the capitalist state whose class and violent character is concealed behind such phrases as 'organised co-operation'. Hjalman Branting's expectations that the labour movement would take over the bourgeois state by 'growing' into it has been exchanged for an assurance that such a development has already occurred. Thus each new state expenditure becomes a step towards socialism and the fact that the expenditures for police in this year's budget proposal have for the first time exceeded approximately 400 million dollars becomes a step towards the 'strong society'.

The confusion regarding the class character of the state makes the road to socialism become a question of slowly working oneself towards abstract ideals.

The objective of equality indicates the direction of policy.

The new magic formula to be used is called 'company democracy':

When company democracy is developed to the extent that employees have acquired real possibilities to influence their own working conditions a turning point will have been reached in the development of industrial society. At that point, employees will no longer be able to be viewed merely as labour power, that is to say, something which is necessary for the maintenance of production.

Thus, exploitation is to be abolished by means of company democracy. Should not the fact that this is simply an old folk party proposal being dusted off (directorship representation for the employees) or the fact that the employers also favour the idea of company democracy, be sufficient for some critical reflection.

With regard to insuring employment in the future, the equality report contains an element of realistic pessimism:

> In any event it is not at all certain that continued industrial development will in fact lead to a large net increase of employment opportunities within industry. Neither is it this which is most essential. What is important, however, is that the total commodity production is too sufficient to cover our common needs of goods and services (including imports).

Instead, the public sector will be used as a source of new employment opportunities. A long preference list is put forward according to which people shall be employed within the youth, neighbourhood and services, improved public transit, and social development work. This optimistic list of new municipal expenditures should be seen in the context of what the finance minister has said in a preface to this year's budget:

> There is much which indicates that municipalities should be able to limit tax increases not only for 1974, the second year in the agreement, but even in the future. Housing construction which is an essential expenditure regulating factor has now entered a calmer stage. The large expansion in the area of youth education seems now to be by and large completed. Even the expansion of medical care services is proceeding at a calmer pace and with emphasis placed on the less costly 'open' medical services.
>
> Taken together this should entail that future municipal expansion need not be as rapid and resource demanding as during the sixties, even while within the framework of this slower pace, one can still take care of basic needs.

Where, within the scope of unaltered municipal expenditures, the money is to be obtained for hundreds of thousands of social and medical personnel for care of the aged, social therapeutists and employees within the neighbourhood services, only the authors of the 'preference' list know. Those who work in practical social work know rather that cutbacks and economic restraints are the current solution.

A further central section of the report deals with the operational form of the party. One self critical piece scrutinises the failure of social democrats to achieve contact with broad groups of people. It is suggested that an attempt should be made to correct this with what is in essence the utilisation of assembly and meeting techniques. Small groups are to replace large meetings. The 'consultation' which is a sort of Gallup study within the party shall in future even focus on non-party members. Efforts are to be made in the form of studies, but not in the first instance as a means for gaining knowledge but rather as contact instruments. Thus there is a desire to spruce up the party's operation in various ways, though there is no question of altering the power structure within the party.

V

The Swedish Labour Party reveals its true character in its business policy programme. The praxis followed by the party in its economic policy with its direct and willing support to big capital is spelled out here, at times through attempts at ideological beautification, but in other instances open and precise.

In one section of the business policy programme, the songs of praise to class co-operation reach an almost unbelievable melodiousness. Is it a 'more difficult climate for Swedish industry' the report asks, and then responds itself by presenting among other things, a breakdown of the development of company taxation in Sweden.

The report bemoans the fact that profits have declined during the sixties. But there has not yet been a decrease of earning in relation to sales volume. Thus 'By means of favourable tax measures, primarily through a use of investment funds, industry's effective tax expend-itures (the tax payment in relation to actual profits) have declined from 50 per cent in 1953 to approximately 35 per cent in 1968'. The report boasts further that 'There are examples of companies which can be brought down to an effective tax expenditure of between 5 and 10 per cent of profits. This calculation applies to stock companies which pay dividends but is not representative for other, for example, family companies'. The group studying business policy has not concerned itself with investigating the number of workers and service personnel who are in the 10 per cent tax bracket. Those favoured by the structure of the tax system are the 'expanding companies', that is to say, large finance. And why are these companies patronised? According to the report it is for three reasons: to promote 'rapid economic growth', to achieve 'full employment' and 'to set the stage for a forceful wage policy from the side of the trade union movement'.

The argument is hardly tenable. If companies which are 'expansive' — which most often are companies which are most highly rationalised or least labour intensive — are favoured at the same time that others are discriminated against, employment is not promoted. Above all not as the owners of 'expansive companies' — big finance — attempt to limit the growth of new places of employment and cause a number of existing companies to be closed down.

The powerful wage policy which is to be carried out is undermined by the Swedish Labour Party itself. As early as in the 1973-74 budget outline this is accomplished. It states, 'In the long run the result of the next contract negotiations on the labour market will have a determining significance on both the domestic price developments and the competitiveness of Swedish industry. It is in the interest of both partners in the labour market that concern for full employment and for the external trade balance of our economy, influences the formation of the coming agreement'. The quotation speaks for itself.

Had the statement concerning the 'powerful wage policy' only been first dismantled in the finance plan several months after the congress, the alterations would have been slow in coming. Therefore, this wage policy was eliminated in the very business policy programme which formulated it. The business policy programme presented three proposals designed to stimulate capital formation. The first is that workers' money in the AP (General Pension Fund) should be used as risk capital in the capitalists' economy. The second was the creation of still another semi-public finance institute. This would purchase stock in small and medium size companies.

The third is the wage policy. The 'powerful wage policy' spoken of is to be an aid to capital's earnings. How can that be brought about? Re-enter, what else? the so called wage policy. It has served as the excuse for the centralisation of the labour movement during the thirties and forties. It served as a support for theories promoting special support for large capital, structural change and population shifts during the fifties and sixties. Now it is to serve as an instrument to support the economising requirements of capital.

The programme states that capital formation 'through wage negotiations can become an important support for and complement to the solidarity wage policy of the trade union movement'. In the expansive companies, solidarity restraint is shown so that 'employees in low wage branches will be able to achieve a wage increase in step with the average for all wage earners.' Thus the full scope for wage increases cannot be taken advantage of within those companies which are doing well. Therefore, there must be a built in element of what is attractively termed collective saving in the wage negotiations. The argument is that the workers should forego demands on these funds so that the money can remain in the company as capital. In this way 'wage earners will share in that capital which remains in the company

37

and cannot be paid out in wages.' With complete impudence, it is said that this should 'contribute to a solution of the distribution problem in connection with the solidarity wage policy'.

What is capital? Social democracy's business experts never trouble themselves with such a discussion. Capital is neither money nor the means of production in and of itself. It is rather the instrument with which owners of capital exploit the working class in order to realise surplus value on the worker's labour. Capital is a production relation. Greater capital formation increases the power of the capitalists. The establishment of minority company directorship positions which lack authority and the suggestion that workers should be petit capitalists in the companies for which they work by abstaining from claiming a portion of — according to the Swedish Confederation of Trade Unions Unions — possible wage gains does not break, but rather strengthens the power of big capital. The ownership democracy of the right wing is just as impossible even if it has the Swedish Labour Party's stamp of approval and is termed 'collective savings'.

The encouragement of capital formation is then combined with proposals for the establishment of a fund for technological development, increased public purchases aimed at Swedish industry, etc. A development block is to be initiated in order to minimise the risk to individual capitalists. Further, branch advisory groups are to be established — a new outgrowth in the flora of class co-operation agencies.

The establishment will then be made more palatable by means of a more effective labour exchange service and measures to influence companies to employ handicapped persons to a greater extent.

To this is added a regional policy made up of general objectives. In this the proposals go so far as to agree to 'try out' business establishment controls. A sample of this regional policy has already been seen in the regional political proposition which was discussed at the close of the 1972 fall sitting of parliament. The proposition contains a statement of general objectives, population limits, a conglomeration of new administrative entities, primary centres, regional centres and other euphonious bureaucratic terms. However nothing is said regarding the creation of the increased number of jobs which are necessary if the outlying regions are not to necessarily be depopulated. In all essentials the legislated national physical plan adheres to the requirements of large finance.

Until now the leadership of the Swedish Labour Party has mastered almost perfectly the art of sitting on two stools simultaneously. They have been able to put through both the pseudo-radicalism of the equality programme as well as a business policy programme which gives open support to capital. Furthermore, prime minister Palme has been able to sing the praises of both women and the monarchy — a monarchy which, to top it all off, is reserved exclusively for the male members of the family — all for increased equality, and the Swedish Labour Party congress approved it.

VI

The main antagonist in the struggle for socialism in Sweden is the capitalist class, and primarily its leading sector: large finance. It is the power of large finance which must be broken and replaced by the power of the working class.

Social democracy is obviously not the major opponent, but breaking its influence in the working class is a necessary condition for the success of the struggle for socialism. This effort must in the first instance be directed at revealing the contradictions in the policy of the social democratic leadership, attacking class co-operation and the party's support of large finance.

The development of the Swedish Labour Party is such that it may not be perceived in its entirety as a potential force for socialism. Nevertheless, there are many members and sympathisers who may be won over to radical demands. These both can and must be transformed to allies in the struggle for socialism.

Note

[1] A leading social democrat of the period.

4 Social Democracy and the Working Class: On the Basis of Reformism

Ingvar Johnsson, E. Tommy Nilsson and Gunnar Olofsson

Five years ago [1] the miners struck in Malmfalten: [2] Svappavaara, Kiruna, and Malmberget. The workers formulated their demands outside formal trade union channels, carried out successful demonstrations and mass meetings, and appointed strike committees which led and co-ordinated the struggle. It was both in fact and experienced by many miners as a thawing, as an opening. The strike was carried out in an area which for a long time has had a strong communist tradition and, naturally enough, many communists were once again on the strike committee.

What were the political consequences of the strike in the mining area? Looking at the situation in the Miners Union Locals in Kiruna and Malmberg, they differ somewhat. In Kiruna the social democrats have secured their grip on the union local while the VPK's (communists) in Malmberget have been able to deepen the lessons of the strike in concrete union policies (such as the termination in the fall, of various forms of co-operation with management). Another expression of political-ideological stance is voting patterns in local and general elections. What was most striking here was the fact that in 1970 the social democrats strengthened their position in relation to the VPK in Malmfalten. This came as a surprise to many. In this article we shall try to show why there was nothing either surprising or strange in this development.

To begin we might illuminate several features of the strikes' development and settlement. For our discussion, the most determining was the role played at the national level by the LO (the Swedish Confederation of Trade Unions) and the Social Democrats, in the person of Kurt Nordgen (at that time vice-chairman of the LO), in the strike committee's discussions and establishment of conditions for negotiations with LKAB [3] (and party friend A.S. Lundberg, the chief of LKAB).

Those successes achieved by the strike and the negotiations were manifest in and formulated through Nordgren's participation. The demands were, so to speak, channelled through the social democrats who were represented on all sides of the negotiation table. The strike's outbreak meant, and provided for a dissociation from the traditionally dominant pattern of negotiations (the 'normal' union and political routine). This dissociation, in the special form it took through Nordgren's central role, entailed a return to older negotiating patterns but in such a form that social democracy, paradoxically enough, came out of the struggle further strengthened. (As the struggle in the strike committee showed, this development was neither automatically necessary nor logically inevitable).

With this example as a point of departure we approach the actual problem of our text: how does a social democratic ideology arise, renew and maintain itself in the working class?

Basic to our perspective is the working class' double determination in a capitalist society. It is on the one hand the exploited and oppressed class — that which produces surplus labour. In principle it is antagonistic in its relationship to the bourgeoisie and the state. On the other hand however, it is renewed within the framework of capitalism, that is to say, within the capital-wage labour relationship. It is forced to continually sell its labour power at whatever price it can get. The duality in the class' situation is reflected in the fact that this struggle is at the same time both a struggle within and a struggle against the existing order. As we shall see, this duality is reflected again in the working class' organisational forms.

The pre-requisites for social democratic ideology

'The production of ideology'

An understanding of the organisational-political situation of the working class pre-supposes a certain comprehension of the manner in which ideology emerges and an understanding of its material moment, that is to say, that ideology is not simply a formulation of articles of faith and evaluations but much more an institutionalised pattern of action which has emerged as a response to objective material conditions. There persists a die hard notion that the working class' ideology becomes bourgeois as a result of ruling class manipulation — ideology is seen to emerge through the indoctrination to which the working class is exposed in schools and the mass media. It may be said that such a conception based itself on the view that it does not require any work to 'discover' the truth, but it does to 'conceal' it. This view even flourishes side by side with the Leninist conception of the party — in spite of the fact that it is based on the opposite — and correct — view that effort is necessary to detect the truth. The working class does not create spontaneous Marxism in the same manner which it spontaneously creates various forms of defense organisations against capitalistic exploitation. The need for such organisations is, so to speak, easily perceived, such is not the case within the basic Marxist truths. The classic example illustrating that a structure or system cannot be identified by a description from a position within that system is the solar system. From our position in the system it actually appears that the sun rotates around the earth, instead of the opposite. Theoretical work is required to perceive that this conclusion is incorrect, and to arrive at the correct one. This incorrect conclusion does not arise from religious indoctrination but through the spontaneous trust in the senses. Precisely the same can be said concerning social structures. From a definite position inside the system, it appears in a definite way — and in the capitalistic system it appears in a manner which in many respects conceals the correct overall picture. To the worker for example, it appears that he is being paid for his work, and not in order to reproduce himself as labour power; or differently expressed, it appears as though capital buys work and not labour power etc. What is involved is to see both sides of the matter. It is not simply that the system spontaneously presents a distorted image of itself. Certain things are visible in the system, for example, that one can fight and negotiate concerning the price of work or labour power, the length of the work day, the work pace, etc. The same can be said concerning the utilisation of the collective organisation of this struggle. It is first in this connection that we shall see the bourgeois/social democratic ideology as a planned system aimed at disorganising the struggle of the working class. However, this aspect of the ideology is secondary.

Two things should be injected here. First: what has been said above does not represent the basis of all ideology, rather only of that which in future will be referred to as spontaneous ideology, that is to say, that which is based upon the conspicuous or obvious. Secondly, what has been said in no way should be taken to imply that workers lack the ability to see through the capitalist mode of production, only that this requires theoretical work — one must go beyond what is immediately perceptible to the workers.

On this basis we can better understand Lenin's notion of spontaneous trade union consciousness. The need for collective struggle (not necessarily defensive) within the existing system of production becomes more or less automatically apparent to the workers, but this does not entail the need and demand for a socialist

42

system of production. It is due to this fact that the primary task of the communist party is to spread socialist ideas within the working class. This means however that the organisation of the working class in a communist party becomes a highly problematic issue. It cannot simply be considered as a question of spontaneous organisation. It has often been claimed that the social democrats represent this spontaneous trade union consciousness, but the currently manifest policy of class co-operation and its theories of stabilisation render this view untenable. Neither can the social democratic parties be viewed as the spontaneous parties of the working class. A spontaneous workers party does not exist!

Reproduction of the social democratic ideology

What then are the more concrete mechanisms which give social democratic ideology such a strong, if not dominant position within the working class in, for example, Sweden? Our thesis is that this position does not depend in the first instance upon its 'inner' strength and logic. Its persuasive strength lies in the fact that it is continually verified through practice in state and municipal administrations, in popular movements in general and, more directly in trade unions activity. The social democratic policy works, it gives results, obvious and concrete in separate instances, and thereby it also 'verifies' the ideology which precedes or accompanies the practical activity. 'If it works it's true' is a guiding axiom in the area of ideology.

What do we mean here by 'verify'? Let us draw an example from union activity. The manner whereby social democratic ideology is spooned out in the trade union movement is not only, or even in the first instance, a question of union courses, etc. (They can however well be important for the development of an *esprit de corps* and the re-enforcement of an already prevailing social perspective, as well as for the orientation of both individual and political aspirations). Day to day union work is itself spontaneous, a 'natural' ideology producing experience. Negotiations and co-operation functions and provides practical results. Co-operation between 'the labour move-ments' political and trade union sectors is manifest in trade union inspired legislation proposals, etc.

Why does union activity serve to 'spontaneously' verify and strengthen social democratic ideology? It is due to the framework in which such union activity takes place. A trade union is an organisation of sellers of labour power and operates within a capital — wage labour relationship. As such, union activity is a participant in the constant recreation of that relationship: it serves the interests of the subordinate partner. However, the framework for union activity, for the spontaneous union ideology, is established by the necessarily very narrow margins of the reproduction process. The trade union struggle is characterised by a number of objectives: the struggle for work, the struggle for the price of labour power and the struggle for the conditions of labour (working hours, working conditions in general, etc.). The framework however is established by the struggle for work, for the reproduction of the individual bearers of labour power. The procedure can be precisely expressed in the formula: 'Rather exploited than unemployed'.

It is precisely this framework — the reproduction aspect — of the trade union struggle, which forms the transition to and connecting link with a developed social democratic/reformist ideology. In the same manner the element of struggle — the contradiction between labour and capital — forms the natural bridge to a communist ideology.

The duality of trade union activity makes it possible that union leaders/cadre can indeed be reformist, 'right wing', but that as such they never constitute the extreme right wing of a social democratic party. (Union leaders almost never leave social democratic parties to move to the right, as with the splintering of the labour party in 1931 when parliamentarians in large numbers established a 'national government' or for that matter when Erhard Jacobsen in Denmark broke away from the social democratic party and built his own'). With regard to communist parties, the trade union cadres are as a rule the more right wing oriented — the more so, the less the party's influence in the trade union is.

However, the ties between the trade union struggle and a developed social democratic ideology (and political apparatus) are neither givens nor everywhere existent. The economic struggle can exist alongside of and fairly independent of an overall political perspective. That is to say that a situation can very well exist in which a radical trade union struggle and policy does not express itself at the political level. An example is the English trade union movement, with a great deal of fight and militance in purely union issues, with many communists who are active in the unions and even as leading cadre, but at the political level this radicalism is not expressed. A similar situation exists in Denmark which for long has had the DKP with a very strong trade union influence, but which not once in an obvious crisis situation has come near a political breakthrough. Thus we easily find a difference between trade union and political radicalism (in the same manner that Leninism more generally points to the potential and 'spontaneous' distinction between union and political struggles).

What is characteristic of the Scandinavian social democrats (the Danish to a lesser degree) is precisely the merging of 'trade union reformism' and state administered political reformism. The trade union apparatus is social democracies' primary instrument for the ideological encapsulation of the working class. The key to the social democrats' success in Sweden lies in the trade unions discipline, subordination and supporting/edifying role in relation to social democratic policy at the state and municipal levels.

The verification of trade unions practice is the central moment in reformist ideology

Another form of 'verification' lies in the municipal political activity. Here hundreds of thousands of people are involved in more or less demanding administrative tasks. It is certainly not their character of paid servants which is central here. In municipal activity reformist ideology is continually verified by 'practical solutions and small steps'.

These two weighty practices — this does not mean that the other 'movement' efforts lack significance, on the contrary — become the very foundation of the ideology of the social democratic apparatus, through and in its 'verification'.

From this perspective municipal and trade union centralisation is not an unconditional boon from a social democratic point of view. This is manifest in the attempts made to re-establish ties with the newly emerging organisational forms. On the one hand this involves deliberation and discussion groups within the party and union, and on the other, proposals concerning expanded layman influence and representation in the administration of municipal institutions as well as spasmodic attempts at resuscitation of SSUs (Social Democratic Youth).

We suggest that all these tendencies reflect the real/sustaining force of social democratic ideology: the verifying participation in an administrative practice — and a successful one. But the 'threat against social democracy' does not primarily lie in the fact that the number of 'administrative participants' is decreasing (even if this is important): rather it lies in the potential contradiction between the progress and demands of the spontaneous trade union struggle and the content and demands of the policies of the social democratic government.

The conditions necessary to permit the spontaneous merging of the union struggle with a social democratic policy and ideology lie in the growth of the rate of employment, real wage developments, and the nature of changes in working conditions. A disciplined, 'restrained' and regulatory trade union movement pre-supposes economic growth and real wage increases. At the same time this economic growth is an overriding objective which motivates a restrained union policy and leaves no room for spontaneous union struggle and local initiative.

A social democratic rationalisation policy in relation to pre-capitalist and pre-monopoly company forms (small farmers, small tradesmen, etc.) together with an elimination of obstacles to the free movement of labour in the labour market can strengthen and lengthen the real wage increase phase. However the other side of the mobility policy is early pensions and objectionable housing conditions for workers (with rental exploitation of the AMS [Labour Market Board] uprooted working class), the other side of technological rationalisation is a frenzied work pace and mental and physical care services for exhausted workers; support to capital intensive industries means fewer jobs, etc. The development of capitalism places the trade union struggle in a new situation and there emerges a clear lack of agreement between the demands of the spontaneous trade union struggle and the content and requirements of social democratic policies.

When the goal of social democracy is the expanded reproduction of the capital/wage-labour relationship and it finds itself in a dilemma between the trade union formulated demands of the working class and capitals demands for guaranteed conditions for capital accumulation, the latter tendency becomes dominant. The formula for a successful social democratic policy has been the uniting of these two tendencially contrary interests. We can witness the conflict between the social democratic government and the trade unions in England for example, concerning the anti-union legislation last year.

Whether the existing objective contradictions between the effects of social democratic policies and the unions' demands become a reality, will be the result of the power relations within the trade union move-emt — the degree of social democratic dominance. It also depends upon what alternative political positions and ideologies exist in material form (that is to say, as parties, political forces which can offer another practice, another policy). A stronger protection of the interests of capital accumulation *vis à vis* the working class is expressed ideologically in the form of a heavier emphasis on either an ideology in direct harmony and agreement with policy (national unity in crisis, moment of truth, home of the people, all in the same boat, etc.) or, by one seemingly the direct opposite, that is to say, a radical ideology in lieu of negotiation, or concealing the nature or existence of an actual policy. As an example one can mention the prevalence of the notion of equality in the sixties seen in relation to the creation of state owned companies and the relationship between the radical foreign policy in the form of proclamations and of practical action, the real content of the tariff policy.

In summary the following may be said in regard to the nature and reproduction of social democratic ideology:

1 The working class does not adopt a position with regard to theory but rather to practice, union and 'political'.

2 Ideology has a material base and should not in the first instance be assessed from without, concerning its logical consistency.

3 The ruling ideology and its practice is continually verified, that is to say the working class can more or less continually see obvious positive results of social democratic policies.

4 This verification contains a 'self-fulfilling moment'. If one says for example that general strikes don't pay, then one opposes general strikes and so it is demonstrated that they in fact don't pay. In concrete issues this involves being able to 'predict' correctly.

Social democracy — 'the two-headed monster'

A striking feature of all the large social democratic parties is their division into left and right wings. It may be said that the left wing represents the spontaneous trade union consciousness or, if one wishes, a pre-political reformism, while the right wing stands for the theoretically-politically formulated reformism which of necessity implies the embracing of one or another bourgeois economic theory — whether it emanates from Keynes or Assar Lindbeck.

Most essential to a comprehension of social democracy is the understanding that its two wings are not at all united in an unholy alliance, rather the opposite, both constitute necessary components in social democracy. This interdependence can be understood in the following way. Assume that an organisation which is exclusively based upon the spontaneous trade union consciousness grows powerful and becomes a significant force. What happens then? When the organisation is not too strong it can fight for the workers' interests without concerning itself with how the whole system functions, but when it becomes stronger the possibility arises that either consciously or unconsciously the organisation can cause a crisis in the entire system. One is then forced to develop a theoretical overview of the system and here there are two alternatives, either one becomes a communist and revolutionary, or one formulates a theoretical-political reformist position or allies oneself to a group that already has one. The left wing creates a right wing. Suppose on the other hand that a little theoretical and political social democratic organisation after much toil acquires a base in the working class. Then the following occurs. The theoretical overview cannot completely put an end to the spontaneous trade union consciousness, but inasmuch as the overview sometimes requires a degree of class co-operation which is so far reaching that it comes into conflict with the spontaneous trade union consciousness, we once again have a party with two wings. The right wing has created for itself a left wing.

What has just been said is not intended to describe how social democratic parties emerge, but rather to illustrate the two moments which are of necessity found in every large social democratic party. Normally the spontaneous trade union consciousness does not form its own ideology but constitutes only an ingredient in an ideology. In reality, in most countries the spontaneous collective organisation of the working class was closely interwoven with a party organisation which then split into a social democratic and a communist party. Nevertheless it may be said that to a surprisingly high degree England exemplifies the ideal type described above. Labour arose through a union of a labour movement based upon the spontaneous union consciousness and small theoretical-political social democratic organisations.

Every social democratic party with a firm footing in the working class contains at the most abstract level, two movements, a right wing and a left wing. The 'left-moment' is noticeably in the trade union sector, and all the more obviously the further down one comes in the union hierarchy. In light of what was earlier said, this situation is quite natural. The 'right-moment' is noticeably among the party's — in the word's true meaning — bureaucrats, that is to say, those persons a bit up in the state and municipal administration. The reasons for this are equally obvious. In a different manner, their position obliges them to adopt a political overview. (To this must of course be added their significant material advantages and wealth compared with that of the working class).

In itself it is not necessary for one to view an individual social democrat as representing either the 'right' moment or the 'left' moment. The most effective social democratic leaders should be those who internalise both moments and themselves embody the dual character of the party. This may explain why it is said that the two pragmatists Harold Wilson and Olof Palme both have their origins in social democracy's left wing. What is central in this connection is that social democracy's actions in different political situations can to a

48

great extent be understood as shiftings between the 'right' and 'left' moments. In certain political situations harmony prevails, in some the tension becomes strong and in others it becomes so strong that the party can split.

In the area of ideology social democracy manifests a peculiarity which becomes intelligible only when one perceives the mutual dependence between the right and left wings. All parties are naturally forced to modify their ideology as capitalism and the relationship between the represented classes (and strata) and the state changes. However certain social democratic parties, the Swedish for example, manifest fluctuations which seem to go far beyond what is normal. From its inception the Swedish party has called itself Marxist. At the end of the thirties, Tingsten stated — correctly — that this characterisation was, so to speak, purely ideological. In practice the party was not at all Marxist. During the fifties it officially rejected Marxism and since then has had approximately the same ideological classification as the Centre Party (one of the three so called bourgeois parties in Sweden — currently the largest — with an ideological position approximating the US democratic party).

They have made small inoffensive attempts to imitate the ideological system of Keynes and social-liberal economic planning but none have successfully taken root, and for the time being they are once again attempting to strike a Marxist tone. The problematic of social democratic ideology is rooted in the fact that the party must project either purely bourgeois theories (right wing) or a lack of long range strategy (left wing). This conflict was seen clearly at SAP's (the Swedish Labour Party) 1972 conference. There the problem was solved with the help of the basic principle of deception: 'the more audacious, the more simple: they separated completely from each other an industrial policy report which contained concrete proposals and an equality report which lacked proposals but spoke instead in generalities of the nature of a good society.'

That the contradiction ridden unity which social democracy represents can in spite of all this and for long periods manifest a great degree of inner harmony — still at the most abstract level — has to do with the relative independence between the political and the economic levels. This relative independence can be simply illustrated in Swedish social democracy's foreign policy. At the same time they have been giving material support to FRELIMO and PAIGC, they have refused to intervene against Swedish investments which supported Portuguese colonialism. The same applies to the relatively all embracing help given to North Vietnam (during and after the conflict) seen in relation to Sweden's membership in the World Bank. It is acceptable so to speak to keep oneself to the left on the political level, at the same time one holds to the right at the economic level. Such a posture obscures the contradictions between social democracy's two wings and consequently is adeptly utilised by the leadership of the Swedish social democratic party.

The earlier abstract picture of the left and right moments can now be concretised. At the political level it is expressed in the positions taken regarding issues such as material support to and recognition of liberation movements, participation in military alliances and the perspective on the European Common Market. Determining what is left and what is right in these questions should not present any problem. On the other hand when it comes to the economic level of activity, separating right from left wing positions and motives is more problematic. The classic characterisation of social democracy states that it intervenes in the distribution of the results of production but not in the production process itself, however this characterisation can obviously not be taken strictly. Governing parties are forced to also intervene in the production process. During the fifties and sixties the so called competition model (= eliminate market disruptions, operate every company and business place according to the profit principle) won a foothold in Swedish social democracy. Rental controls were to be abolished, AMS and numerous other grants were to eliminate workers' reluctance to move from place to place and to be retrained due to altered regional and occupational labour market demands, and the SJ (Swedish Railroad) would not be subsidised. One can distinguish here a 'right' wing line, advocating the competition model and a left wing line rejecting the same position. This manifests what is in fact a general feature. At the economic level the policy of the left wing of social democracy consists of a negation of the right wing policy, but it lacks a positive overview of society. Thus the left takes the form of an 'issue policy'. This is clearly shown in its demands for socialisation. There demands are not integrated into a socialist strategy, but are simply 'issue' or 'point' socialisation which can at best facilitate the maintenance or improvement of the living standard of working class in a capitalist society (most often by socialisation which renders national capital more effective as a unit). The character of the point or issue policy is also apparent in the last year's price freeze policy. The price freeze is of course consciously temporary.

The above describe negative character, or point character, of left wing policy at the economic level which renders such left wing policy more difficult to perceive than is the case at the political level where it is often extremely easy to discern. This partially explains the fact that social democracy is so little shaken up by purely economic crises.

The duality of the working class concerning the capital/wage labour relationship is thus expressed even within social democracy, in its right and left wings. It can as we suggested above, be expressed in a dislocation between 'politics' and 'economy'. If we view social democracy as an organisational arrangement of the relationship between the working class and the dominant state power, we can say that the 'left' moment lies nearer the struggle for the objective interests of the class, while the 'right' moment represents the state's role as a guarantor of the reproduction of the relations of production. It is here that the argument stressing a distinction between social democracy's 'leaders' and 'masses' could have a basis, namely to the degree to which the 'leaders' are supporters of the state's reproduction guaranteeing role, while the 'members' obviously represent the struggle for the interests of the working class. However, this distinction can just as easily be made within the leadership group. This was the case for example concerning the issue of the introduction of labour market laws in England during the Wilson government's first term office in which the government and party stood on one side while the majority of the trade union movement stood on the other. Determining for this division's possibility and growth is capitals development, those conditions under which it can grow, and the corresponding policy pursued by the social democratic leadership and trade union leadership.

At the abstract level which we now find ourselves, we can see the basis of certain possible incorrect communist practical-political assessments of social democracy: a) One looks only at the economic level and consequently has difficulty distinguishing both a left and a right wing within social democracy. The party is then placed in the same category as the bourgeois parties. b) One detects a right and a left wing but does not keep separate the political and the economic level and consequently bases his judgements on the political level — where the two wings of the party are most clearly differentiated. One doesn't perceive the limits of left wing social democracy — it is over-estimated. c) One perceives a left and a right wing but not their mutual interdependence, and thus hopes for a future party splintering which will give rise to a both large and stable left wing social democratic party with which one assumes it possible to have organised co-operation.

Communists, social democracy and the working class

What is specific in the social democratic party's relationship with the

51

working class is that under certain conditions their policy of class co-operation comes into conflict with the spontaneous trade union consciousness. What is specific in the communist parties' relationship to the working class is that their policy goes beyond the spontaneous trade union consciousness. They are the bearers of a future system of production. On the abstract level which we find ourselves, this means that there are no grounds for a division of the party into separate wings analogous to those of the social democratic party. However it perhaps should be pointed out that at a more concrete level it is entirely possible. In certain situations even the communist party can be forced to pursue a policy which comes into conflict with the spontaneous trade union consciousness. In certain 'near revolutionary' situations the bourgeois class wish to have strikes in order to create unrest and break the working class' alliances and ties with other classes and strata.

This oddity in the relationship between the communist parties and the working class entails that at this abstract level there is very much to be said concerning communist parties. One can only formulate the general problem of the communist parties: how can the gap between Marxism and the spontaneous class consciousness be bridged? It is a question which must today be complemented with the problem of 'de-social democratising' the working class. It should be stressed that these are two separate issues. A 'de-social democratised' working class does not automatically become a communistic working class.

Against the background of the views we have put forward concerning the relationship and the mediating mechanisms between the working class and the large social democratic parties, we shall look somewhat at several different strategic conceptions of social democracy which have been and are found among communist parties. We will look at a) the so called class against class policy prevalent during the comminterns third period 1928-34), b) the popular front policy which began to be used in France during 1934 as a defense against fascism, and c) STAMOKAP — strategy, or the theory of advanced democracy, that is to say — an offensive popular front policy aimed at achieving some type of first stage to socialism in which capitalism persists but monopoly's power is broken. It should be pointed out that we have not striven here for a complete under-standing of the respective views, unfortunately they are also interrelated with different conceptions of the state apparatus and of the need for class alliances.

The class against class policy

Against the background of the approaching crisis of the thirties and the possibility for a revolutionary upswing which was assumed to exist in connection with the crisis, the commintern undertook a sharpened critical position towards both social democracies left wing as well as the 'right-deviants' within communist parties. In Stalin's words, the task was seen to be '. . . to sharpen the struggle against social democracy and above all its "left-wing", which is capitalisms social support — by means of the communists so-called new tactic in trade unions ' (from *Theory and Practice*, J. Stalin, p.203). This new tactic within the trade union movement was expressed among other ways, by the establishment of RFO (the Red Union Opposition), and in a tremendous propaganda campaign in which 'social fascists were exposed', that is to say, social democratic leaders. The new tactic contained two moments — in part it was to create at the organisational level a unity of action — 'a grass roots unity front' — with the social democratic workers, and in part, at the ideological level, it was to go to verbally violent attack against the social democratic leaders. This latter moment was presided over completely by the party and was fulfilled to the letter. The first moment on the other hand, was naturally dependent upon the social democratic workers and it failed almost completely. The policy pursued can be theoretically motivated in two different ways, for which there are reasons to keep separate. However both motivations presuppose that one can completely eliminate the influence of the social democratic party in the working class.

1   The first motivation, which lies closest to the factually given motivations, bases itself upon the incorrect view of ideology which we described at the beginning of the article. It is believed that the truth must be consciously concealed by someone in order for the workers to support social democracy. If one assumes that ideology emerges in this manner, so also will one naturally be easily convinced that a social democratic ideology can be broken down and replaced by a communist one with the help of persistent propaganda. The role of party propaganda is tremendously over estimated. The fact that this rationale played a leading role can be detected from all the talk concerning how the verbal radicalism of social democracy tricks the workers. The centrality of this rationale can also be seen in the fact that the failure of the tactic during a certain period was

merely taken as an indication that the propaganda must be intensified and made more acrimonious.

2   There is also another motivation and it was certainly present as a subordinate moment, which based itself in a more knowledgeable understanding of how ideology functions. It has been perceived that the critique of social democratic ideology undermines it no more than to the degree that the basis of the ideology has already been eliminated. The basis of course should not be understood to be as synonymous with various propaganda apparatuses whether they be churches, schools, mass media or social democratic party propaganda, but rather synonymous with the possibility for either agreement or non-agreement between the spontaneous trade union consciousness and social democratic policy. And to reiterate, spontaneous trade union consciousness is not created by any propaganda apparatuses.

To the degree which this rationale provided the basis for the policy against the social democrats during the third period, it must have included the view that the economic crisis would cut away the basis of social democratic ideology. And with this basis cast aside it would have been possible to simultaneously engage in common actions with social democratic workers and strongly attack social democratic leaders, 'social fascists'.

The fact that the class against class policy failed so miserably suggests that there must be some error in both rationales. As we have already pointed out, the first rationale is based upon the erroneous understanding of the emergence and reproduction of ideology, but where is the error in the second? As we understand it, the only possible conclusion is that the view that an economic crisis automatically creates a disjunction between spontaneous trade union consciousness and social democratic policy, is completely incorrect. That the error lies here, also corresponds with our earlier pointing out that social democracy utilises the relative independence between the economic and the political levels, and also that one cannot suddenly go from the economic level to the field of party political organisation. Against the background of the preceding discussion it might prove interesting to ask how those within the commintern explained the failure of the policy pursued. The following statement by Dimitrov should be quite representative: 'The strength which lies in the masses traditional ties with their organisations and leadership was underestimated, and when the masses did not at once cut these ties, they

began to be treated with equal bitterness as their reactionary leaders.'
('Enhetens och folk frontens problem', Dimitrov, p.83). The failure is
also explained by the working class' 'tradition restraint', or put another
way, organisation restraint. The explanation has a superfluous
character of the type, 'sleeping pills induce sleep because they make
one sleepy', rather than a real explanation. The social democratic
workers remained social democrats because they remained social
democrats! Using this 'explanation' it becomes still more incomprehensible why the programme achieved the limited successes it did.
According to this explanation there should have been none at all. The
fact is however, that in most Western European countries, especially in
Germany, the policy became successful within one strata — the
unemployed. What actually should be explained is why those who had
work were 'tradition bound' and why those who were unemployed
were not so. Better formulated, the question posed by the events of
the third period should be: why did the crisis of the thirties result
in a non-correspondence between spontaneous trade union consciousness and social democratic policy among the unemployed, but in a
correspondence among those who had work?

The defensive popular front policy

The policy which followed the 'class against class' policy had the
defensive objective of stopping fascism. As was the case with the old
strategy, it was expected that the new policy would bring about
common actions with social democratic workers at that grass roots
level. What differentiates the policy from its predecessors is the fact
that one now attempted to bring about organisational agreements
with the social democratic leadership, which naturally implied that
one had to contain its critique of that leadership. Dimitrov
formulated the line in the following manner: 'In order to secure the
workers road to unity of action one must . . . strive to attain short
term and long term agreements concerning *common actions with
social democratic parties, reformist trade unions and the workers'
other organisations*, against the proletariats class enemy. In this,
attention must be aimed at developing *local mass actions, which are
carried out by the lower organisations* on the basis of local
"agreements".' (Dimitrov, p.34).
   This altered strategic view of the social democratic party was
associated with at least three things: 1) the above mentioned stress
on 'tradition restraint' 2) the insight that social democracies' class
base prevented it from becoming a purely fascist party 3) the insight

that the issue was not an either/or — question fascism or social democracy. This made possible a policy in which the issue regarding how one should 'de-social democratise' the working class was relegated to a peripheral position. The problem of how one could win the workers to communism without properly attacking the social democratic party was not exactly pressing and so not dealt with theoretically.

The Stamokap (state-monopoly capitalism) strategy

Among the predecessors of the Stamokap strategy it is not possible to find any clearly formulated strategic perspective of the social democratic parties, however the following viewpoint finds support in quite a bit of what the strategy's proponents write and say. They make a sharp distinction between the leaders in the social democratic party and the rest (see for example Hilding Hagberg, a member's critique of VPK's party programme in the buildup to its 1972 congress). Regardless of the fundamental difference in the Stamokap strategy and the class against class strategy both appear to assume a purely manipulatory relationship between leaders and the masses. The latter policy is based upon a completely erroneous understanding of how social democratic ideology is created and reproduced. At least Antti Kasvio — who emerged as a theoretical interpreter of the Stamokap theory seems to have the same erroneous conception, with the difference that he believes that previously, bourgeois ideology emerged spontaneously in the working class but this was completely altered with the emergence of state monopoly capitalism and the socialist states. 'This development means that state monopoly capitalism can no longer to the same extent as earlier rely upon bourgeois ideology's spontaneous emergence, influence and reinforcement among the masses. On the contrary imperialist ideology is in a deep crisis!' (FKS, 2-3, p.36).

Regardless of this similarity of viewpoint with that of the third period, it seems that Stamokap theorists don't believe they can eliminate the social democratic party, but rather that one should achieve organised co-operation with it (compare France). If this is to hang together theoretically one must presumably work with the concept of 'tradition restraint'. They can then say the following: because of their 'tradition restraint' workers will not desert social democracy; one can only count on cleaning out the right wing element, that is to say the present leadership, from the party. One can thus expect to have organised co-operation with the left wing social democratic party which then emerges. In this manner one can successfully unite the viewpoint of the third period with that of the popular front period.

Summary

If we relate this discussion to the three separate principle practical-political misassessments of social democracy which we distinguished, the following may be said: the class against class policy based itself on an erroneous understanding of how ideology functions and/or an over emphasis on the economic level which obscured the perception of the significance of social democracy's division into a right and a left wing — and equated the social democrats with bourgeois parties. The Stamokap strategy also seems to have an incorrect conception of the strength and method of functioning of those mechanisms which maintain social democratic ideology. Furthermore it appears to have completely overlooked the mutual dependence between the two wings in large social democratic parties, apparently hoping for a large 'purely' left wing socialist party. One can perhaps also say that it perceives both a right and a left wing in the party, but does not succeed in keeping separate the economic and political levels and consequently fails to see the limits of left wing social democracy. Here the question arises as to whether or not the limitations of left wing social democracy are not also those of the Stamokap strategy itself, for at the economic level both strategies become 'point' or 'issue' policies.

As we have seen, these erroneous viewpoints evolve around the leader-mass and 'tradition restraint' or 'organisation restraint' conceptions and it is our view that these conceptions are unsuitable as a point of departure for a discussion of the social democratic party's relationship to the working class. It is our hope that this article can serve as the basis for a new discussion of how social democracy can be attacked. We have no finished recipe, but in conclusion we can put forward several suggestions which we consider are in harmony with the abstract but necessary characterisation of social democracy and the production of ideology which have been presented up to this point.

Conclusion

Communist parties have claimed at regular intervals that a crisis in social democracy is near at hand. This crisis theory was and still is based upon an economic interpretation of Marxism. Long range conclusions are drawn concerning developments at the ideological level, on the basis of phenomena at the economic level. They have disregarded the enormous ideology producing power which is created by capitalism's continual re-recreation, and instead viewed bourgeois ideology as an external (deceiving, manipulating) relationship. It has been believed by them that an economic crisis will lead immediately to a crisis for the social democratic party. In reality however, instead of speaking of a crisis in social democracy or reformism, one should be concerned with a crisis in Marxism's understanding of the basis of reformism. It can be objected however that if communists previously too easily predicted crises for social democracy, it now seems that we have landed at the opposite extreme. Social democracy appears unbeatable. Its ideology seems always to be verified in practice. Its creation and re-creation appears predestined. There does not seem to be any possibilities for the communist movement to make inroads in countries where social democracy is strong, as it is for example in Sweden, and where the political situation is relatively stable. It seems one is forced to simply sit down and wait for a revolutionary situation.

This impression results primarily from the fact that we have operated at a very general level; we have chosen to portray a 'motionless' capitalism in order to better view the basic mechanisms through which the social democratic ideology operates. If we move to the concrete level — we set the system in motion — it is then seen that developments are not predestined.

Concrete capitalism develops unevenly. One branch expands, another stagnates; one geographical region is depopulated, another is over populated, one age group is pushed aside, another receives relatively good wages; one sex or race is favoured at the cost of the other, etc. It is this uneven development which creates the basis for a policy which can break large groups of people away from social democracy's grip. We can note how during the parties, the Italian and Finnish communist parties suddenly mobilised completely new strata such as farmers, crofters and day workers. In today's more modern reality we can see how VPK's recent small election successes in the working class are in the new proletarian residential areas with their exploitative rents and inadequate social milieu.

Social democrats often say disparagingly that communist parties are discontent parties which pursue a policy of excessive demands. Regarding the characterisation, 'discontent' party, this was obviously the case. It is when capitalism reveals its unsuitability in both small or large issues, that the objective conditions for a revolutionary consciousness and a revolutionary policy can emerge. The concept of 'a policy of excessive demands' is more difficult. As we earlier pointed out there is in ideologies in general, and in the social democratic ideology in particular, a moment of self-fulfilling. One claims that certain demands are impossible, then fights against them thereby showing them to be unrealisable. Within certain limits social democratic 'representative realism' is a self-fulfilling realism. That which is excessive in a situation with a divided workers collective can, in a situation with a united workers collective, very well be too modest. In the first situation but not in the latter, social democratic ideology is verified (and re-enforced) and the communists appear unrealistic. However inasmuch as it is impossible to precisely judge when and where situations emerge which cause workers to function as a conscious collective, a policy of 'excessive demands' is a necessity.

This self-fulfilling moment always favours the stronger, and in Sweden it is therefore social democracy. If one considers this, in and of itself gloomy relationship, along with what was said earlier concerning capitalism's uneven development, certain hopeful signs may be perceived. This uneven development makes possible breakthroughs into the strata dominated by social democracy, and thus indicates the possibility of consolidating that which has already been won.

Notes

[1] In 1970.
[2] Literally, 'ore area' in Northern Sweden.
[3] The Mining company.

This article originally appeared in Swedish in the Independent Socialist political journal *Zenit* in the early seventies.

5 Post-war Swedish Capitalism

Lennart Berntson

Economic growth and employment

To gain a better appreciation of the background to numerous economic problems it is helpful to begin with a study of: GNP growth in general; the performance of individual sectors in the economy; and changes in the occupational structure.

By international comparison, Swedish GNP growth has stagnated during the postwar years. However, in Sweden as in all advanced capitalism, economic growth during this period has most certainly been greater than during the interwar years. This was especially true for Sweden from 1960-65, when GNP growth was high even by comparison with other OECP countries.

It is nevertheless evident from the table below that the first half of the sixties was an exception to the general postwar growth rate. Of even greater significance is the fact that while Sweden enjoyed the highest interwar growth rate in advanced capitalism, in the years since 1945 it has experienced almost the lowest.

Table 5.1
Changes in GNP in terms of volume

Per cent per year:				
1950-1960	1960-1965	1965-1970	1970-1975	1919-1939
3.4%	5.4%	3.9%	3.8%	approx. 3.5%

Source: L. Jorberg, *Swedish Economy*, p.49; R. Bentzel, *Swedish Economy*, p.85. *Swedish Economy* is edited and published by B. Sodersten. Further, A. Lindbeck, *Swedish Economic Politics*, pp 14-15; 1970-71, pp 12, 21, 24. (S.O.U.)

One explanation of this deteriorating international position is the argument that because Sweden did not have any of its productive apparatus, transportation and communications systems, housing, etc., destroyed as a result of the second world war hostilities, it did not experience the same increased postwar reconstruction demand as did nearly all other capitalist countries. To some extent this argument is correct. Clearly, however, there is no unambiguous connection between postwar reconstruction and rapid economic growth, inasmuch as there are several war devastated countries such as England and Belgium which have had a postwar growth rate even lower than that of Sweden. Switzerland which was a non-belligerent, had a high post-war GNP growth rate. Finally, it follows that Sweden's high comparative position in terms of growth rate during the interwar years must be understood against the background of the first world war which, in principle, should have had the same effect on the relation-ship between demand and growth as did the second world war. Consequently it follows that to a significant degree the worsened growth rate *vis à vis* other capitalist nations, must be attributed to factors other than the influence of the second world war.

The structure of the development of production

In order to gain a clearer picture of the stagnation in the growth of the GNP, a comparison should be made between the growth rates of the various sectors of the economy.

Table 5.2
Changes in production growth in the various economic sectors. Comparison between 1960-65 and 1965-79.
Changes in volume

Per cent per year:

Economic sector	1960-65	1965-70	Difference
Agriculture	−0.8	−1.8	−1.0
Construction industry	7.2	1.9	−5.3
Power production	7.9	5.4	−2.5
Industry	8.0	5.6	−2.4
Retail	5.2	3.3	−1.9
Private services	4.7	3.2	−1.5
Real estate	5.7	4.3	−1.4
Communications	4.3	4.6	+0.3
Public services	3.6	4.6	+1.0
Forestry	0.9	3.6	+2.7
All commodity and power production	6.8	4.5	−2.3
All service industry	4.7	4.0	−0.7
GNP	5.4	3.9	−1.5

Source: Sou 1970:71, p.60

61

As table 5.2 indicates, the growth rate in power production and the retail sector has decreased appreciably more than in the service industries. The bulk of the decrease however can most certainly be attributed to agriculture and the construction industry, but even the stagnation in general industry is notably large.

It is perhaps important here to emphasise the fact that industry had a higher growth rate during the sixties than in the fifties. As table 5.2 shows, this is the result of the high growth rate during the 1960-65 period. In the subsequent years the rate dropped to only half a per cent above the level of the fifties. Within industry the increase in production was 4.6 per cent during the fifties, as opposed to 6.4 per cent during the sixties. If we limit ourselves to looking at the growth of industry and draw a comparison between the fifties and sixties as to how fourteen specially selected branches are clustered in relation to the average rate of growth during the respective periods, we arrive at the following figures.

Table 5.3
Branches of industry respectively over and under the average production growth rate for the 1950s and 1960s respectively. Per cent per year. Fourteen specially selected branches.

Average growth within the fourteen selected branches: during the fifties — 3.7 per cent; for the sixties — 5.0 per cent.

Growth branches	Percentage over the average	
	1950-1960	1960-1969
Chemical/technical	+1.3	+5.4
Engineering industry	+2.9	+3.2
Steel and metal industry	+2.6	+2.0
Rubber goods industry	+2.1	+1.5
Gravel and quarry	+0.4	+1.4
Lumber industry	−2.2	+1.0

Stagnation branches	Percentage under the average	
	1950-1960	1960-1969
Shoes — leather	−5.2	−3.6
Textiles	−4.1	−2.3
Clothing	−2.9	−3.2
Foodstuffs	−1.4	−1.1
Shipbuilding	−0.7	±0.0
Printing	−0.5	−0.7
Mining	−0.3	+1.1
Pulp and paper	−0.1	+1.1

Source: SOU 1971:5, p.55.

It is clear from the above data that those branches of industry which had an above average growth rate during the fifties were even further above the average during the sixties. In those branches however, which had a below average rate of growth, during the fifties, numerous of them experienced a further worsening of their position during the sixties. Put more directly: the gap in the production growth rate between the 'growth' and the 'staganating' branches had increased further during the 1960s.

Of equal interest however, is a comparison between the production growth rate of Swedish industry and that of other advanced capitalist countries.

To be sure, such a comparison makes clear that the trend in production growth in Swedish capitalism fairly well follows the international pattern. More important though is the fact that of those branches of industry which lay below the international average production growth rate, during the 1960-66 period, nowhere did they manifest as low a growth rate as in Sweden. This was particularly the case with textiles, clothing, shoe leather, and with only slight exceptions, in the foodstuffs, pulp and paper, paint and rubber industries. Among those branches of industry with a production growth higher than the international average, the Swedish branches of these industries were significantly closer to the average — the only and important exception being the Swedish engineering industry. [1]

Consequently, such an international comparison makes clear the existence of a not insignificant number of branches of industry that currently no longer play the same important role they once did in the growth of production, employment and investment. For Sweden's part, these branches manifest a greater degree of stagnation than is the case in almost any other advanced capitalist country. Presumably, causes behind this stagnation of production growth vary sharply between the affected branches. This however does not alter the fact that the overall effects of this stagnation hits the working class first and hardest with regard to employment opportunities, scope and possibilities for increases in real wages, worsening working conditions, etc.

Changes in the occupational structure

Agriculture was the only economic sector in which there was an absolute decline in employment during the 1950s. In every other sector of Swedish capitalism there were varying degrees of increase although the growth in employment in the service industries was greater than in retail production. Undoubtedly the most striking change in the employment structure during the sixties was the enormous growth of the public service sector. From 1960-70 the total number gainfully employed in this sector increased no less than 69.4 per cent, or in absolute numbers by 309,000. The next most important shift in the occupational structure was the post-1965 absolute decline by 32,000 of employment in industry. Apart from cyclical variations, it was the first time since the breakthrough of industrialisation that employment in industry had decreased in absolute numbers. According to the governments 'long range study' of 1970, that decline may be expected to continue by a further 55,000 during the first five years of the seventies. This involves a consequent structural change within Swedish monopoly capitalism.

Table 5.4
Total employed within various economic sectors
1960-1970/75, in thousands

Economic sector	1960	1965	1970	1975
Agriculture and fishing	477	347	258	191
Forestry	114	106	87	62
Industry	1108	1157	1125	1070
Construction	301	353	360	364
Retail	447	479	497	505
Communications	254	257	264	272
Private services	372	379	387	404
Public services	445	565	754	939
Others	54	64	74	87
Total	3572	3707	3806	3893

Source: SOU, 1966:1, p.76; SOU, 1970:71, p.63

If one only considers the employment in industry during the post-war period it appears to have increased by 1.0 per cent per year during the fifties, but by only 0.2 per cent annually during the sixties. If we further limit this observation to only a consideration of the sixties it is clear that employment decreased annually in the stagnating branches in the following order: (beginning with the most severe decline) textiles, shoe leather, mining, clothing, petroleum, coal, ship building and pulp and paper. It should be emphasised that what is involved here is an absolute decline within all these industrial sectors among which the ship building, mining, petroleum/coal, and the pulp and paper branches must be counted as belonging to those sectors with both high capital intensity and concentration. The largest rise in employment is accounted for by the engineering and the chemical industries. The increase in these sectors however is considerably less than the yearly decline in the previously listed sectors.

Against the background of these figures on developments in employment in Sweden during the sixties, the driving forces behind the drastically accelerated regional imbalance in Swedish monopoly capitalism became clearer. The closing of smaller farms, rationalisation within forestry and mining, together with stagnation in the sawmill and pulp and paper industries are the basic factors behind the mass unemployment which arose in 'Norrland' (Northern Sweden) during the sixties.

It is often claimed that a reduction of employment in industry is intrinsic to the nature of capitalist development. As an abstract, absolute developmental tendency, apart from all counter factors, this is probably correct. But to claim that such a trend existed within advanced capitalism as a whole during the sixties is a highly dubious assertion. Only three additional countries can lend support to such a statement, specifically USA, Belgium and the Netherlands, the first two of which at least, have been immersed in pronounced economic and social crises. In all other advanced capitalist countries industrial employment has either increased or remained constant. [2] The fact that Sweden is one of the four countries in which industrial employment has declined clearly illuminates the difficulties Swedish monopoly capitalism has run into in recent years. Against the background of the trends in the GNP growth rate, developments in the structure of industrial production, and changes in industrial development, it is clear that the accumulated problems of Swedish capitalism are not of a temporary, conjunctural nature but in all probability associated with deeper changes in Swedish economic structure. The following sections will deal with some of these changes.

The bourgeoisie and the rate of profit

Compared with many other western nations, Swedish capitalism has had a long list of advantages: it was able to maintain an intact productive apparatus through two world wars. The depression of the thirties followed a relatively mild course in Sweden, i.e. through the anticyclical price and commodity structure of export. [3] Further, Swedish monopoly capitalism has received the support of a strong co-operation oriented labour movement. These and numerous other factors have resulted in giving Sweden a comparatively higher growth of real wages and thereby a higher living standard than almost all other advanced capitalist countries. In its turn, the strong purchasing power of this domestic market has provided a base for the expansion of Swedish monopoly capitalism. As Swedish big business grew in size and capacity however, the domestic market became too small to absorb — particularly during the high profit return period of the fifties — the accumulated capital. Due to this and other factors, Swedish monopoly capitalism has been forced to seek new and alternative markets and investment opportunities.

Two further factors have nevertheless attributed to the aggravated situation for monopoly capitalism in Sweden. First, international competition has intensified considerably, not the least the result of the expansion of a small number of giant multi-national corporations, compared to which even the largest Swedish companies are small. Further, the European Economic Community has increased its purchasing strength while at the same time encircling itself with customs barriers.

Direct investment even for large Swedish companies, has become an ever more common way of getting around these barriers. The combined effect of these factors has grown in strength since the early sixties. Almost all the difficulties facing Swedish capitalism which were outlined in the introductory discussion, are associated with these developmental tendencies.

Monopoly capital and the bourgeoisie

If Swedish monopoly capital, through a relative decline in the domestic market and increasing international competition is faced with intensified competitive conditions, then it should be manifest in a falling rate of profit. Before investigating this however, it is important to make clear the internal distribution and relationships of power within the bourgeoisie, and try to evaluate the position of monopoly capital *vis à vis* the other sectors of the bourgeois class. Contrary to widespread opinion, the bourgeoisie is not a united and cohesive class. It is divided into a number of different factions between which of course a high degree of fusion prevails. The latter particularly involves, and has done so for a long time, relations between industrial and bank capital which is more commonly referred to as finance capital or big finance.

Since the thirties, the faction enjoying hegemony within the Swedish bourgeoisie has been monopoly capital. This designation encompasses however a larger grouping than simply finance capital.

Monopoly capital properly includes all capitalists or owner groups who occupy a monopoly position within a certain branch or market, i.e. that group of companies which dominate a particular branch to the degree that they have the final or determining voice concerning the competitive conditions of the branch. Defined in this way, monopoly capital accounts for approximately 150-200 of the largest companies in the country. Within this group, finance capital holds the determining power position. Swedish monopoly capital's dominant position within industry is clear from table 5.5.

Table 5.5

Production value in industry in 1963 given in percentages according to different size categories

Large companies with rank number	
1-50 (private)	37.5
51-100 (private)	8.9
101-200 (private)	6.1
State companies and factories	6.0
Various co-operatives	5.4
Other private companies (approx. 12,500)	36.8

Source: SOU 1968:5, pp 13, 56.

The overwhelmingly dominant position of monopoly capital in relation to the rest of the bourgeoisie is best demonstrated by the fact that the 50 largest companies account for a greater share of the production value than the remaining 12,500 small companies.

In turn the dominant position of finance capital within monopoly is clearly demonstrated by the overview below:

Table 5.6

The influence of finance capital within monopoly capital

Large companies with rank number	Total large companies belonging to finance capital
1-30	24
31-61	19 (43 accumulated total)
61-100	14 (57 accumulated total)
101-200	11 (68 accumulated total)

Source: SOU 1968:5, p.129.

The degree of monopolisation within the various branches of industry is, as the definition suggests, intrinsically related to monopoly capital's influence within the respective branches. Consequently, one cannot only detect the degree or concentration from the table below, but also the industrial base of Swedish monopoly capital.

Table 5.7
Degree of concentration.
Large companies' percentage share of production value. Year 1963.

1	Mining industry	100
2	Metal works	98
3	Chemical industry	91
4	Electro-technical industry	89
5	Pulp and paper industry	87
6	Beverages and tobacco industry	74
7	Transportation industry	72
8	Food industry	63
9	Engineering industry	63
10	Textile industry	56
11	Gravel and quarry industry	50
12	Leather, fur and rubber industry	48
13	Chemical-technical industry	47
14	Saw and planing mills	47
15	Printing industry	40
16	Metal manufacturing	36
17	Sewing industry	22
18	Woodworking industry	16

Source: SOU 1968:5, p.58

Monopoly capital must be viewed as occupying a dominant position down to and including the engineering industry. As is well known, the tobacco industry is controlled by a state monopoly, and within the food industry, farmers' co-operatives hold a strong position. Even within certain markets in the gravel and quarry branches, monopoly capital occupies key controlling positions, although the branch as a whole is not particularly highly monopolised.

In the last analysis, the developmental tendency at least up until 1967, has been towards an increasing degree of concentration within numerous branches of industry. In all probability this tendency has continued after 1967, however there is as yet no systematic data available. [4]

To return to the issue of the development of the rate of profit, there quite naturally does not exist any calculation, according to the Marxist definition of the rate of profit (relationship between surplus value and the fixed, plus variable capital). But quite apart from this factor, it is in the last analysis the current disparate character of available calculations which make such an assessment problematic. Nevertheless, judging by material available there has been a decline in the average rate of profit during the sixties, particularly if comparisons are made with the high profit years in the immediate aftermath of the second world war.

Table 5.8
Operating profit as a percentage of real capital volume.
All industry.

Year	Per cent (approximately)
1953	6.5
1955	6.7
1957	6.8
1959	8.1
1961	7.0
1963	6.3
1965	5.8
1967	4.3

Source: *Wage Growth and Social Economy*, diagram 6:1

Even a somewhat more precise study of all industry in which operating profit prior to taxation was calculated as a percentage of capital in buildings, machines, and stock after estimated depreciation reveals a decline from 7.8 per cent in 1960 to 4.3 per cent in 1967. [5]

The government's own 'long range study' also concluded that an overall decline had occurred in the gross profit margin in Swedish industry. Broken down into individual branches, the profit deterioration takes the form of table 5.9.

Concerning what in the final analysis is a statement of the division of earnings between capital and labour (the so called income factors), the government's long range study suggests that in the first half of the sixties a certain shift has occurred to the advantage of labour, while the latter half of the sixties was characterised by a stabilisation of the proportional distribution of earnings.

Table 5.9
Gross profit as percentage of sales changes between the
periods 1960-64 and 1965-68

Branch	Change between the periods
Metal/engineering	−0.9
Gravel/quarry	−2.3
Lumber	+2.2
Pulp/paper	+0.5
Printing/woodworking	+1.6
Food industry	+0.1
Textile/sewing	−0.6
Leather/fur/rubber	+0.1
Chemicals/chemcial-technical	−1.7
Total industry	−1.2

Source: SOU, 1970:71, p.158

From the figures above it appears that two cautious conclusions can be drawn. Firstly, there has occurred a decline in the rate of profit during the 1960s. According to the chairman of the board of the Commerce Bank (Handelsbanken), Tore Browdahl, beginning in 1965 the actual earnings — dividends plus exchange profits — sank below the rate of interest on bonds.

Earnings in large corporations were approximately 6 per cent, while interest on bonds rose to over 7 per cent. Browdahl estimates earnings for the period 1950-65 at 10 per cent. [6]

It should be noted here that profit volume as manifest in current prices could have risen during the last five years even while the rate of profit declined. Nevertheless it is on the basis of the latter that one must assess the condition of capitalism. Secondly, it seems likely that the fall in the rate of profit will not be as far reaching for Sweden, in any case not for Swedish monopoly capital, as it has been for example for England, Italy and West Germany. [7]

The decline of the rate of profit: effects and countermeasures

Many current problems confronting the working class arise from the new phase which Swedish capitalism has entered since the mid-sixties. Among other things, this new phase is characterised by the fact that Sweden can no longer exploit the exceptionally advantageous conditions it previously enjoyed in comparison with the rest of

Europe — the avoidance of domestic industrial and civilian destruction in two wars and a comparatively milder political and economic crisis during the thirties. The positive impact of these factors however declined at about the same time that the domestic market became increasingly unable to absorb monopoly capital's growing capabilities for investment and commodity production. Parallel to this was the emergence of the special problem of the tariff protected European Common Market and the rise of increasingly keen international competition since the mid-sixties. These new conditions, which to a certain degree Swedish capitalism had in common with many other advanced capitalist countries, have given rise to a situation where the bourgeoisie's rate of profit has begun to decline.

The effects of the decline of the rate of profit and the counter-active measures which were more or less consciously and systematically taken by the bourgeoisie will be analysed below. An important problem here is to assess the degree to which there exists an exclusively economic solution to the present difficulties. In the long run it is dependent upon the comprehensiveness and intensity with which the solutions devised by the capitalist class became the burden of the working class.

The most direct effect of a decline in the average rate of profit is a corresponding drop in the rate of investment, first in industry, but consequently even within the retail trade and private services. And, quite correctly, there has occurred just such a decline in the rate of investment (in the first instance for the entire economy in relation to fixed gross investments as a percentage of the GNP). Since 1934 the investment rate in Sweden has manifest a growth trend. In 1965 however, that upward rising curve was broken and has since that time continued to fall.

On the basis of a comparison between the growth of investment (changes in volume; percent per year), in different business sectors it is clear that for industry's part, there has been a decline in growth during the latter half of the sixties compared to the growth conditions of the fifties. Further, after 1965 there occurred a surprisingly drastic reduction — an absolute decline — of investment volume within the private service sector and particularly in the retail sector. From 1950 to 1965 these two sectors on the other hand, had experienced an incredibly rapid investment growth rate. The only sector which has had an unbroken high investment pace after 1965 is the public sector. [8] Incomparably the most rapid growth during the post war period has been witnessed in municipal investments. The increase between 1950-69 was 37 per cent, which is five times greater than the percentage increase in the total investment volume. [9]

Table 5.10
Fixed gross investments as a percent of GNP.
Yearly volume. Current prices.

Year	Investment rate
1930	16.0
1934	14.0
1935	16.5
1939	19.9
1945	16.7
1947	22.2
1950	20.6
1955	22.7
1960	24.8
1964	25.9
1965	25.7
1969	22.7
1975	21.5

Source: L. Lundberg, *Capital Development in Sweden, 1861-1965*, p.148; Westerlind-Backman, Sv. ekonomis.

The degree of self-financing within a company is intrinsically related to investment development. Since the sixties in particular, this has dropped overall in industry. The decline is especially noticeable in the export industries. The probable cause of this situation is of course the declining profitability of capital. According to the prognosis of the government's long range study the degree of self-financing is expected to sink from 90 per cent (for all industry) in 1965-68 to approximately 70 per cent by 1975. [10] To be willing to finance investors have in the past and will in the future, demand a continually greater degree of external borrowing. The implication of this is partially a negative effect on the willingness to invest and partially the fact that an increasing number of companies will become more dependent upon finance capital.

Foreign expansion

An important index of the waning significance of the Swedish domestic market is the fact that the share of total production going to export sales has increased throughout the sixties. Today, more than 40 per cent of total domestic industrial production goes to foreign markets. [11] Of equal importance however is the fact that the export of surplus money capital has great significance in a situation where the domestic rate of profit either wanes or falls.

There can be no doubt that such a driving force gained a more prominent place during the sixties among those factors which determine capital export. Between 1960-65 for example, foreign investments increased by 80 per cent, a figure which is far above the domestic investment growth rate. During the same period the total number of persons employed by Swedish-owned foreign firms grew at four times the rate as employment in the domestic economy, or, in absolute numbers foreign employment grew from 128,500 in 1960 to 191,000 by 1965. In relation to both employment and investment, the bulk of the growth occurred in the engineering and chemical industries. From this fact and on the basis of other studies the conclusion may be drawn that it has been primarily monopoly capital which has accounted for foreign expansion. To a certain degree, such expansion probably offers significant possibilities for the large company to counteract both the tendencies, as well as the actual fall in the rate of profit. [12] These relationships further emphasise the powerful objective basis underlying Swedish monopoly capitalism's efforts to tie Swedish capitalism to the European Common Market. This is an interest it shares with the medium size companies within certain so called growth branches — metal, engineering, chemical-technical and chemical industry.

A further method which is closely related to the internationalisation of capital, is to allow crisis ridden Swedish companies to be purchased by foreign capitalists. This was the case with the reconstruction of the engineering industry Billman-Regulator in Stockholm. Another example is the transfer of the Oscaria concern to foreign ownership. In the present situation however, this is not a realistic, if even a particularly necessary solution. Further, the Swedish market is clearly not an especially attractive area. Consequently the operations of foreign firms in Sweden are quite limited. In 1962, only 62,000 people were employed by foreign-owned companies and since then there has been no drastic increase in that figure. [13]

Increased concentration of capital

The decline in the rate of profit has been accompanied by an enormous increase in the centralisation and concentration of capital. During the entire postwar period there has been no comparable increase in total amalgamations and purchases of companies to match that which has occurred since the first years of the sixties. In only a few years beginning around 1963-64, more mergers have been carried out than during the entire previous twenty-year period. This involves also a qualitative change in the earlier successive increases of capital concentration.

Table 5.11
Total mergers and co-operation agreements within industry, 1958-66

1958	42
1959	42
1960	92
1961	113
1962	114
1963	147
1964	163
1965	230
1966	296

Source: B. Ryden, *Skandbankens Kvartalstidskrift*, 1967:2 (Skandia Banks Quarterly Publication)

This same tendency can be seen in the total number of persons affected by announced production cutbacks. In 1962 the total number of workers affected was 4,049, a figure which had at that time been relatively constant for some years. Two years later the total affected had in fact declined to 2,852, only to increase one year later to 6,004, and the year thereafter to 9,983. After 1966 both the total number of business mergers and affected workers has increased still more. In 1969 the number of affected workers was 11,000, in 1970 approximately 21,000, and in the first half of 1971 it was an even 14,000. [14]

This increased concentration of the capital has naturally affected the various sectors of the small bourgeoisie most profoundly. From 1950 to 1964 the total number of workshops within industry employing less than 10 workers, decreased by 5,202. [15] With regard to the commercial petite bourgeoisie, this decline can be seen in the total number of retail shop closures. In 1951, there were 69,471 retail shops. Twelve years later the number had declined to 57,158. Of this decrease, grocery stores accounted for 9,200 and the clothing branch for 1,800. [16]

Finally, small agricultural operations declined in numbers during the fifties by approximately 55,000. During the sixties this 'rationalisation out of existence' was further hastened, so that by 1967, more than 70,000 small farmers were proletarianised. [17]

The most important effect of this increased capital concentration is the fact that it is closely followed by a corresponding increase in capital intensity within industry, and thereby an associated rise in productivity.

Table 5.12
Capital intensity and productivity within industry.
Annual change in percentage

	1950-60	1960-65	1965-70
Capital intensity	4.8	5.3	7.2
Productivity	4.0	7.8	7.6

Source: SOU 1970:71, pp 63 and 94

As a consequence of the concentration of capital and as a method of counteracting, in any event in the short run, the decline in the rate of profit, capital intensity has increased continually during the entire postwar period. This has probably led to a situation in which the volume of capital per worked hour is greater than within almost every other advanced capitalist country. This has also meant that the rate of obsolescence and depreciation of old capital has increased, consequently shortening the life of capital. [18] In the short run these conditions contribute to a strong competitive ability for Swedish monopoly capital, *vis à vis* both the foreign and domestic bourgeoisie.

At the same time however, these developments have caused another new and important change in the condition of Swedish capitalism. The rate of increase of employment in industry which during the fifties hovered around 1.0 per cent per year, dropped to 0.2 per cent during the sixties. It is unlikely that this decline is the consequence of decreased growth in the volume of production, for even after the drop in 1965, production growth has still been higher than during the fifties (see page 62). Instead it is more a direct result of the huge increase in capital intensity and productivity. It has now gone so far that during the latter half of the sixties 'absolute employment' decreased by 32,000 and the next five years is expected to witness a further decline of 55,000 workers. The implication of these developments is that a continued emphasis on heavy investment within the growth industries results not in more, but rather in fewer jobs.

The growth of wages

In conjunction with the second world war, Sweden attained the highest wage levels in all Europe, a position it has maintained during the entire postwar period. The relationship between Swedish wages and those of other advanced capitalist countries remained constant throughout the sixties. If anything, this wage differential between Sweden and such countries as West Germany, Austria, Italy, France, England, and Finland has increased somewhat. [19] The high wage level in Sweden compared with other countries has certainly been one of the more important causes of the decline in the rate of profit, just as was, from an international perspective, the high capital intensity. In all probability this has been an active factor contributing to the greater difficulties experienced by Sweden's labour intensive branches, such as textiles, shoes, leather, clothing, etc., than has been the case in numerous other western countries.

From the mid-sixties, Swedish monopoly capital, just as the bourgeoisie in its entirety, has engaged in an increasingly intensive resistance to working class struggles for increases in real wages. To a great degree these counter measures have taken place at the level of wage politics in the interaction between the government, LO (the Swedish Confederation of Trade Unions), and SAF (the Swedish Employers Federation). To briefly summarise these developments, only a few points will be illustrated: in the wage study carried out jointly by the LO, SAF, and TCO (The Swedish Central Organisation of Salaried Employees) an attempt has been made to establish a 9 per cent per year limit on wage increases.

This percentage has been generally adhered to during the 1971 settlements between the LO and SAF. For many years employers have demanded that wage drifts be included in the settlement, it was finally realised in this year's agreements. The prerequisite for an informal income policy is a strong co-ordination and centralisation of wage agreements. During the last three contract negotiations, such a development has become consistently more pronounced. This has also been reinforced by government intervention, the Mediation Institute and the state's own wage policy.

Judging by some statistics, it seems clear that wage increases for the working class and apparently for sections of the middle class as well have been successfully forced down. From 1964 to 1968 the annual percentage increase of the workers' hourly wages including the cost of social services was 11.1 per cent; 9.2 per cent; 9.8 per cent; 6.9 per cent.

The corresponding development for privately employed salaried

workers was 8.2 per cent; 10.0 per cent; 8.1 per cent; 6.9 per cent.
[20]

Whether or not there has been a decline in the real wages of the working class and middle class in the last two or three years is difficult to determine. Nevertheless, certain things do indicate a continued relative wage depression after 1968: the meagre 1969 settlement for large groups within the LO, the regressive tax increases of purchase and municipal taxes, the companies, compensating increases in price levels which indirectly raises the nominal wage level and thus pushes large groups within the LO into higher tax brackets. To what extent these factors have led to a direct wage decline for the working class in total must remain unstated, nevertheless in the last four or five years there has obviously occurred in part a clear stagnation in wage growth, and partially, a transference of an ever greater portion of disposable incomes to groceries and rent. [21] It is clear from this that the consumer price index has risen considerably more rapidly than the price index for all other goods, and further, that within the consumer price index, the grocery and rent components have increased much faster than all other components. Yet another factor which seems to indicate a decline in the absolute real wages for some groups within the working class is the explosive increase in social assistance costs, particularly in the large urban areas. The degree to which it is possible for the state and the bourgeoisie to restrain the growth of wages is of course directly dependent on the strength and determination of the struggle of working class unions. Events of the last few years have shown that even the LO bureaucracy represents an obstacle to that struggle.

Unemployment

The combination of factors which has pressed forward the extremely rapid structural transformation of Swedish capitalism during recent years has quite logically had negative effects on employment as well. For the first time since the breakthrough of industrialisation in Sweden there has been a decline in the absolute number of persons employed in industry. The beginning of this as well as a number of other changes can be located in the mid-sixties. The decline is not the result of conjunctural fluctuations in the business cycle, but rather it is rooted in structural shifts in Swedish monopoly capitalism. The most immediate effect has been an increase of total unemployed as seen in table 5.13.

Table 5.13
Total number unemployed, November 1961-October 1970

Year	Unemployed	Relief work	Retraining	Total
1961	63,000	3,000	9,000	75,000
1963	56,000	8,000	14,000	78,000
1965	46,000	9,000	18,000	73,000
1966	60,000	9,000	22,000	91,000
1967	77,000	13,000	28,000	118,000
1968	76,000	19,000	35,000	130,000
1969	64,000	13,000	38,000	115,000
1970	57,000 (avg.)	14,000	49,000	120,000
1971	99,000 (March)	19,100	54,000	172,000

Source: (AMS) Labour Market Board: *Labour Market Statistics.*
From 1965 the number employed in relief work includes archive work and workers receiving health care.

The rise in unemployment caused by structural factors has its analogue in an incredible increase in government expenditures for the labour market policy. The dimensions of these expenditures, together with some even more important figures are shown in table 5.14.

Table 5.14
Expenditures for Labour Market Policies, 1955-70.
Millions of dollars

Year	Relief work	Workers' services	Retraining	Cash support	Total
1955	5.0	.60	—	—	23.0
1960	40.0	.90	10.0	—	127.0
1965	105.0	40.0	35.0	—	248.0
1970	207.0	25.0	128.0	58.0	492.0

(Note: Expenditures for 1970 probably have part of the costs for workers' care transferred among other things, to retraining).

Source: Budget number 1 for the respective years.

Concerning direct unemployment, it is in all probability greater than what the figures presented reflect. Among other things this is due to the fact that the long term unemployed eventually cease to register as unemployed; and, that unemployed women do not seek employment or register themselves as unemployed to the same degree as do men. In spite of the scarcity of statistics it is nevertheless clear that an increasingly large industrial reserve army has been created. Its presence and growth is certainly one of the most important causes of the worsening of the real wage growth of real wages. The higher unemployment, the more effective is the Swedish bourgeoisie and the state at restraining the wage increases primarily of the working class but even of the middle class as unemployment increases in that sector as well.

From the social democratic point of view, the increasing government expenditures in the area of labour market policy, are particularly necessary to dampen the political consequences of unemployment. On the other hand, the frequent claim from certain social democratic circles that the business policy can absorb the rising unemployment in a positive way by means of new industrial investments, is extremely improbable. This may be best seen perhaps in the changes in employment within government owned companies.

Table 5.15
The number employed within state owned companies.
Total and for industry

Year	Total	Industry	Industry in Norrland (Northern region of Sweden)
1955	34,385	15,745	13,034
1960	39,462	17,251	15,219
1965	44,970	22,186	14,545
1970	61,316	23,413	14,189

Source: Statistical Yearbooks, 1955-1970.

The rise in the total number employed between 1965-70 is almost entirely explained by a greatly increased shareholding position in SAS. With regard to industrial employment by government companies however, there has been a clear stagnation in the latter half of the sixties. Considering that even government businesses will now be subjected to so called rationalisation, it is most probable that a further decline of employment may be expected.

The increased intensity of exploitation

In the last few years an increasing number of reports have come forth indicating a worsening of the work milieu in companies — an increased physical and psychological exhaustion of the labour force. The

79

response of the social democrats to these deteriorations has for the most part been an increased demand for workers' participation and co-operation within the framework of individual companies. However, against the background of the facts presented above it should now be clear that the deteriorated work environments are the effects of more structural changes in Swedish monopoly capitalism during the sixties — the declining rate of profit, the stagnation of industrial investments, the greatly increased capital intensity and related to that the new technical work routines, etc. In short the companies' worsened financial situation has led to increased demands being made on the performance of the labour force exploitation of the employed has increased. The consequences of this may be seen in a series of changes in the production processes within individual companies.

Above all, these changes have been felt in an increased work pace with an accompanying expansion of piece work. In 1956 piece work accounted for 61.2 per cent of all man hours within industry, in 1960 it was 63.4 per cent and in 1964, 64.4 per cent. [22] In connection with the introduction of new techniques, there has come to be a more rigid regulation of the labour process, a growing specialisation and increased monotony in individual labour functions. What is more, these changes have ushered in new occupational illnesses and a rise in the number of injuries on the job. [23]

Another index of the worsening profit margins in industry is the growing necessity to exploit even fixed capital to greater degrees, partly through the introduction of shiftwork and partly through staggered employee vacations. In 1965 approximately 8 per cent of workers within industry were involved in double shift work while only four years later the percentage had increased to 13.0. The corresponding figures for three-shift work was 5 per cent and 9.5 per cent respectively. [24] It is sometimes suggested that the worsened working conditions are the result of higher demands made by workers, the implication being that they now are better off. There is more than convincing evidence however (see especially Jepsson and Ågren in this reader) that what is involved rather is an objective, real worsening, which is not attributable to technical developments as such, but rather to the manner in which capitalists have exploited these developments in a tight profit situation. During recent years working class resistance to this deterioration of working conditions, or increased exploitation, has clearly grown in strength. To the degree that this trend continues it will not only become difficult for the bourgeoisie to continue along those lines, but it will also become even harder for the social democrats to confine their counter measures within the framework of individual firms.

Economic policy and the public sector

Currently Sweden has the highest percentage of its GNP going to public expenditures of all capitalist nations. This leading position was first attained in the postwar period, and particularly during the rapid expansion of the public sector during the sixties.

In 1950, at a time when at least five other nations had higher public expenditures (calculated as a percentage of their GNP), Sweden's was 22.4 per cent. By 1960 Sweden had already achieved its top position, with public expenditure totalling 29.4 per cent of the GNP, a lead which has further increased during the sixties by an additional rise to 40 per cent of the GNP in 1968. [25] If one looks at the distribution of these expenditures as manifest in the public investments expenditure patterns, housing, roads, administration, education, health and social care accounted for 74.5 per cent of total public investments. The major part of the enormous increase in the public sector must be attributed to municipal investments and consumption. A comparison involving the volume of growth in per cent per year between municipal and national investments during the postwar period is striking: in the period 1950-60, national investments grew by 4.6 per cent per year, and the municipal by 6.7 per cent; during the 1960-70 period, the corresponding yearly figures were 2.7 per cent and 10.0 per cent respectively. [26]

The increase of public expenditure has had a direct counterpart in the continual and rapid increase of taxes. The share of the GNP accounted for by taxes and other national and municipal fees, including indirect taxation and subsidies, was 25 per cent in 1950, 33 per cent in 1960 and 45 per cent in 1969. On the other hand, as table 5.16 indicates, the transfer of income from the state to households has not increased anywhere near this rapidly.

Table 5.16

	1950	1960	1965	1969
Direct taxes/fees	16.9	22.0	26.1	30.3
Income transfer to households	5.3	4.6	5.1	5.6
Difference	11.6	17.4	21.0	24.7

Source: Westerlind-Beckman, op.cit., p.78.

It should be added here that it is also the indirect taxes, together with the proportional municipal tax which has increased most drastically during the sixties. With these facts in mind, it is certainly no exaggeration to state that the scope for new tax financed reforms in the present economic situation is almost non-existent. An extremely important question, in this context, which cannot be answered here thoroughly enough, is the connection on the one hand between changes in the rate of profit, investment rate, employment, etc., and on the other, the unprecedented increase of public expenditures. For example, has the expansion of the public sector during the sixties required resources to the extent of limiting the growth of private investment? Or has the increase in public expenditures acted as a compensation for, or counter to stagnation tendencies within the private sector?

As far as it is possible to judge, public expenditures have generated a demand for capital and labour power which would otherwise have remained unused. The most obvious are those related to employment, here labour market expenditures in part and partially expansion within the areas of education, health care, etc., have absorbed labour power which Swedish capitalism's weakened expansion power was incapable of employing. Further, it appears the social democratic business policy, through among other things, the use of the investment bank, has come to function as a social and employment buffer within regions and branches hit by crises.

More important however, is the fact that the government's economic policy, just as the LO's so called solidarity wage policy, has very consciously aimed at driving forward an increased capital concentration and degree of monopolisation within industry in its entirety. With that objective in mind company taxation has been designed, investment funds used, and research expenditures, military orders and export credit guarantees distributed. While this cornerstone in social democracy's economic policy has certainly partially counteracted the decline in the rate of profit and maintained monopoly capitals international competitive strength, during recent years it has led to a point where the support and subsidies to big capital have begun to have negative effects on employment along with the political consequences this can entail. If social democracy continues to pursue an economic policy along these general lines, it will in any case be at increased political and social costs.

Political conclusions

Any very precise political conclusions can in principle, never be based simply on economic development tendencies. The economic situation does not stand in direct and unmediated relationship to the political struggle. For a safer assessment of this, it is necessary that the political, organisational and ideological situation of social classes be studied and this is not within the scope of this investigation of the economic structure of Swedish monopoly capitalism. However it is possible on the basis of those facts which have been revealed to establish certain general and objective limitations to the political actions of the bourgeoisie state and the social democratic government; limitations on political actions which previously in the postwar period have not emerged on the same scale and to some degree of difficulty. The first of these constraints has to do with the scope for consumption and wage increases. Due to the decline in the rate of profit, waning investment volume and production development, the general economic scope for real wage rises and consumption increases has decidedly declined. What is more, the high wage levels of Swedish capitalism relative to other advanced capitalist countries, has led to an increasingly more open income policy executed in the co-operation between the LO, SAF and the government during wage negotiations. The decreased scope for 'real' wage improvements, along with the LO's self-appointed role as guarantor of social-economic balance will most certainly lead to an increased division between the LO bureaucracy and the mass of the working class.

The waning, and seen from an international perspective, low production growth of Swedish monopoly capitalism, combined with the exceptionally heavy tax burden which is primarily borne by the working class — has given rise to a situation where the scope for social reforms has been radically reduced. In spite of this, the need for new and expansive reforms is nearly inexhaustible within for example such areas as preschools, working milieu, nature conservation, day care centres, city planning, dental care, motoring, etc. The predicament of social democracy is made even more critical by the fact that no really politically mobilising reform has been carried out since the general supplementary pensions scheme (ATP) was pushed through in 1957-58.

Thirdly, for the first time since the breakthrough of industrialisation in the 1870s, Swedish capitalism has entered into a situation where the employment within industry has begun to decline in absolute terms. This by the way is one of the more important indexes indicating the new turn taken by monopoly capitalism in the sixties. The causal context of this is complicated but a couple of the driving factors seem clear: stagnation within certain labour intensive branches has gone further in Sweden than in almost all other western capitalist countries, with consequent cutbacks in employment. This change has coincided with a more greatly increased capital intensity within the so called growth branches of Swedish industry than in numerous other late capitalist societies. New and costly investments in these branches result in ever fewer employment opportunities. Since the mid-sixties the interplay between these two factors has resulted in a tendencial rise in unemployment which has hit older workers, women, and untrained young workers especially hard.

Both these tendencies, in conjunction with the so called rationalisation of mines and forestry, together with the state initiated closure of small farming, has hit the economy of Norrland (the Northern region of Sweden) especially hard. The political effects of these developments have not failed to become manifest: the working class and the agrarian petite bourgeoisie in Norrland, especially since the LKAB strike, [27] has put up an increasingly strong resistance. Overall the regional antagonisms have been sharpened during the latter half of the sixties, a development which has entailed greater political stress for the social democrats. This trend may be expected to continue regardless of attempts to ease the strain through growing labour market and localisation policy expenditures.

The above described effects of the decline in the rate of profit and the accumulated measures taken to counteract the fall and once again raise the rate has had the important and much discussed consequences of bringing about a real worsening of the work milieu in one work-place after another. The social democratic sector of the labour movement has selected these as the most important issues of the seventies and attempted to confine the solution to the framework of the individual companies. However, the important point here which because of their class function they have either chosen not to or been unable to perceive, is that not only a fundamental solution to these problems, but even a temporary alleviation necessitates intervention into the power relationships of monopoly capitalism. Such a policy however is a far cry from the renewed call for labour/management and government co-operation proposed by the leaders of the social democratic party in the fall of 1971. Just how practicable this approach is in work milieu issues will to a great degree be determined by the size of public expenditures and the general situation of the bourgeoisie and monopoly capital. Considering the narrow economic limits, this approach for LO/SAP's (Swedish Labour Party) part, will in all probability be filled with obstacles and setbacks.

This new phase in Swedish — as well as international — monopoly capitalism however, has led to a more basic dilemma for social democracy and the LO. During the latter half of the 1930s, LO and SAP embarked on an expressed policy of co-operation with bourgeoisie in general and monopoly capital in particular. It is fair to say that subsequently a political alliance emerged between social

democracy and monopoly capital. Manifestation of this were the
Saltsjöads agreement, the post-1935 halt of reforms with consequent
increases in the rate of profit, and the 1938 Göteborgs conference
between big capital and the government. The key point in the social
democratic policy of co-operation has been unwavering support for
the so called structural transformation which Swedish capitalism has
undergone during the last three decades. The favourable political
results of this policy of co-operation for SAP — forty years of
unbroken government [28] — has rested on high and growing
industrial employment, coupled with a rapid growth of wages and
consumption, along with new social reforms.

Since the mid-sixties however, the structural changes in Swedish
monopoly capitalism have entered a new phase characterised among
other things by, declining industrial employment, decreasing real
wage rises and diminishing consumption possibilities together with an
almost non-existent scope for new social reforms. With that, the
fundamental basis for social democracy's policy of co-operation with
monopoly capital has been shaken to its foundations. Due to
external objective conditions the major direction of three decades of
political activity has reached an impasse. Several signs of this have
already been suggested: SAP's efforts to make large companies even
larger and more powerful results today in ever fewer employment
opportunities. The LO's line on wage politics, to consciously attempt
to eliminate smaller and middle size companies having poor wage
conditions, is leading to growing regional and structural unemployment. The same applies concerning the government's support for a
monopoly capitalistic rationalisation of farming, forestry and mining.
For reasons mentioned above, alternate employment opportunities in
the so called growth branches, are becoming increasingly less common.
The only thing that is increasing — and this like an avalanche — are
expenditures for labour market and localisation policies.

Social democracy's traditional policy of co-operation has
consequently been thrown into a crisis, which can be seen in SAP's
declining figures in opinion polls and the rise in the number of
'wildcat' strikes.

SAP/LO are looking for various ways out of this situation. One of
these is the inflated investment efforts in the area of work milieu,
although enough has already been mentioned above concerning this.
Another and related approach, is the company-democracy line which
has gained renewed currency in social democratic ideology. There is
much which indicates that this line has partially altered in character
as a result of the union's organisations and representatives increased
integration and co-operation with the employers. To the degree that

this is the case, the gap between the workers and the union bureaucracy will certainly increase further, in any case if the dominant
economic tendencies continue.

At the 1967 social democratic party conference the widely
discussed business policy was launched. It was claimed that the state
would become involved in those branches of industry where private
capital did not have the ability or could not alone carry the risks with
new investments. In this manner, a growing state company sector,
coupled with the new investment bank would ensure employment in
branches and regions where private capital was incapable of the task.
However, the reality has become something quite different. The
figures relating employment in state owned companies shown above
speaks a truer language than social democratic demagogy. Employment opportunities within state owned companies in industry have
stagnated since 1965, and in Norrland they have in fact declined. To
a great extent, both state companies and the investment bank have
been forced to enter into stagnating branches and crisis ridden
companies: the Karlskrona wharves, the Uddevalla wharves,
Göaverken, Junex, Kalmar factory, and Durex are only a few names
which testify to the setbacks for SAP's business policy. The first
thing that may be expected in the attempt to breathe new life into the
policy will most probably be increased caution and a sharpened
demand for profitability. Nevertheless, there are unlikely to be any
new and fresh sources of employment for the working or middle class.

One further current avenue which the social democratic leadership have steadily moved towards is to attempt to tie in Swedish
monopoly capitalism as closely as possible to the European Common
Market. Even if the association with the European Common Market
can somewhat improve monopoly capital's conditions of
competition, it will not decrease the political pressure on social
democracy.

The conclusion that can be drawn from this abbreviated overview of
social democracy's various attempts to find a way out of the impasse
it has landed in, is that none of the approaches attempted in the last
few years has provided a solution to its dilemma. For obvious reasons
social democracy has been unable to grasp these structural changes
brought on with this new phase of monopoly capital. To what degree
the limitations established by the new stage of development will give
rise to a more deep-going political and ideological crisis within the
entire movement depends to a great extent on the capacity, unity and
fighting power of those political forces which are still found to the
left of the reformist apparatus.

Translator's footnote

The economic trends depicted in this essay have continued in exacerbated form during the past few years. The further intensification of international economic competition has had numerous profound consequences for the structure and development of Swedish capitalism. Some of the more important are the following.

— There has been a spiralling increase in the degree of capital intensity in Swedish industry. The direct results of this have been, growing occupational insecurity, a declining growth rate of industrial employment, rising structural unemployment, deteriorating work milieu, and increasing worker militancy — this latter development may be seen in the relatively large number of 'wildcat' strikes and sporadic 'break aways' from larger unions by more local and specialised sectors.

— The accumulation and concentration of wealth in the hands of Sweden's top fifteen families has continued and with government approval and support the number of annual mergers has increased. The position of finance capital in the Swedish economy has always been strong with the fifteen leading families clustered around three major banks. During recent years these financial institutions have extended their control over the most expansive sectors of industry both in monopoly and non-monopoly branches controlled branches. In the realm of finance itself, concentration through mergers is characteristic. In 1972 the number of dominant banks was reduced from three to two with the merger of the Skandinaviska Banken and Stokholms Enskilda Banken to form the new Skandinaviska Enskilda Bank accounting for 33 per cent of total deposits in Sweden surpassing the powerful Svenska Handelsbanken with 28 per cent of deposits. Also in the finance sector, the early seventies saw the merger of Göteborgs bank and the Smålands bank to form the new Götabank.

— Recent years have also witnessed an increased rate of inflation, stagnation of real wages, a rapid growth (until very recently) of the public sector and a steady rise in public expenditure. Since the 1960-70 decade, Sweden has had the highest rate of public expenditures as a percentage of the GNP of any advanced capitalist country and all indications are that it has maintained this position in recent years.

In summary then, the trends suggested in this essay of declining real wages, increased capital intensity in industry, frequent and widespread occupational and geographical displacement of the work force, growing capital accumulation and concentration, declining employment in industry, and increased public employment and expenditure have continued unabated in recent years in Swedish capitalism.

Notes

[1] Source: SOU 1971:5, p.57.
[2] Source: SOU 1971:5, p.17.
[3] See E. Lundberg, *Konjunkturer och Economisk Politik.*
[4] Source: SOU 1968, pp 5, 129.
[5] Op.cit., p.125.
[6] *Vekans Affarer*, 27/1971.
[7] See NLR, NR 66/1971, p.14.
[8] See SOU 1970-71, p.64.
[9] See Westerlind, Beckman, *Sveriges Economi*, p.67.
[10] SOU 1970:71, p.217.
[11] H. Swedberg, *Svensk Utrikshandel*, p.11; EFO report, p.9.
[12] Much information has been taken from H. Lund, *Svenska Foretags Investeringari Utlandet.*
[13] H. Lund, op.cit., p.15.
[14] TU 1/7/71.
[15] B. Ryden, op.cit., p.51.
[16] SOU 1968:6, p.53.
[17] O. Guldbrandsen, A. Linkbeck, *Jordbruks Politikens Mal Och Medel*, p.21 'The Goals and Methods of the Agricultural Policy'.
[18] SOU 1970:71, pp 212-3.
[19] SOU 1971:5, p.49.
[20] Edgren-Faxen-Odhner, *Wage Growth and Social Economy — Lonebildning och Samhallsekonomi*, pp 32-3.
[21] For price index development see Edgren-Faxen-Odhner, op.cit., diagram 3:2.
[22] The Labour Movement and Technical Development, p.168.
[23] See Olle Jepsson and Gunnar Agren, 'Work Milieu' also included in this reader.
[24] *The Trade Union Movement*, op.cit., p.150 and SOU 1971:5, p.72.
[25] Westerlind-Beckman, op.cit., pp 120-1.
[26] SOU 1970:71, p.60.
[27] A long and bitter wildcat miners' strike in 1970-71 period.

[28] Until 1976 and then only marginally over the nuclear power issue.

This article originally appeared in Swedish in the Independent Socialist political journal *Zenit* in the early seventies.

6 The International Dependence of the Swedish Economy

Karl Anders Larsson

According to liberal theory [1] it is assumed that foreign trade and the international division of labour which arises from it are the result of the particular and distinct conditions of different countries, their so called comparative advantages for an international market. From this perspective, reducing these international relations becomes merely a question of 'technical' substitution, a restructuring of the economy which in turn results in reduced production efficiency and growth because the advantages of international specialisation can no longer be utilised. [2] The government seems to be confronted with the choice of international dependence on the one hand, which implies difficulties in achieving objectives of full employment and price stability, and on the other, a greater degree of independence in achieving these objectives, while at the same time being confronted with a lower growth rate.

A concept such as international dependence cannot be defined within the framework of liberal political economy. [3] Nevertheless, the concept appears often in economic debate. There, however, 'dependence' is not considered as a sociological relationship, but rather within the scope of political economic policy issues arising from balance of payment problems in a system with fixed monetic exchange rates. From this point of view it is supposed that Sweden's foreign dependency would decline significantly if the kronor was allowed to 'float' in relation to other currencies. [4]

From a Marxist viewpoint these perspectives are inadequate because they fail to take into consideration the capitalist mode of production. The prevailing international division of labour is not the result of comparative advantages but rather of the historical development of the capitalist system. To be able for example, to comprehend Sweden's present international economic dependence, requires a theoretical understanding of the world capitalist system with its complicated relationships of dependency and domination. It is of particular importance to make clear the role of the individual states as integral parts of the capitalist system with objective functions to be fulfilled, and not simply as sovereign entities free to choose between independence and growth.

Consequently, it is somewhat meaningless to speak of Sweden's 'economic' dependence, as opposed to its political, military and cultural dependence. The location of Sweden's position within international capitalism requires the clarification of all these types of dependence. That of course, is a very long range study and the present enquiry can be understood only as a pre-analysis on the economic level. I have concentrated primarily on an attempt to empirically illuminate various aspects of the Swedish economy's international dependence, especially the relationships of domination. Also discussed are different forms of capital export and the competitive power of Swedish capitalism. The handful of large Swedish export companies which occupy an exceptional position in both these contexts are brought into relief in a special section and in summarising, their steadily increasing independence from the state is discussed.

Commodity export and capital export

The traditional form of internationalisation of capital has been commodity export. Calculated on the basis of current prices, it is clear from table 6.1, that exports share of the Swedish GNP during the postwar period has been fairly constant. Calculated in fixed prices however, there has been a clear increase. The same phenomenon is observable with reference to the share of the GNP accounted for by imports, the reason being that price increases on domestically sold goods have been higher than on those going to international trade. With regard to commodity export and calculated in 'real' terms, the conclusion can be drawn that Swedish capital has become more international.

The development of the trade balance like a qualitative analysis of foreign trade, offers further information regarding the position of a particular social formation within the system of international capitalism. But should it be concluded for example, that the more finished products a country exports, the higher its position in the hierarchy of international capitalism. Such a procedure is debatable, of Canada's total 1969 exports for example, 62 per cent were processed as finished products, while the comparable figures for Brazil was 70 per cent. Furthermore it is questionable whether this type [5] of vertical division of labour in general, has any meaning or significance for the definition of imperialism and exploitation. Even if it does offer significant insights, [6] it is probable that new types of imperialism can render the old 'raw material imperialism' irrelevant (at least in statistics). [7]

Table 6.1
Export and import per cent of Swedish GNP 1950-70

	1950	1955	1960	1965	1970
Export in percentage of GNP current prices	24.2	24.8	23.1	22.0	24.6
Export in percentage of GNP 1963 prices	18.9	19.3	21.2	22.9	28.7
Import in percentage of GNP current prices	23.5	25.5	23.7	22.9	25.2
Import in percentage of GNP 1963 prices	17.1	20.3	22.1	24.1	29.0

Source: OECD, National Accounts.

The most advanced form of capital internationalisation however, is capital export. Even though world trade is increasing, the relative role of exports in large companies is decreasing. Of the sales growth of 197 Swedish companies in the period 1965-70, 45 per cent of the increase of the 'large companies' was accounted for by intershipment to and sales from foreign located subsidiaries, whereas 26 per cent was increased export. For 'small companies' the corresponding figures were 13 per cent and 23 per cent respectively. [8] There is therefore a pronounced difference between the larger companies which above all expand via foreign subsidiaries and the smaller which expand via commodity export.

Table 6.2 reveals a strong increase in direct Swedish foreign investments during the sixties, both in relation to domestic investments and to export. Sweden's 'direct investment balance', that is to say, the balance of direct Swedish and foreign investment in Sweden, has according to table 6.3 been negative in most years, i.e. Swedish companies have placed more foreign investment than foreign investors have placed in Sweden. As would also be expected, total profits returned to Sweden were greater than those taken out of the country. In this respect it also appears that Sweden's position has strengthened during the sixties.

The foreign owned companies in Sweden are increasing both export and domestic sales substantially more rapidly than Swedish owned companies. However, it appears that foreign subsidiaries of Swedish

Table 6.2

Swedish direct foreign investment as a percentage of
domestic gross investments and export in current prices

	1962	1963	1964	1965	1966	1967	1968	1969	1970
Direct foreign investments as % of gross investments in domestic industry (manufacturing and mine industry	6.0	6.5	10.8	10.0	10.1	9.4	3.9	19.8	12.6
Direct foreign investment as % of export	1.4	1.5	2.1	3.1	2.3	2.0	0.8	3.0	2.9

Source: IMF, Balance of Payments Yearbook; OECD, National
Accounts.

Table 6.3

Balance of direct foreign investments returned profits from
direct investments respectively for Sweden in millions of dollars

	Balance of direct investments	Balance of returned profits
1962	−4	?
1963	23	?
1964	−55	31
1965	−15	26
1966	21	34
1967	−9	30
1968	−59	21
1969	−82	34
1970	−87	30
1971	−91	15

Source: IMF, Balance of Payments Yearbook.

companies (at least subsidiaries of the larger companies) have expanded
more rapidly than foreign companies in Sweden. [9]   The greater
aggressiveness of Swedish foreign subsidiaries than foreign owned
companies in Sweden is also suggested by the fact that during the
period 1946-69, 240 foreign based and owned companies were taken
over by Swedish companies, while only 130 Swedish owned domestic
companies were acquired by foreign companies. [10]   This suggests

93

that Sweden as an individual social formation in the system of global capitalism is 'more dominating than dominated'. This impression is in no way contradicted by international comparisons.

As we see in table 6.4, there are significant differences between the degree of foreign investments' share of domestic investment, and of their share of export. The reason is of course that economies have different degrees of 'openness'. This depends primarily upon the economies' size, but is also influenced by economic policy. Here we are primarily interested in knowing how 'dominating' different countries are. Consequently, it is the second measurement which compares direct investment with export which is most relevant; it reflects the extent to which foreign expansion has occurred in its most advanced form (which affords the greatest possibilities for control and domination).

Table 6.4

Direct foreign investments in percentage of domestic investments in manufacturing and mining industry (1), direct foreign investments as a percentage of exports (2), and the balance of direct investments in millions of dollars (3), for 1970

	(1)	(2)	(3)
USA	11.4	17.5	−5927
Canada	9.6*	2.4*	+474
Japan	1.7	1.9	−261
France	3.3	2.0	+249
Italy	1.8	0.8	+497
Netherlands	19.4	4.7	+24
Great Britain	30.4	9.4	−50
Belgium	10.1	1.6	+162
Sweden	12.6	2.9	−87
Finland	2.7	0.8	+16
Denmark	4.5*	0.5*	+109
Norway	3.4*	0.7*	+12*

Source: IMF Balance of Payments Yearbook; OECD, National Accounts.

*1969.

Sweden is one of the few countries whose companies invest more abroad than foreign companies invest domestically. The USA has, of course, an overwhelming dominance in this respect, and the tendency seems to be the same for Japan (there, however, it seems to be

94

primarily the result of traditional regulations restricting foreign investments in that country). After USA, Great Britain and the Netherlands, Sweden occupies fourth place with regard to share of export accounted for by foreign investments. This ranking presumably gives quite a good picture of Swedish capitalism's international position.

One should not however draw overly hasty conclusions from these figures. In the first place they reflect capital flow for only one year and this could have been an exceptional one in one way or another. Further, direct investments are financed only to a lesser degree from the country in which the head office of the company is located. In the case of American companies the amount is calculated to be 25 per cent. [11] The remainder is financed in part by foreign borrowing, and also through reinvestment of previously earned profits. In the Swedish balance of payments statistics, even these items are included with the information on direct investments. This also appears to be the case for France, Japan, Great Britain and the USA. The information regarding other countries is unclear, consequently the possibilities for comparisons are limited.

Thirdly, even if accurate direct investment information is available, it is still necessary to differentiate between different forms of direct investment by means of an analysis of the position occupied in the imperialist hierarchy by individual countries. In very general terms it is possible to differentiate three types of direct investments:
1) Market exploiting, 2) Raw material exploiting and 3) Labour power exploiting.

In addition, a differentiation should be made between those direct investments which are part of a company's global expansion strategy, (these may be called 'offensive'), and those direct investments which have a more 'defensive' character. A defensive market exploiting direct investment is made in order to retain a market which would otherwise be lost due to trade restrictions or demands for the domestic production of state orders. The earliest direct investments of large companies were often of this type [12] and even today it continues to be a common type. Even companies with global expansion strategies are of course at times obliged to pursue such direct investments.

Offensive market exploiting investments however, aim at carving out new markets, or achieving a more intensive penetration of existing ones. At an early stage of a company's internationalisation process, such investments merely involve the establishment of sales subsidiaries abroad, while at a later stage it entails foreign based production as well. The highest stage of this internationalisation process is characterised by the companies' establishment of some form of international division of labour between its units in different countries. Direct investment at this later stage of a company's development can hardly be accurately related to any of the above three categories.

Labour power exploiting direct investment is most often defensive in the sense that it offers the only opportunity for a company to continue production when domestic wage costs rise. It should be noted that this type of direct investment is not normally market exploiting, but rather, the largest part of production is exported back to the capital exporting country. Finally, raw material exploiting direct investment can hardly be classified as being generally offensive or defensive.

Unfortunately, on the basis of available statistics it is impossible either at the aggregate or branch level to discern these different types of direct investments. At the micro-level the primary question should be whether or not a particular company has a global strategy. In the final analysis, this can only be determined by studying the company's internal organisation, a task which for obvious reasons is near impossible from the outside. However, a general perception can be acquired from the information available concerning the number of countries in which the company is established in various forms (sales companies, branches, franchised production, partial or wholly owned production subsidiaries). Later we will discuss these conditions as they exist in several large individual companies.

Information concerning internal shipments and transfers between central and subsidiary companies in different countries can also provide data on the international status of capital. Such shipments and transfers account for a significant and rising share of total international commodity shipments. A study carried out by Sweden's Industry Association, concluded that the share of such internal shipments among Swedish companies rose from 22 per cent in 1965 to 27 per cent in 1970. [13] The same study revealed that in 1970, the foreign owned companies in Sweden manifested an even stronger integration with sectors of the company located outside the country, 57 per cent of their exports from Sweden were 'internal' shipments. Inasmuch as companies should be compared from the same perspective (i.e. internal shipments from either the central or subsidiary company) these figures are not equatable. Nevertheless, it appears that international companies are becoming increasingly more strongly integrated and that a greater share of international commodity shipments (as was the case at an earlier stage with national shipments) takes place within individual concerns rather than via the market.

The international economic competitive power

The Swedish economy is usually separated into a sector which is exposed to international competition and a sector which is protected from it. [14]   The sector exposed to competition is partially the area which competes through exports, and partially the sector which competes domestically with imports from other countries. Common to both areas are the severe limitations in the area of price setting. Consequently, the growth of profits has come to be almost entirely dependent upon growth of production costs (in the first instance wages) and the growth in productivity. If wage developments proceed at the same pace as the growth of productivity and external prices, then the wage/profit ratio will remain constant.

In Marxist terminology the wage/profit ratio is most closely represented as the rate of surplus value. The rate of profit, which is the critical factor influencing capitalists investment behaviour, is however not simply dependent upon the rate of surplus value, but also on the organic composition of capital. Two English Marxists have found cause to draw the conclusion that:

> The dramatically falling rate of profit in Britain does not seem to have been caused to any significant extent by the increasing organic composition of capital but rather by an increase in labour's share of the product (very roughly the equivalent of a decrease in the rate of exploitation). [15]

Unlike Great Britain, the changes have not been as drastic in Sweden (see table 6.5), but available data indicates that the tendency can have been the same. [16]

Capital in the sector exposed to competition (and especially within the export sector) is also the most internationally flexible, and therefore foreign investment is often an alternative. Unfavourable developments in wages and productivity within this sector would bring about the slow down or closure of Swedish domestic industry and the consequent relocation of a high degree of production in foreign countries, a development which in its turn would result in a greatly worsened trade balance.

The protected sector has a greater possibility of independently determining prices. The result seems to be that this sector has parallel wage and profit growths with the sector exposed to competition. [17] At the same time however, this sector has a significantly slower rate of productivity growth so that the growth of prices in relation to productivity has become disproportionately more rapid than in the sector more directly exposed to international

Table 6.5
Developments in wage share of the product in
several different industrial countries†

	50-54	55-59	60-64	1964	1965	1966	1967	1968	1969	1970
Britain	64.9	67.6	69.2	69.1	70.1	72.7	70.8	72.2	75.2	76.6
USA	69.2	70.7	71.5	70.2	68.8	69.3	70.8	70.8	72.2	
West Germany	59.6	60.3	61.5	62.1	62.1	63.7	63.6	60.7	61.9	
Italy	53.6	67.8	61.7	65.3	62.8	60.9	63.4	62.7	63.7	
Japan††				39.6	41.8	41.0	40.3	41.3	40.9	41.3
Netherlands	54.6	56.6	60.2	62.5	62.8	64.5	63.6	63.4	64.2	
Sweden	66.5	67.1	70.1	69.4	69.3	70.9	71.0	69.9	69.0	

Source: Glyn-Sutcliffe, *British Capitalism, Workers and the Profit Squeeze*, Penguin 1972.

†Wage share is defined as wages and employer paid fringe benefits as a percentage of domestic gross production.

††Large companies.

competition. Inasmuch as a portion of the 'protected' sectors production goes to the 'unprotected' sector as component commodities this fact is not without significance for the international competitive position of Swedish capitalism.

Naturally these relationships continue for a period even after internationally flexible companies have relocated production abroad, but only until a new system of subcontracts has been established in the new locale. For companies under pressure from the growth of production costs in Sweden, but which for one or another reason are unable to relocate outside the country, an alternate possibility is the utilisation of foreign subcontractors. In this manner, the industry of neighbouring Scandinavian states act to an increasing degree as subcontractors for Swedish industry. [18] An illustration of the increasing commonplace of this strategy is the increased proportion of imported component commodities in the Swedish export industry, from 15 per cent in 1957 to 18 per cent in 1964 and 20 per cent in 1968. [19] The consequences of this development is a worsened trade balance and increased difficulties for small and medium sized Swedish industry.

The intensification of international competition during the sixties and early seventies is primarily the result of two factors:

1   Increased competition from countries with low wage rates and intimate state/industry economic co-operation. For the export industry this competition has come primarily from Japan, for those competing with imports, heightened competition has come as well from such countries as Hong Kong and South Korea.

2   The growth and development of technology and communications has enabled the large companies to become more internationally flexible and thus to more intensively penetrate each others markets. In its turn, the intensification of international competition has pressed forward in various countries the creation of larger, more effective and efficient companies within the economic sectors exposed to this competition. Inasmuch as the domestic market has shown no appreciable growth, expansion must be affected through (a) the concentration of capital in the home country, or (b) expansion into foreign markets. For companies located in countries with small domestic markets, (a) is a precondition for the more expansive degree of (b).

In principle, the concentration of capital can proceed in two ways: through mergers and co-operation or by means of the more rapid growth of large companies and the consequent gradual elimination of smaller ones. Studies already conducted reveal that there is hardly any positive relationship between company size and growth rate, rather the relationship appears to be negative. [20] This implies that capital involved in foreign competition must attain greater concentration by means of mergers and co-operation, and this is precisely what has occurred.

During the sixties, merger activity throughout Europe and the USA has increased greatly. [21] It is typical of this process that it has largely taken place within individual states, especially when it involved co-operation between companies of fairly comparable size. [22] This indicates that the process has in the first instance been an effort to develop a stronger national base for foreign expansion, but it has also been due to the energetic encouragement given to such merger activity by the individual states. [23] The paradox of course is that in an effort to prevent a worsened trade balance and the foreign purchase of domestic industry, the state support for the creation of strong internationally competitive industry makes it increasingly difficult for it to control the actions of the large domestic companies as they gain international flexibility and to a growing degree view investment abroad as an alternative to domestic investment.

Table 6.6
Profitability within Swedish industry from 1960-71, calculated as gross surplus prior to reserve stock adjustment through deduction of estimated depreciation in terms of fire insurance value of machines, buildings and stocks. Percent.

1960	1961	1962	1963	1964	1965	1966	1967	1968	1969	1970
7.8	7.5	6.2	6.1	6.9	6.6	4.7	4.3	4.5	6.0	5.5

Source: EFO Report, together with SAF's (Swedish Employers Federation) brochure, 'Facts about Profits'.

Table 6.5 reveals a certain increase in the wage share within manufacturing industry since the fifties. Further, it can be seen that this increase in the wage share has risen most significantly in England, but also in the Netherlands and Italy. Compared with developments in these countries, the Swedish increase is rather moderate. In fact, there appears no reason to make the general claim that wage increases in Sweden have seriously threatened capitalism's competitive strength.

It is apparent from table 6.6 that during the sixties there has been somewhat of a decline in profitability in Swedish industry. Even in the high conjuncture year of 1970, it was no greater than 5.5 per cent While it is indeed true that profitability information is not easy to interpret, there is nevertheless no reason to doubt that the rate of profit has actually declined within Swedish industry during the sixties. However, considering the development of the wage share of profits, it can be assumed that this phenomenon has also occurred in other comparable countries.

Table 6.7 shows the growth of production and productivity in Sweden and a few other comparable countries for the periods 1960-65 and 1965-70. It can be seen that during the first period, excluding Japan, Sweden occupied a leading position both with regard to rate of growth of production and productivity. During the second period Sweden had dropped back, especially in the area of production growth. Due to the rationalisation introduced in this period, Sweden was able to maintain nearly the same level of development of productivity. It is one of the three countries where industrial employment has declined during the 1965-70 period (the others are the Netherlands and England).

Table 6.7
Developmental production and productivity within industry in
some of the more important industrial countries 1960-70.
Annual change in per cent

	Production 1960-65	Production 1965-70	Productivity 1960-65	Productivity 1965-70
Canada	7.0	4.0	4.0	3.0
USA	6.2	4.3	4.8	1.5
Japan	11.6	16.7	7.0	14.0
Denmark	6.1	5.0	4.3	3.9
Finland	6.3	7.4	5.1	6.0
Norway	5.5	4.6	4.1	3.3
Sweden	7.4	4.9	6.0	5.2
Belgium	6.5	5.9	4.4	5.1
France	6.5	6.7	5.9	6.5
Netherlands	6.1	7.6	4.9	8.3
Italy	6.7	8.6	5.2	6.2
West Germany	6.4	5.7	5.0	4.8
England	3.3	2.6	2.9	3.3
Austria	4.5	6.0	4.1	5.8

Source: SOU 1973:21, p.313

As mentioned above, capital in a small country must be more highly concentrated than in larger nations if it is to have effective competitive strength on the international market. Table 6.8 makes clear that studies conducted have verified this proposition; the largest companies control a significantly greater share of the markets in small countries such as Belgium, Switzerland and Sweden than in countries with very large domestic markets. An undeniable characteristic of the Swedish situation is that a small number of large internationally flexible companies — the core of monopoly capital — determine what may be called Sweden's competitive strength.

Some of the biggest companies presently have such a large percentage of their production established abroad, that they may be considered totally internationalised. Their foreign expansion appears beginning to reach a saturation level and it is now primarily certain smaller companies which are increasing their foreign production. In 1965, fifteen of 197 companies studied accounted for 92 per cent of new investments and 88 per cent of foreign production. By 1970 these proportions had dropped to 90 per cent and 83 per cent respectively and plans up until 1973 indicate a continued decline. [24]

Table 6.8
Comparison of the degree of concentration in different countries.
Vaiues refer to the production share of the four largest companies
in the different branches, then calculated together for a national
average which is compared to the value for USA.
Information is based upon investigations carried out in the
respective countries during the period 1961-65

Belgium	1.66
Switzerland	1.63
Sweden	1.54
Netherlands	1.23
Japan	1.14
USA	1.00
West Germany	0.94
France	0.93
Italy	0.89

Source: Pryor, 'An International Comparison of Concentration
Ratios', *The Review of Economics and Statistics*, May 1972.

Even though it is in the first instance the situation in the largest
companies which determine the competitive strength of the Swedish
economy, the significance of developments in other sectors should not
be underestimated. The larger international concerns are dependent
upon a number of smaller companies as subcontractors. Also,
conditions within the other smaller sectors have significance for wage
developments in the entire economy. Finally, even these other sectors
are moving towards internationalisation. This is being effected partly
as smaller and often specialised companies compete by means of
export and even through direct investment for expansion on the
foreign market, and is partly due to the fact that increased
competition from imports make the situation for import competing
industries an even more important factor in the international position
of the Swedish economy.

Where is Swedish capital expanding?

Relatively large changes occurred in the geographical distribution of
Swedish foreign trade during the sixties. Table 6.9 indicates clearly
that the creation of the European Common Market and the European
Free Trade Association played an important role in this development.

There has been a particularly strong increase in imports from other Nordic countries, a development that may be partially explained by these countries' function as subcontractors for Swedish industry. This increase may also be explained by the establishment of Swedish companies especially in Finland in order to take advantage of the lower wage levels which, combined with low transportation costs and the absence of import taxes made it more profitable to produce for the Swedish market in Finland than it would be to produce in Sweden. The extensive interlacing of the Scandinavian economies is revealed also in the fact that no less than 19 per cent of Norway's 1970 imports came from Sweden, with a corresponding figure for Denmark and Finland of 16.5 per cent. [25]   As a comparison it can be noted that of Sweden's imports for the same year, respectively 6.8 per cent and 5 per cent came from these countries. [26]

Table 6.9
Different regions share of Sweden's export and import
for 1961 and 1971

	Export 1961	Export 1971	Import 1961	Import 1971
Scandinavia	22	26	10	20
Other European Free Trade Association countries	14	20	16	19
European Common Market	33	26	40	33
USA, Canada	5	8	12	9
East Europe	1	4	4	5
Underdeveloped countries	11	9	12	10
Others	11	7	5	4

Source: Department of Trade and Commerce.

From table 6.10 indicating the distribution of Swedish companies abroad, it is clear that by far the largest number are located in Europe while the majority of those established in the third world are located in Latin America. Further, it is clear that the EFTA companies are distinctly smaller than the average, a characteristic which is especially true of companies located in neighbouring Scandinavian countries. This is largely due to the fact that it is most natural for smaller companies to first expand into nearby countries, primarily in Scandinavia. However, these countries do not have domestic markets large enough to make large scale production operations profitable.

103

Table 6.10 also reveals that there exist no outstanding differences between the distribution of assets and the distribution of employees. A fact which indicates that there are no great differences in capital intensity in different areas. The one exception to this pattern is Asia which has 8 per cent of the total employees but only 2 per cent of total assets. It seems evident however that expansion in Asia and Africa is relatively insignificant and future developments appear to be moving toward an even lower proportion of total Swedish foreign investment in these areas. Since the LAMCO project raised the figures in the early sixties, investments in Africa especially have stagnated. Half of all subsidiaries on that continent are located in South Africa. In Asia, India occupies a nearly identical position of dominance. [27] Latin America occupies the leading position for overall Third World investment. Subsidiaries in this area are somewhat larger than average and have average capital intensity. It is typical of companies investing in Latin America that they tend to be even larger than companies investing in other foreign areas. [28] Further, the number of production subsidiaries in this area is greater than in any other. [29]

Table 6.10
Swedish subsidiaries abroad.
Percentage distribution 1970 and percentage increase 1965-70

	Total 1970	Assets 1970	Increased assets 1965-70	Employed 1970	Increase of employed 1965-70
(EFTA) European Trade Association	45	20	155	23	37
Scandinavia	27	8	163	10	65
European Common Market	30	51	141	46	21
North America	8	12	63	7	-16
Latin America	8	11	192	12	90
Africa	2	0	-16	0	0
Asia	3	2	0	8	4
Others	4	4		4	
Total	100				

Source: Hornell-Vahlre, 'Swedish Subsidiaries Abroad Increase Heavily', *Industry Association Magazine* 7/70, SOU 1972:90, p.163.

Latin America is also the area showing the most rapid growth of assets and employees during the 1965-70 period. Scandinavia too has been the location of a rapid expansion, while in North America it has been insignificant, with the total number of employees even declining. It may be noted that there exists a difference between the development of export and direct investment. In general, it is difficult to see any effect that the customs tax elimination with EFTA has had on the distribution of direct investment. If trade restrictions were an important cause of direct investment then EFTA's share should have declined, but on the contrary, this area and especially the Scandinavian countries, has been the recipient of one of the highest rates of Swedish capital investment. There is even a difference in the case of underdeveloped countries: while exports to these areas show a relative decline, direct investments are more or less unchanged. Underdeveloped countries, Latin American in particular, are far more significant as recipients of Swedish capital than of Swedish commodity export. This may be partially due to the fact that investments in underdeveloped countries is of a different nature than in industrialised countries, specifically, they are to a higher degree defensively market exploiting or raw material exploiting.

The rapid expansion into Latin America during the last few years indicates however, that it is not simply trade restrictions which have prompted Swedish companies to establish themselves there. It undoubtedly has a great deal to do with the fact that the largest countries (Brazil, Argentina and Mexico) have begun to be attractive markets for industrial commodities. During the last fifteen years these three countries have received 82 per cent of the total investments in Latin America, with Brazil alone drawing one half. [30] During the last few years however, Brazil's share has declined while above all Argentina, but even other smaller countries have increased their share of investments received.

The internationalisation of monopoly capital

As mentioned above, the internationalisation of Swedish capital through direct investment in foreign subsidiaries is almost entirely accounted for by a very small number of large companies. An important aspect of the international dependence of the Swedish economy is consequently directly related to the internationalisation of a handful of companies and it is necessary therefore to identify and study more closely their development. The twelve that have been selected for closer study in this paper are those companies, which according to *Veckans Affarer* [31], had the largest number of employees in their foreign operations in 1971. (Together, these companies accounted for approximately 70 per cent of all employees of Swedish companies located abroad). Table 6.11 presents some of the basic information about these companies. It can be seen that there are clear differences between the twelve companies. Some (SILF and STAB for example) have an overwhelming proportion of their production located abroad and proportionally little export. Other companies (ASEA and Volvo for example) have only a minor part of their production located abroad and have instead large commodity exports. These differences are due partially to the nature of the products produced by the companies, and partially to historical circumstances.

Table 6.11
International operations of some large Swedish companies. 1971

	Employed abroad	Employed abroad in % of total employed	Total invoicing abroad in % of total sales	Export from Sweden in % of total sales	Earnings on working capital (total operation)
SKF	52,141	78.5	91.5	15.2	6.8
LM Ericsson	37,700	56.4	76.7	36.5	10.9
STAB	25,400	75.1	74.1	12.2	8.5
Electrolux	18,489	59.0	68.8	17.7	9.6
Alfa-Laval	9,869	64.5	85.2	29.1	5.7
Atlas-Copco	9,276	64.5	89.3	—	10.9
AGA	8,834	62.4	66.3	8.5	6.8
Sandvik	7,532	40.1	87.1	49.4	7.9
Granges	7,300	29.2	39.6	29.9	3.8
Asea	6,166	16.3	50.2	33.5	5.4
Volvo	5,219	12.7	68.5	50.1	8.1
Svensk Flakt	4,581	53.0	77.2	12.7	6.8

Source: *Veckans Affarer* NR.27/72 together with Sweden's 1000 largest companies.

The companies which today dominate foreign operations are in general the same ones that have always been Sweden's leading large international companies. With the exception of Wicanders which was the first Swedish company to establish itself abroad in Abo, Finland, in 1871, the picture has been completely dominated by those companies which shall be studied here. [32]

In table 6.12 I have attempted to give a view of developments during the twentieth century. However inasmuch as the table is derived from many differentially calculated sources, often with contradictory information, it should be read with reservation. It is clear that as early as the twenties, the massive foreign expansion occurred and that by 1930 still more companies had built up international organisations. In addition, all the subsidiaries had branches and agents in a further large number of countries. Some companies even had extensive international production; in 1930 L.M. Ericsson for example had producing subsidiaries in no less than twelve countries in addition to Sweden. [33]

Typical of these Swedish companies which were internationalised early was the fact that they had a specialised production which was often built upon Swedish inventions (Winquists' ballbearing, Laval's separator, Dalen's matches, etc.) From the very beginning the Swedish market was too small for such production and foreign expansion was necessary. This occurred in the first instance via commodity export, but it soon became obvious that it would be advantageous to establish sales firms abroad to maintain better contact with customers and authorities.

One of the companies which internationalised most rapidly and which is today the most international of all Swedish companies is SKF. [34] The company was formed in 1907 and already by 1920 had established subsidiaries in nineteen countries including production operations in five foreign countries. Ten years later it had subsidiaries in thirty-two countries. [35] In 1971 SKF operated production subsidiaries in twelve countries. Remarkably enough SKF (like Electrolux and Alfa-Laval) had government permission not to give a separate account of stock holdings in its foreign subsidiaries. For this reason it is not possible to attain more detailed information concerning the actual situations.

It is characteristic of SKF that it both has for a long time had an international expansion strategy and has also chosen to focus on a very specialised line of commodities and thus expanded vertically rather than embarking upon entirely new types of production (SKF owns steelworks at Hofors and Hallefors). Currently however, this policy is under review and plans exist to diversify production. Subsidiaries of SKF have seldom been granted any great degree of independence following instead a centrally developed strategy. Typical of this approach is that the profitability of individual subsidiaries are never considered in isolation, but rather viewed in relation to the subsidiaries' function within the overall operation of the company.

SKF has also implemented an ever greater international division of labour with the consequence that within the next five years all parallel production of the same types of goods in Europe will cease and production will be co-ordinated from a new office in Brussels. In

107

Table 6.12
Foreign subsidiaries of large Swedish companies.
Total countries where the company is represented by majority owned subsidiaries

	1900	1910	1920	1930	1940	1945	1950	1955	1960	1965	1971
SKF	–	3	19	31	31	32	32	37	–	–	–
LM	0	5	–	21	22	21	20	20	30	24	28
STAB	–	–	0	31	27	24	23	19	19	22	22
Electrolux	–	–	–	–	–	25	23	23	24	26	33
Alfa-L	2	5	8	11	11	–	–	–	–	–	–
Atlas	0	0	2	2	4	4	11	14	20	24	21
AGA	–	2	14	20	22	–	–	–	–	29	27
Sandvik	0	1	7	–	–	8	12	14	15	25	34
Granges	–	–	–	–	–	2	3	3	3	9	9
Asea	2	2	6	13	16	15	18	21	19	25	22
Volvo	–	–	–	–	–	2	2	2	7	9	15
Sv. Flakf	–	–	0	0	1	–	–	7	12	16	18

Source: Diverse company monographs and anniversary magazines together with various issues of *Svenska Aktiebolag.*

1942, SKF had 72 per cent of its employees abroad, [36] by 1971 the proportion had risen to 79 per cent. This international mobility has naturally been used against the working class. As early as the twenties SKF began to practice the strategy of moving production from companies hit by strikes to corporation companies in other countries. [37] In 1972 SKF had approximately 22 per cent of the Western world's market for rolling stock and was clearly the leading producer in the world. In the last few years, however, competition has increased, particularly from Japan. It is from this perspective one should view the definite new trend towards new areas of production.

Another of Sweden's large international companies, Volvo, is in m many respects the opposite of SKF. Volvo has only a very small share of the world market for cars, not even in the Swedish market is its share larger than 25 per cent. It is still a typical commodity export company with the bulk of production carried out in Sweden. This does not mean however, that Volvo lacks other types of international contacts. The largest assembly plant, in Gent, Belgium, is expanding continually and Volvo even has factories in such far flung countries as Peru and Malaysia in which automobile parts are assembled. In the last few years Volvo has become tied more strongly to the international automobile industry. In 1971 it began a co-operative effort with Renault and Peugeot for the production of motors at a new factory in Northern France. The following year Volvo acquired one-third ownership in the Dutch automobile firm

DAF's passenger car company. At an even earlier stage, Volvo had worked together with DAF, the French company Saviem and the German KHD on the production of trucks. At present, Volvo plans to establish an assembly plant in the USA.

L.M. Ericsson finds itself in a situation which differs from both SKF's and Volvo's. The world market within the telecommunications industry is dominated completely by a small number of large companies, of which LM is the third largest after the American ITT and the German Siemens. LM has approximately 10 per cent of the world market outside the USA and its production is almost totally concentrated in Western Europe and Latin America. The foreign establishment of LM has been dependent upon those special factors which are involved in the production and sale of telephone systems. Often it has been involved in the granting of concessions for the expansion of telephone systems in individual countries, an activity which has frequently been tied to a demand for local production. In several cases LM has even been involved in the running of telephone companies, a business which has now been completely liquidated. For these reasons it has been more difficult for LM to put into practice an international strategy than it has been for a company of the nature of SKF. Today however, the largest part of resources go to keeping abreast of the rapid technical developments in the area of tele-communications and thereby to maintaining or increasing its share of the market in industrial countries. This does not prevent LM from taking part in the ever intensifying competition for the development and expansion of telephone systems in those countries which have not yet fully developed such communications networks. Of the remaining companies AGA and Atlas Copco have patterns of development which are like that of SKF in the sense that it is intimately related to the exploitation of technical knowledge. AGA expanded abroad early by the establishment of foreign subsidiaries. As opposed to SKF for example, such foreign production was pursued from the very begin-ning, above all due to the difficulties of transporting gas long distances. [38] This factor was especially critical in Latin America where the company expanded rapidly. Atlas Copco on the other hand did not really begin its internationalisation before the end of the second world war because the company concentrated completely in the area of compressed air.

ASEA's development has quite naturally had certain similarities to LM's inasmuch as the company is engaged in the same area of production. Nevertheless, the Swedish domestic market has been relatively more significant for ASEA than for LM. This characteristic is partially due to the division of labour which exists between these two Wallenberg companies. Of all foreign markets, the neighbouring Scandinavian countries have been more important for ASEA than for any other large Swedish company. During the 1960s however, a markedly increased internationalisation has taken place into, among other areas, Latin America. ASEA has also begun to work jointly with such American companies as General Electric, American Electric Power and Control Data Corporation (CDC). [39]

Sandvik, STAB and Electrolux have a broader range of commodities produced than any of the companies mentioned above. Sandvik's production can be divided into special steel and hard metal products of which, it has been the latter which largely represents the area in which the company has expanded and internationalised. Electrolux is distinct from the other electrical companies (L.M. Ericsson and ASEA) in that its production is almost totally geared to consumer goods. Originally, vacuum cleaners were the dominant commodity produced, but at present the company sells a wide assortment of consumer goods. Further, the company owns a number of cleaning firms in different European countries.

The match company (STAB) as is well known, has its own special history: it was the central unit in the Kreuger corporation (to which even L.M. Ericsson belonged). Around 1930 it probably had the most comprehensive foreign operations of any Swedish company. [40] The collapse of the Kreuger corporation involved the liquidation of many of STAB's enterprises, but the international character of the company remained. Today it is perhaps the one large Swedish company which most clearly approximates the character of a conglomerate and at present building materials account for both a larger and more rapidly expanding share of sales than do matches. The firm is even beginning to expand into the furniture industry. In every area, only a very small part of production is sold on the Swedish market.

Alfa-Laval which through its predecessor AB Separator was the first large company to establish subsidiaries abroad, has continued to produce for the agricultural sector, above all dairy equipment. Even Svenska Flaktfabriken, previously a subsidiary of ASEA, is expanding rapidly abroad on the basis of specific technological knowledge. Finally, Granges represents an exception in that its foreign operations are almost totally concentrated in its participation in the LAMCO project in Liberia. Apart from the types of involvement outlined above, Swedish capital has very seldom made direct foreign investment in raw material exploitation and in this sense differs markedly from, for example, American capital.

The new role of the state

Because it occupies a relatively autonomous position the state is seen to be capable of acting against the short range interests of capital. [41] But how is it with the large internationally flexible companies? Can the Swedish state actually take action against their short range interests? And if not, can the state continue to fulfil its overriding function of guaranteeing the continued supremacy of capital?

In general it may be said that the strength of the state relative to monopoly capital depends upon two factors: the size and rate of expansion of the domestic market and the international flexibility of monopoly capital. [42] For Sweden's part, both these factors suggest that the position of the state is weak: the domestic market is small and Swedish monopoly capital has a high degree of international flexibility. However, the power relationship is also dependent upon more specific factors.

In an earlier article, I categorised the state's economic functions into four main groups: [43]

1   Short range stabilisation of the economy
2   The furnishing of 'inputs'
3   The acceleration of the concentration process
4   The maintenance of social balance.

To gain a better picture of its possibilities of pursuing a political programme which counters the short range interests of monopoly capital, we shall now look more closely at the manner in which the Swedish state carried out these functions — and in doing so we will limit ourselves to the first three.

There is no doubt that individual nation states are experiencing increasing difficulty in implementing a market policy which includes monopoly capital. This is partially due to the possibilities for companies to adapt production to international economic situations and partially to the internationalisation of the credit market. The task is also made generally more difficult by the demand to maintain the value of the national currency. [44]

The second function, the furnishing of 'inputs', can be carried out in a variety of different ways. In this discussion I shall only touch lightly on the two most important 'inputs', labour power and credits.

The furnishing of labour power involves among other things, the following: 1) education; 2) measures for promoting mobility and flexibility; 3) the guarantee of 'calm' on the labour market (a function which is partially carried out at the ideological level;

4) the furnishing of a reserve army of labour.

In large measure, the Swedish state has carried out these functions in an exemplary manner, but inasmuch as monopoly capital is becoming increasingly international in character, its relative dependence on the Swedish labour force declines and the adeptness of the Swedish state in furnishing the necessary labour force becomes a less important strength factor. There is however another function which the Swedish state can fulfil to 'bind' monopoly capital closer to it, namely, the supplying of research and higher education. If the state is to be able to do this, it naturally entails the restructuring of the entire education policy to meet the demands of large companies, a development which as in many other countries, is occurring at present in Sweden.

Earlier in this paper it was noted that there was a decline in the rate of profit in Sweden during the sixties. This development hardly applied to monopoly capital, but inasmuch as there has been an intensification of international competition, one should not draw the conclusion that 'enormous' profits are being earned by this sector. The degree of self-financing in industry has decreased during the sixties which implies the increased reliance on external financing. In this context the state, through its control of the growing capital in the General Pension Fund has the possibility of increasing its relative strength. Until now the General Pension Fund has been used above all to finance housing construction, but developments are moving in the direction of an ever greater proportion of these funds being loaned to industry. [45] It is perhaps this factor which has given the government the resolve to oppose the short range interests of monopoly capital and propose the purchase of industrial stock with funds from the General Pension Fund.

It has been the heightened degree of international competition which has given emphasis to the state's function in facilitating the process of capital concentration. This involves in the first instance encouraging mergers and co-operation and in other ways supporting monopoly capital in relation to other capital so that large companies will acquire a larger share of Swedish production within their respective areas. Secondly it entails structural changes which concentrate resources in the areas in which monopoly capital is primarily active. Even in this area there are numerous methods to choose from. As is well known, this process has been pursued quite far in Sweden, primarily because smaller industry could only mobilise a weak opposition. However, it might possibly be a policy which has outlived its usefulness. It has succeeded in making Swedish monopoly capital strong and internationally flexible, but now that it has reached that level and become less dependent upon the Swedish economy, monopoly capital's need of such a policy is also diminished.

The conclusions which may be drawn are roughly the following. That capital which is internationally flexible has a strong position in relation to the Swedish state. Today, however, there are scarcely more than a few companies which are really internationally flexible (above all SKF and STAB). Other companies are still dependent enough on the Swedish economy that the state should be able to counter their short sighted interests. However, this possibility decreases with increased internationalisation and consequently the state will experience increasing difficulty in moderating class conflicts in society. Workers' demand for control will increase, and if the state cannot link them to undisruptive channels (which implies that it goes against the short range interests of monopoly capital), the long range interests of capital will be seriously threatened.

In such a situation the Swedish state can in a variety of ways bind monopoly capital to it through a more effective implementation of certain functions than other states or state structures. In this context we have suggested education policy and the General Pension Fund as possibilities available to the Swedish State. But above all, individual nation states will be forced into co-operation to create international institutions in different areas which can carry out functions on behalf of international capital.

Translator's footnote

All available evidence clearly suggests that the developments outlined in this essay have persisted. There has been a steady decline in the relative importance of the Swedish domestic market for most expansive sectors of industry. This, as well as higher than average international wage costs, in the face of intense competition on the international market have encouraged capital concentration, capital intensity and the further shift towards capital as opposed to commodity export. Swedish capital continues to expand abroad at a higher rate than foreign capital is expanding into Sweden. In short Swedish capital has increased its dependency on foreign markets and investment opportunities.

Notes

[1]   J.O. Anderson, *Till Kritiken av den liberal a utrikeshandels teorin*, HFKS 5/1972.
[2]   G. Eliasson, *Diagnosis pa 70-talet*, p.19.
[3]   See G. Hemberg, *Kring omoligheten av 'utsugning' i den nyklassiska national ekononin*, HFKS 1-2/1968.
[4]   See for example, S. Grossman, 'Valfard pa spel', *Dagens Nyheter* 7/3 1973 and N. Lundgren, 'Vardera upp Kronan', *Dagens Nyheter* 14/6 1973.
[5]   UN Yearbook of Trade Statistics. See also, J. Galtung, 'A Structural Theory of Imperialism', *Journal of Peace Research*, 1971.
[6]   Compare A. Emmanuel, *Unequal Exchange*, Monthly Review Press 1972, p.362.
[7]   Annerstedt-Gustavsson, 'Mot en ny arbets-fordelning?', *Zenit 30*, November-December 1972.
[8]   Or Fahlen, *Foretagstillvaxt och internationalisering*, Sveriges Industriforbund, Stockholm 1972, p.27.
[9]   Fahlen, op.cit., p.45.
[10] B. Ryden, *Fusioner i. svenskindustri, Industriens Utrednings-institut*, Stockholm 1971, p.50.
[11] R. Vernon, *Sjalvustandigheten hotad*, Stockholm 1972, p.138.
[12] See for example, M. Wilkins, *The Emergence of Multinational Enterprise*, Cambridge, Mass., 1970.
[13] Fahlen, op.cit., p.8.
[14] Edgren-Faxen-Odhner, *Lonebildning och samhalls ekonomi* (the so called EFO report), Stockholm 1970.
[15] A. Glyn and B. Sutcliffe, *British Capitalism, Workers and the Profit Squeeze*, Penguin 1972, p.231.
[16] Edgren and others, op.cit., p.125.
[17] Ibid., p.19.
[18] G. Eliasson, 'Multinationalla foretag och integration', *Ekonomisk Revy 8*, 1970.
[19] Figures for 1957 and 1964 taken from G. Eliasson, *Diagnos pa 70-talet*, Industriforbundets forlag, Katrineholm 1971. Figures for 1968 calculated from 'Input-output tabeller for Sverige 1968', *Statistiska Meddelanden N 1972: 44.*
[20] R. Rowthorn, *International Big Business 1957-67*, Cambridge University Press, 1971.
[21] Ryden, op.cit., p.65 ff.
[22] C. Tugendhat, *De Multinationella, Prisma, Falkoping 1972*, p.84 ff.
[23] Ibid., p.68 ff.

[24] Fahlen, op.cit., p.35.
[25] SOU 1973:21, p.200.
[26] Handels department, EEC information.
[27] Hornell-Vahlne, 'Svenska dotterbolag i utlandet okar starkt', *Industriforbundets tidskrift* 7/70.
[28] SOU 1972:90, p.160.
[29] Hornell-Vahlne, op.cit.
[30] Ibid.
[31] A Swedish business magazine of the nature of USA's *Fortune Magazine*.
[32] H. Runblour, *Svenska foretag i Latin Amerika*, Uppsala 1971.
[33] H. Johansson, *Telefonaktiebolaget L.M. Ericsson*, 1953.
[34] Information on individual companies is, unless stated otherwise, taken from articles in *Dagens Nyheter, Svenska Dagbladet* and *Veckans Affarer* along with various annual issues of *Svenska Aktiebolag.*
[35] B. Steckzen, *Sk.F. — en vensk exportindustris historia, 1907-57*, Goteborg 1957.
[36] Ibid.
[37] Ibid.
[38] Runblom, op.cit.
[39] *Foretag i utveckling*, Till Marcus Wallenberg October 5, 1969.
[40] Runblom, op.cit.
[41] See for example, L. Berntson, *Sverige och 'Korporatismen'*, HFKS. 6/70.
[42] B. J fr. Rowthorn, 'Imperialism in the Seventies "Unity or Rivalry", *New Left Review 69*, September-October 1971.
[43] *Kapitalets internationalisering*, HFKS 5/72.
[44] See for example, C. Levinson, *De multinationella foretagen och inflationer*, Uddevalla 1972, p.32 ff. See also Eliasson, *Diagnos pa 70-talet* which shows that credit restrictions during the high conjuncture period 1969-70, primarily affects the smaller and medium size company slinvestments.
[45] SOU 1970:71, p.164.

7 The Swedish Arms Industry and the Viggen Project

Jan Annerstedt

1   During the post war period there has been an extremely strong militarisation of Swedish state research efforts, partially through a concerted channelling of research grants into private industry, and partially through percentage increase of the state research and development (R & D) efforts within the exclusively military area. Concurrently, a military strategy perspective began to pervade the more civilian R & D efforts, for example in the areas of computors and atomic energy (where in certain periods, they have been crucial).

2   The largest research project ever engaged in by the Swedish state has been the so called Viggen Project — a military aircraft. Preparations for and the decision concerning Viggen have been reserved to a small circle of leading people in large industry, the military and the social democratic party (in close co-operation with the bourgeois parties). The VPK (the Left Party Communist) represented in the Swedish Parliament, was however not included in these discussions or decisions.

3   The militarisation of research has corresponded to militarisation of the technologically most expansive sectors of industry. The concentration of research on military objectives has contributed to a situation in which the advanced technological developments occurring in a number of large Swedish companies outside the arms industry, more often have application to the military rather than civilian areas.

4   A special characteristic, an intimate and ill concealed high level co-operation between industry and finance capital on the one hand and the state bureaucracy and top politicians on the other, has been a prerequisite for this militarisation. The state interventionism in the economy of the Wickman, Strang/Palme variety is nothing new. It has been an essential ingredient in social democratic political praxis throughout the entire post war period.

5   The interlacing of Swedish and foreign industrial capital has been especially strong within those industries where the state military effort has been most marked. This interlacing is manifested foremost in licencing, production, and co-operative research agreements. Within the area of civilian technology there has emerged an increased foreign dependence.

6   In the area of foreign policy, these economic alterations in Swedish capitalism have brought with them a closer coupling to NATO countries. Swedish military strategy is developed in close connection with the so called 'threat image' used as the point of departure for NATO strategy. It is probable that to a greater degree than earlier in the post war period, the Warsaw pact nations perceive the Swedish military defense as a part of NATO's northeastern flank.

7   Economic and other ties between the Swedish and foreign defense industries have permitted some foreign countries a thorough insight into the most intimate details of the technology of the Swedish defense system. Through American companies the CIA has a complete knowledge of Swedish military defense. In addition, the decision making process behind the largest military research projects have been mapped out by a German born political scientist now working with a CIA financed institute in the USA.

Military strategy and the decision concerning Viggen

Sweden has effected a very rapid modernisation of its war machine during the post war period. New types of weapons have been introduced into the Army, many at a relatively rapid pace. The airforce is in a class by itself. An extremely advanced air defense system has been built up in which increasingly refined types of aircraft are the most important element. Next to Israel, Sweden today has the largest fleet of military aircraft in the world, calculated in relation to the country's size and GNP. During the latter part of the sixties the Swedish state has invested between 1 and 1.2 billion dollars annually in military defense (current rates). Each year approximately 250 million dollars has been spent on the acquisition of military air equipment, above all for the latest military plane, Viggen.

   Swedish military defense may be called an invasion defense. In other words, it is based upon the 'threat conception' of an enemy which intends to invade the country by one or two massive troop landings. In this situation the primary task of the navy and coast artillery is to ward off (or delay) these invasions. The airforce will function in the first instance to resist or delay the invasion, but also for a limited number of days to assist the army to resist or delay the enemy's occupation. It is anticipated that the airforce will have a very short life in a war situation. This in turn leads to the notion that the airforce will be capable of a powerful and concentrated contribution during the opening stages of the war. A large number of planes are required during the first days. It is then that the airforce can play a key role, partly by forcing the enemy to employ massive air support for its invasion (and thereby discourage an invasion from taking place at all) and partly by destroying such large parts of the invasion force that the army would be capable of slowing down the occupation and hopefully force it back.

This is not the place to critically assess the basic notions underlying Swedish military defense posture. To be sure, this is a very simple task, which is done by even civilian employees within the defense department who specialise in studying more modern attack strategies on a small country than the regular invasion model of the second world war. What is important to note in this context is that the 'invasion threat conception' which underlies the defense posture and strategy is almost without exception based upon the notion of a Soviet invasion force, not one from NATO countries. The entire air defense system, STRIL 60, concentrates its information gathering concerning military and noteworthy civilian activities, in the air over the socialist countries. STRIL 60 which has a somewhat different technical configuration than NATO's air defense system, is an excellent complement without being directly coupled to it. Interferences aimed at NATO-defense's electronics can be avoided by STRIL 60 and vice versa. In reality then, the north east flank of NATO achieves a double air defense system because of Sweden. This fact has been noted with gratitude in Nato publications.

Normally Swedish military strategy is never discussed publicly. The excellent manner which this strategy complements and strengthens that of the NATO system as noted above, is intimated even less often. If it is an issue at all in election campaigns, defense discussions are pursued in terms of such notions as, 'strong defense' and 'better neutrality protection'. During the entire post war period however, the social democratic establishment has carried out such discussions with a select number of people within the opposition parties (SKP — Swedish Communist Party and VPK — Left Party Communist, excepted). These discussions have taken the form of the 'defense committees' which regularly establish military expenditures for a fixed number of budget years. It has been this exclusive circle which has carried out military strategy discussions with top military personnel and leading directors in the arms industry, in order to decide the direction to be taken in Swedish arms development. Normally no debates concerning military strategy have been permitted in the parliament. (At the end of the fifties and into the early sixties there was however, a public debate on the issue of atomic weapons).

By the time the Swedish parliament took the Viggen project under serious consideration in 1964, the defense committee had already made the decision to go ahead (in 1962). Party representatives on this committee worked out and formulated the decisions concerning the military defense system, which were later endorsed (without debate) by the parliament, SKP representatives excluded. Since 1936 all decisions concerning military defense have been made without parliamentary insights into these studies. On only one occasion (1968, when the representatives of the bourgeois parties and the social democrats on the defense committee were at odds) has this decision making process failed to function.

The Viggen project, the most expensive arms acquisition undertaking ever engaged in by the Swedish defense organisation was set in motion by a series of non-parliamentary decisions. This is by no means unique for the Swedish armed forces. The entire military apparatus was designed in detail without insight or debate, a characteristic which does not apply to the same high degree for state actions taken outside the military sector. The motivation for this secrecy and non-parliamentary subterfuge is not due to security requirements no matter how exaggerated they may be. Rather it must be sought in the political system itself which is based upon a small circle of people controlling the economy and thereby determining the frames of reference in which the political action of the country must be carried out. Apart from all political controversies, this situation is re-enforced by an increasingly advanced arms industry at the base of Sweden's economy. Enormous profits have been earned and investments made in this sector of industry. This explains why it has been the capitalists' special interest parties, the right wing and the FP (People's Party), which have pressed hardest for the Viggen project, as they had earlier with the acquisition of military aeroplanes. However, as the more progressive managers of capitalist production relations, the social democrats too, have perceived the possibility of stimulating the economy by means of large long term military orders. Never before during the twentieth century have the key industries in the Swedish economy, such as electronics, telecommunications and heavy industry, been so closely tied to the production of military armaments as they came to be during the sixties.

Military aircraft industry: international arms

Sweden is one of the few countries which develops and produces its own military aircraft. Besides Sweden, only England, France, USA and the Soviet Union have their own such industries. China is in the process of developing its own. By international comparison the Swedish aircraft industry is not especially old. After the 1936 decision concerning a strong increase of Sweden's military forces, Saab (Svenska Aeroplan Aktiebologet, 1937) was established, which later purchased the Aeroplane division of the Railroad Factories in 1939. Since then, the new company together with Bafors has been the nucleus of the Swedish arms industry.

Saab's existence has been and continues to be dependent upon large scale military orders. From the outset the Swedish state has stimulated and encouraged the creation of a domestic monopoly in the development and production of military aircraft. By granting long term military contracts to Saab with no form of tender-letting, the state has created a type of hot house environment in which the company has been able to grow and expand. This relationship between a state and a single aircraft industry is quite unique.

Apart from several insignificant companies, there is in France at present a state aircraft industry and a private owned concern which specialises in military aircraft (Dassault). The wholly state-owned SNIAS was previously two independent operations (Sud Aviation and Nord Aviation) each having different production aims. When the French state plans to acquire military aircraft, it endeavours, to as great a degree as possible, to stimulate competition between the domestic companies. This competition does not simply occur on the drawing board (by comparing the different basic plans), but also by means of laboratory and flight tests of the competing prototypes. The French state also achieves greater security in its judgement of the aircraft prior to the signing of the purchase contract, permitting the development of fewer types of aircraft. During the post war period, Dassault for example has developed only two aircraft fuselages which have been used for no less than nine different models of aircraft (including the atomic weapons equipped strategic bomber). During the same period Sweden has developed four completely different aircraft fuselages having unusually few similarities.

The English experiment at a state acquisition policy for military aircraft was terminated during 1955-64. In 1957 the government decided to focus on the development of missiles and rockets instead of conventional military aircraft. This was opposite to the development which occurred in France and Sweden during the same period. To be sure, English military aircraft were to be produced in England, but research and development work would take place in close co-operation with the USA. The acquisition policy was incorporated into other areas of NATO co-operation. In the beginning of the sixties the aircraft industry was shaken by a series of scandals (among others, the Skybolt affair in 1962) through which it became clear that in such a milieu, the entire arms industry could operate with enormous profits due to the ambiguous texts of government contracts.

The British aircraft industry has now been reconstructed. The state has forced ahead mergers between companies in order to create a domestic monopoly. The objective however is not to reconstruct the production capacity upon a solely British base. Rather, several European Common Market countries together with England, have invested in a common military aircraft project (MRCA 75).

USA's aircraft industry and the largest electronic corporations represent the nucleus of the military-industrial complex. The largest ten or so companies account for the major part of production capacity in industries producing military products. These are the companies with greatest significance for USA's armaments.

As in France, the aircraft industry in the USA operates in a certain degree of competition. Following government directives, new projects are worked out by the companies and then compared both on the drawing board and in the air. Formally no monopoly exists, only varying forms of cartels and oligopoly co-operation. Only McNamara has experimented with something other than the traditional so called 'fly before you buy' policy. Upon his suggestion during the post war period, the American government purchased a military aircraft before it was completely finished, (the F111). It proved to be a mistake; the F111 did not match the proposed requirements (material failures, etc. were discovered during final tests).

Remarkably enough, the Soviet Union also has conditions of domestic competition. There are independent construction bureaux (the most well known being Mikoyan and Sukhoi), which put forward proposals on the basis of government specifications. Different prototypes are produced also. Production does not begin until testing has been completed. The essential difference between the USA's and Soviet Union's aircraft acquisition policy is that in the Soviet Union, all aircraft are produced in the same factory and with the same personnel. In the USA, when an aircraft company fails in its bid to secure a large military contract, and sooner or later this happens, thousands of workers and technicians are laid off.

The military aircraft industry: Swedish arms

Against this international background, the conditions in the Swedish
arms industry take on a more accurate dimension. Specifically, the
Swedish aircraft industry has numerous noteworthy features. The
monopoly situation of Saab has already been mentioned. During and
after the second world war, the Swedish State has as good as placed
all orders for military aircraft with Saab in Linkoping. (Malmo aircraft industry has received several special orders during the post war
period). Together with several other suppliers listed below, Saab has
developed four war planes since 1945: The Tunnan (which flew for
the first time in 1948), Lansen (1952), Draken (1955) and finally
Viggen (1967). These four generations of aircraft have been developed
in a protected environment, without observation and competition and
with intimate co-operation with top airforce personnel. This special
form of union between military leaders and industrial leaders
characteristic of Sweden's acquisition policy, differs markedly from
that of other countries.

   The Swedish aircraft development programme, dominated
completely from the beginning by concentration on military requirements, has on only one occasion concentrated on a large civilian
aircraft (the twin engined Scandia of which ten were produced after
the war). The aircraft technology which developed in Sweden during
the four large aeroplane projects has been exclusively military and in
no way has the state stimulated the development of civilian aircraft.

   The Swedish pattern differs from others in yet another respect.
The new types of aircraft which have been developed each represent a
distinct aircraft generation shift in Sweden. The French acquisition
model — two aircraft fuselages for use in completely different aeroplanes, with increasingly advanced technology and performance — has
not been attempted despite the fact that it has been demonstrated
safer and less expensive in the long run. Also, the Swedish State has
gambled with high stakes each time it has invested hundreds of
millions of kronor on a completely new type of aircraft, having no
initial guarantee whatever that the investment was made in a technologically feasible project. For research and development work alone,
Lansen and Draken cost 430 million dollars (1963 rates). Viggen's
research bill alone reached approximately 500 million dollars (current
rates). Had any of the planes been technically malconstructed it would
have entailed a catastrophe for the entire acquisitions programme and

adversely affected the nations military strength. As a result of the state's promotion of a domestic monopoly, it completely eliminated possibilities for securing technological guarantees, by means for example of having alternative prototypes to choose between. Because of the huge costs involved in developing a new aircraft from the drawing board to the finished prototype, the little nation of Sweden (with approximately 5 per cent of its GNP within the military sector; a high percentage by international comparison), chose to produce aircraft for different military purposes, i.e. fighters, bombers, reconnaissance, etc., using a common fuselage and motor assembly. Larger countries have the possibility of developing different aircraft for different purposes. When the state now invested in frequent aircraft 'generation' shifts, it at the same time entailed still less economic scope for experimentation with the prototypes. This in turn involved increased risk of technical failure. Saab and the other industries engaged in the aircrafts' development — with the sanction of the state — have solved this dilemma by coupling its development work by means of licences and other co-operative agreements to that of NATO countries. The aeroplanes for example are equipped with foreign produced motors; Lansen and Draken have modified British Rolls Royce motors, with Viggen's coming from Pratt and Whitney in the USA.

Arms industry: the Swedish model

As mentioned above, the formation of Saab was the immediate result of the Swedish arms build up in the mid-thirties. It was meant also to be a heavy investment in a Swedish airforce. The objective was not the development of a Swedish war-plane. In 1937, the same year Saab was established, contracts were signed for the licenced production of foreign aircraft. Several years after the outbreak of the second world war, it became clear that the continued purchase of foreign planes and licences was impossible. A Swedish aircraft industry, based primarily on domestic technology was to be established.

Primarily through profitable contracts (1937 production agreement, 1940 six year general agreement), the Swedish State gave strong economic support from the outset to Saab's establishment and growth, guaranteeing also to purchase a fixed volume of aircraft. In 1941 after two years' construction work, the State Air Technology Experimental Station (FFA) was opened with equipment from, among other places, Germany and the USA. The FFA continues to operate as a state organisation which subsidises Saab's development work in the area of experiments of technical strength, etc. Saab anticipates investments up to 25 million dollars in the FFA; this too, indicates the magnitude of previous government support.

During the forties Saab expanded very rapidly. Stock capital grew by approximately one million dollars annually. Seven years after its establishment the company was registered on the stock exchange. Today Saab is one of Sweden's largest companies with a stock value of 40 million dollars (1968) and reserve funds of 9 million dollars. Profits before taxes in 1968 were 18 million dollars. Towards the end of the second world war Saab had a work force of 4000 persons and by 1967, the company's aircraft division alone employed 6500 workers. During the last three years, with the production of Viggen beginning in earnest, the total employees in this latter division has increased sharply. It has been calculated that more than 10,000 of Saab's 14,000 employees, (both in the parent plants and subsidiaries) are engaged in filling military orders of one or another type. During recent years between one half and three-quarters of Saab's business was within the military sector. Of all large Swedish companies, it is the most dependent upon military orders.

The largest share of Saab is controlled by the Wallenberg family. Marcus Wallenberg is the chairman of the board of directors, Eric Boheman, earlier ambassador to the USA and Folk Party (Liberal) member of parliament, is vice chairman. Apart from Wallenberg, the largest amounts of shares are held by Skandia and Folksam (a co-operatively owned insurance company), SAF and the Bonnier family. Also registered as a share holder is Bofors, traditionally Sweden's most important defense industry. Volvo-Flygmotors (aircraft motors), now one hundred percent Volvo owned subsidiary, was previously one-third owned by Bofors. Flygmotors builds, as the name suggests, motors for Saab's military aircraft. The establishment and expansion of Flygmotors is to an equally high degree as Saab's, coupled to military orders. At present the company has a little over 2000 employees and annual sales of 50 million dollars. Volvo is primarily owned by Handelsbanken (The Bank of Commerce), Skandinaviska (Scandinavian Bank) banken, Skandia (insurance company), Hansa (insurance company), and the Bonnier, Brostrom and Wallenberg families. Folksam and SIF (Industrial Service Personal Union) also have stock holdings.

Bofors which manufactures among other things, guns, missiles, military vehicles and tanks, is still the key industry within the military sector. Approximately half of its sales during the past ten years have been military, to a great degree, foreign. The company is for the most part controlled by the Wallenberg family.

With L.M. Ericsson, also a Wallenberg family-owned company, approximately 25 per cent of the business of its Swedish based operations are concerned with filling military contracts. The company has a special military division located in Molndal; Svensk Radio AB is a subsidiary of LM and the British Marconi company. The subsidiary has specialised in producing military equipment. Through its subsidiary, Marconi has entered into the Swedish military market and has a complete insight into and overview of parts of the Swedish air defense system, STRIL 60.

This insight is shared by another company, Standard Radio and Telephone Company (100 per cent owned by the American ITT corporation). SRT was a major supplier to the Swedish air defense system STRIL 60. Among other things SRT supplied the central computers for the top strategic command of Lansen, Draken and Viggen. In 1964, SRT made public the technological principles underlying STRIL 60 in a public relations article published in two trade magazines resulting in a certain stir in military circles.

By threatening to close down its military development laboratory in Sweden, the ITT concern forced the government's Industry Department in September 1970 to open to them Saab's (!) advanced hospital care data processing section. A new company, Stansaab (ITT's SRT and Saab) was established during the autumn which means that ITT can presently utilise the relatively advanced research results of a Swedish company central to the production of Swedish air defense equipment.

Svenska AB Philips (100 per cent owned by Philips of Holland) is one of the foreign electronics companies which have ties with the Swedish military defense establishment. Its subsidiary Arenco Electronics (including Swedish Computer) is a supplier of military electronic equipment.

Before one can refer to the Swedish variant of the 'military-industrial complex' a few further companies should be mentioned. Kockums (including Landsverk) is responsible for a large part of ship construction for the navy, as well as tank production (under licence from Bofors). Approximately 10 per cent of the company's business is in the military sector. Gotaverken and Eriksberg also have military orders to fill. The only state operated industry for military materials is Forsvarets Fabriksverk, which includes a group of companies with partially advanced production.

Concerning the Viggen project, Saab is the major supplier. This implies that Saab is responsible for the largest share of the project's developmental work. For the Viggen project, Saab has established a system of co-, parallel, and subcontractors, depending upon which technological and economic role the respective companies play. Co-contractors are AGA, Arenco (Philips of Holland), Bofors, Flygmotor, LM Ericsson, Philips, Svenska Radio (CM Marconi, England), Standard Radio (ITT, USA), Honeywell (USA), Sundstrand Aviation (USA), General Electric (USA). Parallel or collateral suppliers with special status are Flygmotor, Bofors, Saab (subsidiaries) and AGA. Finally, Asea, Motala Verkstad, Svenska Metallverkan, Habia and Trelleborg plastics are subcontractors.

These companies in turn have their own network of suppliers. Altogether there are approximately 200 companies in Sweden and abroad involved in the Viggen project.

Viggen's performance

The Saab 37 Viggen is the fourth generation advanced war plane produced by the Swedish Arms Industry. It differs from its three predecessors, Tunnan, Lansen and Draken, primarily in that it is based on a 'common platform'. This means that the base construction (the fuselage and motor) after modification can be used for the production of completely different types of aircraft, i.e. as a fighter, bomber and reconnaissance plane. Until now Viggen has only been produced as a bomber, but plans exist for a fighter version.

AJ 37 Viggen is an extremely modern military aircraft. It is comparable to the most advanced planes of the superpowers such as the latest model of the French Mirage, USA's Phantom (perhaps even the F111) and the Soviet Union's Mig 23. But even though Viggen is comparable to these, it does not mean that it is superior, for example in air combat. That remains to be seen.

Viggen is a full 16 meters long, almost 11 meters wide and 5.6 meters high on the runway. It has a unique nose wing, which provides greater lift force. With normal armament the Viggen weighs 16,000 kilograms. It can take off and land in approximately 500 meters. It has a high altitude speed of just over two times the speed of sound and just over one at sea level. The engine is a military version of those used in DC9s or Boeing 727s. The attack version is equipped with, among other things, two missiles developed in Sweden and two produced under licence (Sidewinder and Falcon).

Five hundred million dollars to Viggen

Viggen represents the most expensive research task ever undertaken in

Sweden. It is also 'probably the largest and technologically most exclusive project ever actualised in any context within Swedish industry'. (M. Stahl in the 1964 parliament). It has been Swedish industry and above all some of the largest companies, which have reaped the benefits in the form of increased profits by operating in a state protected 'greenhouse' environment. Military money has guaranteed the expansion of these chosen companies and has — by definition — militarised some of the economically, and technologically most important branches of industry in Sweden's advanced capitalist economy.

Close to 500 million dollars of state money has been pumped into the development of Viggen, that is, for the research and experimental development (R & D) of one of aircraft type. There may still be 50 million more dollars added to that sum. Specifically, Viggen requires advanced missile equipment which is partially developed in Sweden. More important expenses are also absorbed by the research team which is working on the further development of the air defense system, STRIL 60. The system was constructed at the end of the fifties and is now being adapted to Viggen.

A probable total figure for all research and development work for and around Viggen would certainly be at least 625 million dollars. Nearly the entire sum has been spent during the sixties. To these millions of dollars must be added the purchase costs for the assembly produced Viggen. That sum will be many times larger than the amount already expended.

It should be noted that there exists no official compilation of Viggen's total costs. The Swedish government has chosen not to make available detailed reports regarding the project's economic aspects, still less the profit margins of the companies involved. The government operated Central Bureau of Statistics, which regularly conducts studies of capital investments in Swedish research, are referred by the companies involved to questionnaire responses not detailed accounts. A (provisional) account of the state's investments is shown in table 7.1.

One important qualification must be made. Saab and Volvo-Flygmotor make use of a special development system which results in the costs of other activities also being included in R and D figures. Parallel to the production of the first seven Viggen prototypes, special instruments and machinery which would later be used in the assembly production of the aircraft, were also developed. In other countries production and research operations are completely separate. Consequently, this makes international R and D comparisons some-what uncertain when Swedish R and D figures include costs which in other countries fall under the category of production.

Table 7.1
State R and D — authorisations for Viggen project 1960-70
(million Kronor, current values). For certain years only fuselage,
motor and other equipment is included, for others, R and D for
armament and surface combat direction is included.
Note a US dollar is approximately equivalent to 4 Swedish kronor.

			dollars (millions — approx)
1952/60		17.3	4.0
1960/61		17.7	4.0
1961/62		39.7	10.0
1962/63		61.0	15.0
1963/64		192.6	48.0
1964/65		244.5	61.0
1965/66		283.2	71.0
1966/67		267.0	67.0
1967/68	approx.	350.0	87.0
1968/69	approx.	250.0	62.0
1969/70	approx.	235.0	60.0

1960/1970 approximately 1,940,7

Source: 1952-61 from Saab, 1960-63 from the Department of
Finance, 1963-70 information from public publications, primarily
from parliamentary publications. It should be pointed out that
appropriations to the Viggen project do not reflect the real expenditures, partly because the military leaders for a fixed number of years
are granted the authority to place orders, and partly due to the fact
that sums of money have been channelled from different sectors of
the defense establishment into Viggen (financed by the top military
commander, in that up to 1960/61, he alone administered
appropriations for the Viggen project. One example is that during
1967/68 more than 100 million dollars was paid by the airforce sector
for R and D, which means that the figures cited above (as well as for
other budget years) are probably too low).

   A very high proportion of total state research expenditures in
Sweden goes to military R and D. In 1960/61 approximately
65 million dollars of an approximate total of 133 million dollars spent
in the state sector was used for military R and D, (calculated on the
basis of planned state research expenditures). The average annual

military research expenditure during the sixties has been a little more than 100 million dollars.

The relative proportion of military research has varied, but not to such an extent that the overall picture of a continual militarisation need be modified. Compared to other capitalist countries (even the USA) Sweden invests very heavily in military research.

Viggen: the five silent years

In spring 1963, political leaders in parliament were informed for the first time that a new aeroplane project had commenced. The notification took the form of a single paragraph in a government bill (NR.108, 1963) concerning increased military expenditures during the coming seven budget years. The chief of staff of the airforce had requested material for just over one and three quarter billion dollars for the period 1963/1970 (1962 rate). Recommendation for this proposal came from both the 1962 defense committee as well as the government. Still another in the long series of defense agreements had paralysed parliamentary debate and excluded all insight into the basic discussions of principle involved. The public was presented with an accomplished fact. The Viggen project was formally approved at Sweden's highest political levels. Prior to this however, much had transpired.

During the fifties, the Lansen, designed as a fighter and bomber, was serial produced (final deliveries took place in 1960). Draken, originally a fighter, was further developed by Saab in a new version, the Draken F, which was produced from the beginning of the sixties. Parallel to the development of Draken F, preliminary studies were being carried out between 1952-58 for a new military aircraft, which would later become known as Viggen. Among the alternatives evaluated was the so called 'Stor-Viggen' (large-Viggen). It was to be a strategic bomber armed with atomic weapons and capable of reaching Leningrad and Soviet cities near the Baltic coast. The Stor-Viggen project was shelved when Sweden decided to put off for the time being, the development of nuclear weapons.

The parliamentary defense committee which preceded the 1958 decision concerning military expenditures during the next few years, was not informed of the Viggen project other than in the form of very loosely sketched plans for air defense in the seventies. The same year however, the military chief of staff, and the Flygforvaltning (aircraft administration) presented the aerotechnical specifications which would lay the basis for Saab's developmental work during the sixties. In October Saab organised a project group within the company, to be responsible for work on Viggen. Therein, the Viggen project had begun. Ten years later Saab had spent approximately 300 million dollars on the project.

Inasmuch as no parliamentary decision was made concerning the Viggen, there is reason to wonder from what source Saab received the necessary funds. Together with Svensk Flygmotor (later Volvo-Flygmotor), the company spent at least 24 million (and probably more), prior to the parliament's decision in 1963. The answer is that the military chief of staff through funds administered by him, was able to transfer military funds to these projects. This is how Viggen expenditures for 1960-61 were registered with the finance department. (See table 7.1).

During the 1958-60 period the Saab group worked intensively on detailed sketches of the new military plane. Viggen began to take on definite form. During 1959 the government appointed an aero-technical advisory group made up of Saab directors and military personnel, submitted recommendations to the parliament for more intensive efforts in aerotechnical research. During that period, Flygmotor's and Saab's ten year contract expired. Other factors too suggested new possibilities for a complete reconsideration of continued Swedish arms preparation in the aerotechnical area.

In this situation and in customary secretive manner the 1960 defense committee met to decide upon military expenditures and future arms preparations. The committee, which worked for six months, was composed, among others, of three persons who would become key figures in the Viggen project. They were Manne Ståhl (Folk Party-Liberal), Gösta Bohman [1] (right wing Conservative) and Lars Eliasson (Centre Liberal/Conservative): these three would appear in more defense committees and in parliament giving continual support to the military leader's and Saab's Viggen plans. They pressed the government into compromises which excluded attempts to break off the entire project. Even though the 1960 defense committee had received a summary presentation of Viggen plans, no discussion of the basic rationale and principles involved in the project took place in parliament. The Viggen group within Saab was able to continue its work without disturbance or disruption.

On 13 June 1961, a full half year after the defense committee's decision and several months after the formal parliamentary defense decision (in which Viggen was still not specifically named) the military chief of staff decided to give total support to Viggen. This decision was the result of several months' discussion among top military leaders and between them and the directors of Saab. Saab at once embarked on the detailed planning of the coming undertaking.

In September 1961 the 'Flygforvaltning' (aircraft administration) signed a continuing basic agreement with Saab. It entailed among other things, a guarantee from the military leadership of a specified annual scope of expenditures for Saab's R and D work during the coming three years. Saab had now received a guarantee for three years' work on the Viggen project. The government was only informed long after the agreement had been signed. An *ex post facto* approval of the agreement was passed by the government in February 1962. Immediately thereafter, defense minister Sven Anderson publicly criticised the procedures followed by the military leaders, but nevertheless felt obliged to approve the move. Parliament was not informed that the agreement involved a completely new aeroplane project.

Ties to NATO, 1

The special agreement with Saab was not the only one entered into independently by the military leadership. Viggen not only required a new fuselage construction but also a larger motor than Draken's. The possibility of Flygmotor designing and producing a completely new aircraft motor was seen to be small. Consequently in May 1962 the aircraft administration signed a contract with the aircraft manufacturing firm they saw as most suitable — the American firm of Pratt and Whitney Aircraft (it has not been possible to uncover the precise motivation behind the military leaders' choice of this particular company). The aircraft administration's licence agreement with PWA included a clause which stipulated that if the agreement was broken before 31 December 1965 for reasons other than technical quality, PWA would be compensated with between 5 and 20 million dollars depending on the termination point. On even this occasion the government was confronted with an accomplished fact as the agreement was never submitted for its approval. In spring 1964, Defense Minister Sven Andersson 'discovered' the agreement with the American company and the economic consequences of a contract termination which were involved. The government's criticism satisfied itself by 'finding it noteworthy the agreement had not been submitted to his Royal Majesty, the King.' [2] The fact that Viggen was to be equipped with a motor produced in Sweden under license from a US company was not mentioned, even less, the name of the company involved. This was the first step for the USA towards a complete insight into the technology of the Viggen project.

The feverish activity on the part of Saab and the military leadership to set all parts of the project in motion as soon as possible before the political agreements were arrived at is to say the least, noteworthy. It suggests that they trusted their political channels would continue to function as effectively as they had in past years. So sure were they of their case that while the 1962 Defense Committee was still in the midst of its deliberations, Saab and the military leadership signed a detailed contract which was to regulate all subsequent Viggen agreements. Specifically, in April 1962 the aircraft administration and Saab agreed that Saab was to be the major contractor for the Viggen project. Subcontractors no longer signed contracts concerning the supplying of aircraft material with the Swedish State but rather with Saab. To ensure that the entire research and development of the Viggen would run smoothly, Saab was to have overall responsibility through an 'operations centre' (CB37) within the company. As previously Saab was thereby given a unique position within the Swedish arms industry. The possibilities for state control (especially over the company's profits) was reduced.

During that year, the 1962 Defense Committee with Bohman, Eliasson and Stahl as leading members received the first detailed military reports concerning Viggen. They went on a study visit to Saab and travelled to an aircraft exhibition in England. Even though there was disagreement within the committee concerning the necessity of a military apparatus equipped with ultra-modern warplanes, by the end of the year the committee had for its part (and thereby also for parliament) approved the Viggen. They presented their position on the nation's largest military acquisitions project ever, in approximately one page of a 130 page report. [3] The 1962 Defense Committee had established the direction and scope of Swedish military defense for the next five years.

After noting its existence in a few sentences in a 1963 government bill, the parliament approved the Viggen project. No public account of the project's content and planned dimensions was ever given. After five years and at least 29 million dollars the project for the first time received parliamentary approval.

Ties to NATO, 2

The following two years, 1963 and 1964 were to be the most dramatic in the entire history of the Viggen project. To be sure Viggen was already at a very advanced research stage, which had only been approved after the fact by a poorly informed parliament. But the uneasiness amongst the top personnel in the defense department was above all due to the estimated cost increases of the project. This uneasiness and doubt concerning the realisability of the project was not made public for approximately one year. It was only then, early in 1964, that the press and radio informed the Swedish public of the nature and size of the Viggen project. After six years, official silence had been broken.

In mid-1962 the defense staff itself made the first military assessment of the research costs in the project. 255 million dollars was the estimate. It was calculated that the total cost of each Viggen would be one and a half million dollars — 1962 rates. These were the figures presented to the 1962 defense committee. In retrospect they are ridiculously low and as we shall see, would be doubled. But even then, the estimates were appreciably too low as it was definitely in the interest of the military leadership to hold down these figures. Saab was most conscious of this need when they furnished the basic data for the military's calculations.

In autumn 1963 after parliamentary approval had been granted, new cost calculations were carried out. The conclusion was (in 1963 rates) 323 million dollars for R and D, and a per-plane production cost of one and three quarter million dollars. A year later the finance department calculated the R and D costs (in 1963 rates) to be approximately 400 million dollars. The per-plane production cost rose to approximately 2 million dollars. These figures were still a long way from what was to be the final cost.

Regardless of the rapid cost increases, which could have been anticipated had someone other than Saab or the military leadership analysed the project in detail at its inception, the question of reconsidering the undertaking was never an issue. Saab and the Swedish arms industry would be guaranteed expansion and continued profits throughout the sixties and seventies. Viggen was the prerequisite for this state support. There were already too many political ties involved in the project to make reconsideration possible.

During the spring of 1963 approximately 200 persons including thirty five civil engineers in Saab's Viggen department were working on the project. By January 1964, following the beginning of construction of the first prototype several months earlier, this same project group consisted of approximately 1,000 persons. Saab which was at the same time the central contractor for the entire project, was unable to cope with this rate of expansion still less with that which was planned for the future. The aircraft administration which was itself having internal problems adapting to the new contract form, foresaw this at an early stage. From the very beginning, other sectors of the Swedish defense industry hesitated to sign long term contracts with Saab. Many companies, especially the foreign owned subsidiaries, wanted to continue to do business directly with the military. This had proven to be the most profitable procedure in the past.

In this situation the military leadership through the Flygforaltingen decided to establish a company to assist Saab in the organisation of an overall administrative planning system to correlate and integrate the production programmes of all subcontractors involved with those of Saab. PERT as the system was called, was the key to the Viggen project. In addition to this, Saab also had significant difficulties with Viggen's electronic guidance system (including the central computer which on Saab's advice was to replace Viggen's navigator). The aircraft administration selected Honeywell for the task, an American company tied into that country's military-industrial complex. (Honeywell has long been the most important electronics company in USA's military sector. 37 per cent of the company's sales in 1968 were military contracts — approximately 440 million dollars).

As early as the beginning of 1963, a Honeywell group then working on a NATO project in Europe, was informed of Viggen's technical data. This was done through Honeywell's Stockholm office which in turn had received the information from L.M. Ericsson. In December of the same year the Honeywell group arrived at Saab to spend the next few months acquiring a complete insight into the project and in practice become primarily responsible for Saab's project planning. Honeywell was also granted the contract for Viggen's guidance system and for the central computer, CK 37. The Viggen project — so secret that the Swedish public had not been informed of its existence any more than in the form of brief news announcements — was now turned over to one of the key companies in the US military-industrial complex.

Unofficial doubt/official involvement

About the same time that Honeywell was informed of the technical details of the Viggen project, the financial details were being discussed within the Department of Finance. During the 1964 budget discussions concerning the military sector many social democrats within the department perceived the economic weaknesses of the project. One of them, Ingemar Stahl, decided to break the official silence surrounding Viggen. In an editorial in *Tiden* (a social democrat magazine) he questioned the entire project, primarily for economic reasons, and presented his own cost calculations which reached three and three quarter billion dollars; (double the official estimates). By the time the entire project was completed (including

R and D, production and operation) by the end of the 1980s, Stahl estimated it would have cost six and three quarter billion dollars. (Even this was probably too low a final figure).

The reaction was tremendous. Newspapers which had consciously repressed all information concerning the project were now forced to take up the issue. The military leadership utilised the 'slicksters' of *Svenska Dagbladet* (a leading right wing national daily newspaper) to completely dismiss Stahl's article in *Tiden* as loose speculation. Saab let it be known that thousands of employees would be laid off if the project was abandoned. In official pronouncements it was stated that the situation represented only a temporary disunity in the social democratic party. The State Secretary in the Defense Department, Karl Frithiofson, assured the defense industry that the project would continue. It was the task of the aircraft material preparation board to ensure that the Viggen project functioned within an acceptable economic framework — it was not involved in a reassessment of the project. (Among others included in the aircraft material preparation board were Krister Wickman, Bengt Dahlberg — key military man in the project, Hans Hakansson — in finance — and presently in the department of industry as head of technical and scientific research).

One year later in March 1965, the group was already with its first report. In close co-operation with Saab, Flygmotor, L.M. Ericsson, and other important suppliers, it had by then gone through all the details of the project. They had studied the alternative of purchasing aircraft from one of the NATO countries. (No investigation of possible purchase from the Soviet Union was conducted). In a new contract, the aircraft material preparation board pressed through certain economising measures with Saab and others. By means of a postponement of the entire project, the project's smoother future development could be guaranteed. However, more than 125 million dollars had already been pumped into the project, consequently the preparation board concluded that it could continue.

In the spring of 1965 the preparation board's proposal was presented to the parliament in the form of a bill. Viggen had weathered its first storm. A majority in the parliament thought it pointless to terminate the project and the leading representatives of the defense industry could now breathe more easily. Even though it had been clear from the outset that the social democrats would not abandon the project out of consideration for the interests of industry, there remained reasons for caution inasmuch as the public could have reacted negatively to the enormous Swedish armament undertakings.

Parliamentary efforts to stop Viggen

Several members of parliament had reacted to these developments. In March 1964 when the government was forced to present its first detailed account of Viggen, several motions were subsequently presented aimed at stopping the project entirely. These motions, drawn up by a joint social democrat and communist parliamentary group, were aimed at reducing Swedish armaments. The government had recently expended more than 125 million dollars for the purchase of missiles. Since 1947 a total of 2,535 million dollars had been spent on military aircraft equipment. Now the government was proposing an annual expenditure of more than 250 million dollars for the forthcoming years. It would entail the most rapid and expensive armament expansion during the post war period.

The spring parliament approved both the general scope of increased armaments and for the second time, the Viggen project itself. In his first of May speech of the same year, the country's then Minister of Foreign Affairs, Torsten Nilsson declared: 'On the international scene, arms reduction is the most urgent question of our time.'

In October, renewed action was taken in parliament by Gösta Bohman and Manne Ståhl, the most avid promotors of the Viggen project. Bohman had received military information that the aircraft material preparation board had carried out an extremely thorough evaluation of the project, so thoroughly in fact that one might suspect it was being re-evaluated. For its part Saab became uneasy because the government through the influence of the preparation group did not approve all requested expenditures for the project.

These were expenditures not included in the economic framework originally approved by the parliament. After consultation with several co-contractors, in August 1964, Saab issued a direct threat to the aircraft administration: if funds for the requested expenditures were not forthcoming before 1 October, the consequence would be lay offs in Linköping and enormous difficulties for the carrying out of the entire Viggen project.

Bohman put the question to the Minister of Defense in the parliament with the result that the government yielded to Saab. Without consulting the parliament the government had laid out an extra 14 million dollars at the request of the military leadership. In reality the government had held back on these expenditures precisely because they had not yet been formally approved by the parliament. Bohman on the other hand wanted the funds paid out immediately upon request; 'we know that the concerned industries were uneasy' [4]. Stahl declared forthrightly that the reason for the action was 'uneasiness in Saab'.

In 1965 a new attempt was made to terminate the Viggen project. A motion put forward by the communist party (VPK) called for decreased funds to, among other things, military aircraft material. Another motion proposed by the same party did not go quite as far. It suggested that, 'it would be best to have a pause in the continued work on the aircraft 37 Viggen', partly because a defense committee needed to be appointed and partly because the resources were required for housing, care of the sick and aged, and communications. [5] These motions to slow down or halt the Viggen project completely were defeated in the 1965 parliament.

The military chiefs of staff and Saab could now signal that the danger was past. The aircraft material preparation board continued to function as the finance department's control organ, but it was only from 1 July 1965, seven years after the project's inception that a state project directorship for Viggen came into being. All energy was employed to complete the project as quickly as possible. As a result of Frithiofsons' influence, the top man in the government's Viggen group was Lars Brising, a technical director with Saab. Brising was an excellent representative of the generation of technicians who had primary responsibility for the growth of armaments in the airforce sector since the end of the second world war. Since 1938, with but a few years between, he had altered between the private aircraft industry and the military aircraft administration. Since the beginning of the sixties he had administered important assignments in the state's research planning organisation. Brising is in fact one of the persons most responsible for the militarisation of Swedish research.

Internal skirmishes

In 1965 a new defense committee was appointed with the traditional task of allowing the four large parties in the parliament to reach a settlement on impending military expenditures. Outwardly the Viggen no longer appeared to be a controversial research project. Saab and the other sectors of the Swedish and foreign defense industry involved in the project continued their work with unwaning energy. Internally however, within the finance and defense departments, opposition was not completely subdued. Within the aircraft material preparation board the project continued to be discussed as if it were still possible to halt it. It was reasoned that 500 million dollars invested in research and development for an aircraft body, the

137

rebuilding of a civil aircraft motor, two missiles and an entire attack command system, need not necessarily lead to further billion dollar investments in the form of the assembly produced fighter plane.

One employee in the finance department assembled a series of economic and military strategic arguments against the project in a memorandum which was discussed in January 1966 within the military leadership. The memorandum which was classified secret because it contained information concerning the 'operational life' of current aircraft (and thereby the combat strength of the Swedish air defense), concluded with a proposal for a total reconsideration of the entire Viggen project. Even this attempt to stop the project failed. As late as 1968, after Viggen had been test flown (1967) and after 100 Viggen aircraft had been ordered, at the highest levels within the government departments concerned there remained doubt regarding the wisdom of completing the project.

There is a difference however between doubt and direct opposition. Throughout the entire sixties the government pursued a defense policy which directly supported the Swedish defense industry. On the issue of large military investments, the last decade has no counterpart during the entire post war period. The Viggen project — the largest Swedish research undertaking ever — has been complemented by the further development of Draken (F-version), missile development and production (numerous completely different types), the development of a completely new tank (model S), a new armoured personnel carrier, and more. The Swedish military is technologically more sophisticated than ever before. Among those smaller countries which are building up armaments most intensively, Sweden's place is self evident.

Triumph for the arms industry: the Viggen is purchased

As early as 1967, before the then convened Defense Committee had reached its decision, parliament, on the government's initiative, took the position to purchase Viggen aircraft. The military chiefs of staff had proposed a series order of 83 Viggen of the fighter bomber version and 17 of the training version. The cost would be two and three quarter million dollars per plane; 275 million dollars total. To this would be added the annual development costs of the Viggen project — at that time 115 million dollars. The only party which acted against the order of the Viggen was the VPK — some of the party members wanted to stop the project completely. Nevertheless, nine years after the project's inception the first Viggen order was passed by parliament without debate. The first plane was to be delivered in the summer of 1971.

In 1970 Saab announced that production capacity was able to accommodate further orders. The government proposed parliamentary approval for the purchase of 75 more Viggen planes within a cost framework of 450 million dollars. In the summer of 1970 several months after the latest Viggen order was placed, the 1967 Air Defense Study (commissioned by the military chief of staff) issued two reports. One was classified as secret while the other was publicly distributed. The public report contained a series of conclusions abstracted from the military strategy considerations of the secret portion. In short the summary was as follows: STRIL 60, despite the continuous reconstruction and expansion which annually cost millions of dollars must continue its further technological development. Those foreign companies primarily responsible for its design and development should continue their work. Viggen will be the key ingredient in the Swedish air defense and a new fighter version must be developed on the basis of Saab's first Viggen construction. Enormous investment must be made in the new version of Viggen which will replace the remaining Lansens and Drakens. The traditional anti-aircraft defense system should be completely dismantled. And finally, the report concluded that the defense industry should be kept busy with new research, and experimental development of new production series, activity which was to cost hundreds of millions of dollars annually.

CIA furnished with a double insight

It has been mentioned earlier how closely the Swedish military apparatus is linked to those of NATO countries, particularly the USA. The Swedish arms industry has long been tied to the USA's not only through licences, co-operative agreements, etc., but also through the direct involvement of American companies in Swedish military projects from the planning stage through to final production. Thus, the Viggen project was no anomaly in this respect.

In addition to this, knowledge of the decision making process involved in weapons acquisitions is itself of great significance for foreign powers. That the CIA or the State Department for example has technical insight into the Swedish military defense is not sufficient. The total defense strategy, the airforce's role together with the weaponry chosen to fulfil that function is, from an intelligence point of view, of equal significance. There are military and political security interests in acquiring a knowledge of which persons occupy key positions, command real power and have complete overviews of the Swedish defense system. Because Sweden has embarked on a new top secret aircraft project, there also exists military-industrial interest in acquiring the same intimate knowledge and evaluations.

Since the mid-sixties a German born researcher, 'D', has been engaged in specialised studies of the Swedish aircraft industry 1945-70. His doctoral dissertation, financed by the Riksbankens (the Swedish State Bank) Anniversary fund, will analyse the Viggen project as it has developed behind the scenes in the light of military strategy. 'D' has had access to the working papers of the aircraft material preparation board project studies and papers from Saab and other industries, together with – and this is also worth noting – a series of top secret documents on the project from the finance and defense departments. When a Swedish social researcher approached the finance department in the spring of 1970 in order to attain some general information regarding the aircraft material preparations board, he was told by a high level employee: 'It is much easier to ask "D". He has a complete overview and can lay out in detail the entire project.'

It is however, not easy to ask 'D'. For several years now he has been at the Centre for International Affairs (CFIA) at Harvard, and only comes to Sweden occasionally to gather data. CFIA is no ordinary institution at an ordinary university. Harvard belongs to that group of American Universities which have the closest ties with the State Department and the White House. Since the mid-fifties professors and researchers have streamed from the faculty outside Boston to Washington DC. Eisenhower's staff in later years was characterised by 'Harvard men'. Kennedy, Johnson and Nixon have all chosen their closest most trustworthy advisers from Harvard; Henry Kissinger for example, came directly from the CFIA at Harvard to the White House.

The CFIA was established on the initiative of the then Secretary of State, Robert R. Bowie and McGeorge Bundy (later adviser to Kennedy) of Harvard. A key original and continuing purpose of the institute was to provide further education for key State Department and CIA personnel after extended periods of service. Another objective was that the CFIA, through close ties to the research resources of a leading university, could carry out special operative studies of foreign policy problems for the US government and intelligence service. The CFIA has carried out such special studies, especially in regard to Vietnam and has also given advice to rulers in

140

Argentina, Greece, Iran, Pakistan, Indonesia (during the mass murders), Malaysia, Ghana (after the coup), Liberia and Columbia. It is not only lower ranking personnel from the CIA and other organisations who take part in courses and seminars at the centre. On one occasion USA's Secretary of State has taken part in discussions regarding the government's policy towards China. CIA money finances research assignments and travel. In the fall of 1970, after revelations of increased CIA operations with CFIA, parts of the institute's library was destroyed by a time bomb. 'D' is involved in the section within CFIA which deals among other things, with military strategies in Western Europe. His study is the first to map out in detail the highest level of internal defense policy decisions in a Western European country. When the draft of the Viggen dissertation reached department personnel in Sweden in Augumn 1970, it was discovered to be so detailed that it even referred to the contents of classified secret documents from the defense department. Needless to say it caused a degree of internal nervousness.

The present situation: preparations for 'FPL 80'

In the spring of 1971 Saab and other arms industries were working under heavy pressure. Viggen must be delivered to the military units by the summer. Other production continues; according to plans, 175 Viggen of the attack version must be delivered within the coming ten years. Saab will probably receive increased orders when the Airforce acquires the fighter version of Viggen. STRIL 60 is now being adapted to Viggen.

At the same time the Viggen project is entering a new phase, Saab and the military leadership have made preparations for a new aircraft project now under the code name 'FPL 80'. According to studies conducted within the defense department the 'FPL 80' will make its initial flight in 1978. Saab's first deliveries are expected to take place in the beginning of the 1980s.

Preliminary planning operations have already begun. Investments in a new wind tunnel at the Aerotechnical Experimental Station are expected to reach 25 million dollars. If it is decided to continue working with the basic Viggen construction, which is likely according to current plans, wind tunnel testing alone will cost approximately 12 million dollars. The military leadership have hinted that the decision will involve not only a heavy attack aircraft to replace Viggen, but also a new 'light' attack plane.

One thing is certain, the 'FPL 80' is already at the same stage that

Viggen was in 1960/61. The first millions have already rolled into Saab's designers.

Translator's footnote

After some minor discussions in the early seventies concerning the future nature of Swedish defense and the consequent armament emphasis, the state's previous long standing commitment to advanced air defense technology and its domestic research and development has been reaffirmed.

Saab has not been successful in securing any major foreign sales of its Viggen.

Research and development and further prototypes of military aircraft continues, and while the enterprise is being partially reassessed by the new coalition government it appears unlikely that there will be any reversal of government commitment to larger expenditures on the purchase of domestically produced military aircraft. This is all the more likely considering rising unemployment and the fact that Gösta Bohman, leader of the Moderate party and from its inception, one of the strongest and most outspoken advocates of the Viggen project, is now Minister of Finance and in the view of some, the most powerful person in the new coalition government.

Notes

[1] Gösta Bohman is now finance minister and one of the most powerful members of the new bourgeois coalition government.
[2] Prop. 136/1964, p.13.
[3] SOU 1963:5.
[4] AK Nr 32, 1964, p.27.
[5] Motion AK 882, 1965.

This article originally appeared in Swedish in the Independent Socialist political journal *Zenit* in the early seventies.

8 Swedish Class Structure

Goran Therborn

Marxist class analysis has two primary tasks, 1) to show the effect society's structure and mode of functioning upon the social relations among the people in society. This means that the Marxist classes are no *ad hoc* arbitrary categories created for special occasion (as, for instance, 'classes' of income size or educational level, which might be relevant in certain investigations) but are grounded in a theory of society and its historical development, i.e. in historical materialism. As Sweden is a capitalist country, the analysis of the classes in Sweden is based on the Marxist theory of capital, wage labour, bourgeois state, bourgeois ideology, etc. The first main question for a Marxist analysis of class is not — like in the social liberal discussion of equality and in the academic sociological interest in 'stratification' — how much people have of this and that. Rather the question is, in what type of society they live and what tasks have they in that society, above all their position in production. Herein lies the possibility of explaining why some are poor and some are rich; 2) to present the pattern of social contradictions and the forces in society which strive either to preserve or to change it. In short, the objective is to show: 'who are our enemies? who are our friends?', as a distinguished Marxist Mao Tsetung, has expressed it in a class analysis of his society. This studying of the objective conflicts of interest and forces of change based upon them — rather than an uncritical acceptance of professed political good will and egalitarian values — is another line of demarcation between Marxian and prevailing views on equality and stratification.

Exploitation and class society

The relationship between a society and the classes in it might be illustrated by a house and the people who live in it. The house is the structure of society. It can remain, while the people in it are born, grow up, grow old and die, while some move in or out, while some move up and some move down. How and where the people live in the house determines their relationships to other people, whom they belong together with, who have the interest in one day tearing the old house down and building a new one.

But it is not in all societies that people are related to each other as different classes. Marxism also speaks of a classless society. What then, defines a class society? What kind of house confers the character of class relationships upon the social relationships of its inhabitants? To answer this question we must introduce a basic distinction made by Marxist social theory, that between necessary and surplus labour. Necessary labour is the labour necessary for the sustenance and reproduction of human life, food, shelter, clothing, etc. including sufficient for the rearing of a new generation. Marx emphasises that what is necessary sustenance is not only biologically but also historically determined. However, in all societies beyond a very primitive stage, more is produced than is necessary to sustain those involved in production and their families. Surplus labour is performed, resulting in a surplus product. This can be used both for the consumption of those who do not produce — chieftains, shamans, warriors, priests, landowners, capitalists, officials of various kinds — and for investment.

Surplus labour can be appropriated in different ways. According to Marx it is the manner in which surplus labour is expropriated from the direct producers which represents the fundamental difference between different kinds of societies and between different modes of production. It can be achieved through slavery, through the obligation to do a certain number of workdays on the landowner's land, through turning over to him a certain part of the harvest, etc. It can be effected by the direct producers receiving wages for their necessary labour, while the capital owners receive their profit from the surplus labour of the wage workers. A society is also possible in which the workers themselves collectively appropriate the surplus product. A society is divided into classes (in the Marxist sense) when the tasks of performing surplus labour and of the appropriation and determination of the disposal of the resulting surplus product are separated. This is the essence of exploitation, one class appropriates the fruits of another class' labour.

To ask about the way in which surplus labour is expropriated is to ask about the relations of production. The relations of production is a key Marxist concept denoting the determination of: (a) the position and relationship of the direct producers to the means of production (the distribution of the means of production) and to those who appropriate the (eventual) surplus labour (the social relations of production); (b) the orientation and character of the process of production. Capitalist relations of production, for example mean that one class of capital owners own the means of production and appropriate unpaid surplus labour from a class of wage earners who sell their labour power as a commodity, that the work process is carried out under the direct control of the capital owner (or his representatives), and that production is for profit and is oriented towards the accumulation of capital.

The relations of production are based on, and in their turn affect the development of the technical-organisational conditions of production, the level of the productive forces.

Compared to the economic relations of production juridical property relations are of subsidiary importance only. The economic structure is the determinant moment of society and the relations of production therefore provide the basic determination of its classes. But the latter are also the effect of the ideological and the political — the state and the power relationships in the economic process itself — structures of society. An empirical class analysis has also to take them into account.

A social system, a mode of production, which is based on exploitation is always divided into two classes, one of exploiters and another of the exploited. However, at any given point in time a concrete society as a rule contains more than two modes of production, and therefore more than two classes. How many classes there are in a given society then, is to Marxists an open empirical question. Inasmuch as one mode of production is usually dominant, two classes generally constitute the two main poles of the society.

Besides the production and direct appropriation of surplus labour there are also other necessary tasks in a society. The people who perform them constitute no specific classes but are attached or tending towards one class or the other. Included here are categories with specialised political and ideological functions. Another example of this sort are the large 'white collar' groups in modern capitalist society. According to the Marxist theory of value, they produce no surplus value, but on the other hand, it is not they who directly appropriate and decide over the surplus value produced by the workers. (Cf. the bailiffs and scribes of feudal society). These groups do not constitute a class but a stratum. Because of their position between the working class and the bourgeoisie they are often called middle stratum or strata.

With several classes, which in turn can be subdivided into sections, strata and special categories, the social pattern becomes rather complex. It is effected by the development of the social structure through the ever present struggle between the classes. For the analysis of the class relationships at any given point in time, one therefore has to take into consideration not only the structure of society but also the nature of class struggle during the previous period.

Sweden is a capitalist country. Thereby, the social relations are polarised between bourgeoisie and proletariat (working class). This corresponds to the capitalist mode of production based on capital and surplus value producing wage labour. In Sweden there is also a third class, expressing another but subordinate mode of production, simple commodity production. That class is the petite bourgeoisie, self employed without any (or at most a few) employees and selling their products on a market. Moreover we have also to deal with a growing middle strata and with special categories attached to the bourgeoisie — a bourgeois bureaucracy, a bourgeois army and police, a bourgeois intelligentsia, etc.

The statistics

The basic statistical material used here are census data of those gainfully employed. The latest census of which the data are available is that of 1965. (The first findings of the 1970 census are not beginning to appear). As far as possible, efforts have been made to incorporate post 1965 tendencies, which in several cases represent to a certain extent a turning point. A number of other sources have also been used, other official statistics on agriculture and industry for instance, the Swedish Lexicon of Occupations, published and unpublished statistics from trade unions and from the Swedish Employers Confederation, interviews with officials of unions and trade organisations and with insightful people in various occupations and positions in order to avoid getting lost in the labyrinths of statistical headings and categories.

The working class

The working class or the proletariat in the strict sense comprises the workers who produce surplus value for the capitalist economy as a whole, that is, industrial, construction, mining, forestry, agricultural, transport and warehouse workers. On the other hand a shop assistant provides profit for the owner of the shop through his labour, however, no new surplus value is thereby created in the economy, but the shop owner does receive part of the surplus value which is produced. That part increases the more he can press down the costs for the wages of his employees. (This role of the 'circulation workers' is perhaps more easily seen in the similar case of the work of those employed in the sales department of a factory). There might be other employees who contribute to the production of surplus value, engineers and various kinds of technical and research personnel. But because of their position in the political and ideological structure of capitalist production they do not belong to the working class. To many of them is delegated part of the power of capital over the workers (powers of supervision and control), and 'control' of the ideological structure thus severing intellectual from manual labour which in turn separates them from the direct producers.

In order to understand the place of the working class in the structure and functioning of capitalist society it is necessary not to gloss over the fundamental, strict definition of the working class. The working class is the class which, subject to the political and ideological domination of capital, above the value of its own wages produces the riches which another class, the bourgeoisie, appropriates and disposes of. The enormously increased productivity of the workers' labour has made possible the rapid growth of the public sector and the private white collar strata, which we have witnessed in modern times. In the narrow sense then, the working class includes two main types of workers, those manufacturing (including repairing) goods, whether in industry, construction, mining, forestry or agriculture, and those engaged in the packing [1], storing and transportation of goods (warehouse workers, lorry and engine drivers, seamen, postmen, long-shoremen and so on).

Table 8.1
The working class in the strict sense 1930 and 1965

| | Thousands | | Percentage of those gainfully employed | |
	1930	1965	1930	1965
Manufacturing workers	1040	1120	36	33
Storing and transport workers	150	200	5	6
Sum total	1190	1320	41	39

Source: Census of 1930 and 1965.

147

Thus, there is little in the data to indicate any drastic decrease in numbers of the working class. In absolute figures it has even increased after the depression and during the post war years. In the 1966-68 period the number of industrial workers in Sweden declined rather significantly, whereas in 1969 it increased slightly, though not so much as to offset the previous drop. According to the official statistics on industry, the figures of which are not directly comparable with those of the census, the number of industrial workers decreased from 742,000 in 1965 to 700,000 in 1969. [2] This should not too readily be taken as the expression of secular tendencies. Whereas the number of industrial workers in 1959 was roughly the same as in 1949, the sixties as a whole was a period of increase in the number of workers in industry, from 665,000 in 1959 to 700,000 in 1969.

Capitalist society also contains people who while not being producers of surplus value, live and work under the same or similar conditions as the proletariat. They are wage earners, their wages are determined in the same way as those of the working class proper. Their position is completely subordinate, they have not been delegated any part of capital's power of command. Many of them work under partially and increasingly proletarian conditions, having no opportunity for individual decisions and initiatives. In a broader, extended definition of the working class these groups should also be included.

Among these are charwomen, janitors, caretakers, hospital assistants (including those employed for cleaning and cooking for elderly and sick people outside hospitals), canteen personnel in schools and industries, waitresses, children's attendants and maids. Two substantial groups are problematic in this context, shop assistants and typists and other routine office employees. None belongs to the working class in the strict sense, but none is barred from becoming part of it in a looser and broader definition. In the contemporary Swedish situation it seems appropriate to include the former but not the latter. The distinction between the office and the shop floor is still an objective reality, whereas the outcome of unionisation (highly successful in Sweden in terms of percentage organised) is an index of the difference between the two groups. From the 1930s on it has been possible for the organised storing workers and the workers who delivered beer, milk, etc. (proletarians in the strict sense) to organise the shop assistants in Handels fackforening (the trade union of commercial employees affiliated to the confederation of manual workers, the LO). On the other hand, the industrial workers (now belonging to a white collar union and confederation). Even in a broad definition however, the shop assistants should be divided up. Those occupied in the prevailing ideological structure of luxury and fashion should in fact be included with the middle strata, but available data do not make that possible.

Table 8.2
The working class in the broad sense 1930 and 1965

	Thousands		Percentage of those gainfully employed	
	1930	1965	1930	1965
Working class including shop assistants	1590	1840	55	53
Working class excluding shop assistants	1530	1695	53	49

Source: Census 1940, 1965.

The great number of jobs performed by the members of the working class in the broad sense might be divided into five categories, the basis of their position in the economy. Two of these are the ones which create the surplus value producing working class: workers engaged in any kind of manufacturing of goods (including: construction, mining, wood cutting, farming and repairing), and transport and storing workers. Two other categories of jobs derive their wages from the sum total of surplus value produced in society: the circulation workers (shop assistants, gas station attendants, ticket collectors on railways and buses), whose economic function it is to realise the surplus value that has been produced: the workers who provide various kinds of services to persons, enterprises, and public authorities (cleaning, tending to houses and to children, haircutting, washing, waitresses, etc.). Finally, there is a category of workers whose primary task it is to furnish production with a healthy and well adapted labour force: hospital assistants [3], canteen personnel within educational and other institutions and within enterprises, and public offices. Their work is geared to the reproduction of the labour force. Thus they are neither producers nor consumers of surplus value but are paid out out of the sum total of variable capital, an increasing part of which is no longer paid out by the individual capitalist enterprises directly in the form of wages but rather in the form of taxes levied on the individual enterprises which is paid out via the state budget.

With reference to the ideologies of the post-industrial 'service society', it is perhaps worth special note that the only part of the working class, which has declined in absolute numbers is the service

149

workers. This fact is mainly due to the disappearance of most of the maids and other domestics, that is, of the generally most subservient part of the working class in the broad sense.

Table 8.3
Occupational groups of the working class
in the broad sense 1930 and 1965

	Thousands		Percentage of those gainfully employed	
	1930	1965	1930	1965
1 Manufacturing workers	1040	1120	36	33
2 Storing and transport workers	150	210	5	6
Sum 1-2 productive (surplus value producing)	1190	1330	41	39
3 Circulation workers	70	170	2	5
4 Service workers	260	200	9	6
Sum 3-4 nonproductive (surplus value consuming)	330	370	11	11
5 Workers in the reproduction of the labour force (reproductive	60	130	2	4

Source: Censuses 1930, 1965. Rounded figures.

The classes exist in polarised relationships of conflict and struggle, which might be more or less manifest and might take a number of forms. With this in mind, another division of the working class in the broad sense is of great interest and importance, that is, according to the degree of the workers: independence from the pressure and influence of bourgeois society. This is of course affected by the particular experiences and traditions of class struggle in different places, regions and occupations. However in this context we are only concerned with the general effects of characteristics of the workers' position in society.

Two basic criteria will be used to define and to estimate the size of the core and the periphery of the working class. One is the type of work, ranging from surplus value producing work (the working class proper) to sales and personal service work. Another is the size of the workplace, from the plants of the large export industries with thousands of workers down to the single shop or domestic assistant. Besides these two criteria we need to take into consideration at least one more factor, that is, the possibility for social mobility — the change of becoming self employed. If these chances substantial to a category of workers, then they should be regarded as belonging to the outer periphery of the class. To lorry drivers, to radio, television, car and bicycle repair mechanics and to rather large groups of construction workers of various kinds, the petite bourgeois perspective of becoming 'one's own boss', or a partner is significant.

With the help of these criteria the working class has been divided into four groups: the core, the outer core, the inner periphery, and the outer periphery. The core includes industrial and construction workers in workplaces with more than fifty workers. The outer core comprises the same occupational groups in medium size workplaces — 21-50 workers — forestry workers and transport workers, except in small enterprises. The inner periphery includes productive workers in small enterprises (with the exceptions mentioned below), hospital assistants, cleaning and canteen workers. The outer periphery is composed partly of those who are close to the middle strata: shop assistants and other circulation workers, waitresses, maids and other workers in personal service, partly of those who are close to the petite bourgeoisie, repair mechanics, artisans in the construction field and in other occupations. Of the latter groups only crude estimates can be made.

Table 8.4
The core and the periphery of the working class 1965

	Thousands
Core	580
Outer core	280
Inner periphery	560
Outer periphery	420

Sources: Censuses 1965 and 1960 (more complete than the one in 1965). SOS Industry 1965, Swedish Employers' Confederation; list of size of member enterprises, interviews with trade organisation officials and trade union officials and militants.

The most reliable figure of these estimates are those referring to the core group. It constitutes about a third of the working class in the broad sense and 17 per cent of all those gainfully employed. With the concentration and centralisation of capital the core of the proletariat has increased since 1930, relatively as well as in absolute figures. No figures for construction workers in large enterprises are available for 1930, but there were then only 322,000 industrial workers in plants employing more than 50 workers, and should the construction workers in the same category have been as many as in 1965 (which they certainly were not), the core would even then have constituted less than a quarter of the working class and about an eighth of the gainfully employed.

The bourgeoisie

Who are the bourgeoisie? The bourgeoisie are a personification of capitalism, the functionaries of capital. The bourgeois represents the capitalist process of production, the appropriation of surplus value from the labour of the wage earners, and production geared towards continuously increased profits and capital accumulation. It follows that a member of the bourgeoisie can be either an owner or a manager of a capitalist enterprise employing wage workers. The purely legal distinction between owners and managers is not significant in this context. Secondly, the definition of a bourgeois implies that an employer with a single or but a few employees should not be included in the bourgeoisie to the extent that the enterprise and the profit of the entrepreneur is not wholly or overwhelmingly founded upon the surplus labour of the employees, but to a significant extent upon the entrepreneur's own labour. To some extent an exact demarcation must always be arbitrary; the division between the bourgeoisie and the petite bourgeoisie has been made according to the categories used in the registers of the non-agricultural employers by the Swedish Central Bureau of Statistics. Therefore, the bourgeoisie for our present purposes consists of businessmen having at least five employees.

The 1965 population census reveals that there were 385,000 individuals in business on their own account; of these 300,000 had no employees. Among the remaining 85,000 we must distinguish between the bourgeoisie and the petite bourgeoisie. According to the *Yearbook of Agricultural Statistics*, in 1965 only on farms of 100 hectares and more is the major part of the work performed by employees. Using this criterion the Swedish agrarian bourgeoisie in 1965 comprised a good 2000 gainfully employed people.

Apart from agriculture there were 11,755 individually owned enterprises having at least five employees. During the latter half of the 1960s the number of such enterprises decreased rapidly. Around the turn of the year 1969-70 they were only 8.664. Because of their economic function all *en gros* dealers with employees will be counted among the bourgeoisie, even if they have less than five employees. That makes another 2,000.

The total number of people employed by these small bourgeois (to be distinguished from the petite bourgeoisie is rather small, about 90,000 in 1969. The most important part of the modern bourgeoisie are not the self employed businessmen but the juridically employed managers. Non-owner of managers in 1965 numbered 29,000.

To complete the picture of the (occupationally active) bourgeoisie we need also to add the 'helping family members' of the owners. They constitute a few thousand.

Table 8.5
The bourgeoisie in 1965

	Thousands
Owner-employers including helping family members	20
Other top managers	29
Sum	49
Percentage of gainfully employed	1.5

Sources: Census 1965, *Yearbook of Agricultural Statistics 1966*, Enterprises with employed personnel 1963-65.

Compared to that of 1965 the 1930 census gives a much fuller picture of the bourgeois class, and makes possible a breakdown by sectors. (The agricultural classifications of the census have been changed to make them comparable to the 1965 table, in 1930 the limit for major use of employed labour was farms of 50 hectares. Farmers with more than 50 hectares are thus counted among the bourgeoisie).

The strength of the bourgeoisie lies not in its numbers but in its ownership of capital and thereby its control of the means of production. Thus, census data are of limited use for a proper study of the bourgeois class and its sections, big monopoly capital, the middle and the small bourgeoisie, banking (finance) and industrial capital, etc. What we have done here is only to delineate the bourgeoisie from the common categories of professionals, managers of all kinds, and self employed.

Table 8.6
The bourgeoisie 1930

	Thousands
Agrarian bourgeoisie	16
Industrial (including construction) Commercial	11
Mercantile	14
Financial	1
Rentiers	10
Sum total	52
Of which businessmen on their own account	24
helping family members	8
other managers	9
Percentage of the gainfully employed	2

Sources: Census 1930, Agricultural census 1932.

Secondly, there is the state apparatus, of which there is one (primarily) administrative sector directing the administration of society and the economic and other interventions of the state necessary for the expanded reproduction of capitalism, and one repressive apparatus with the function of maintaining 'law and order' and of taking care of national 'lives and property' and 'national interests' abroad. The former comprises the top echelons of the bourgeois bureaucracy and high level state officials. The repressive personnel include the judiciary, the police and the professional military (officers and non-commissioned offices; Sweden has no standing army).

Finally, there are the directors of the ideological apparatus, those responsible for seeing to it that the population has an appropriate and 'correct' attitude to the existing society and to their roles in it. This bourgeois intelligentsia is made up of the heads of the various educational establishments, from the elementary school to the university level and the officials of the central educational bureaucracy, chief and political editors in the mass media, directors of advertising and so called public relations. Precisely who are a part of this leading intellectual category depends on the specific character of the ruling ideology. In this respect there seems to have occurred a shift since the 1930s. The traditional 'cultural heritage' — both religious and secular — has lost much ground to a more technocratic, bureaucratic, and commercial ideology. The content of the educational reforms in the 1960s are indicators of this change. Because of this, and also because of their altered situation due to the enormous expansion of higher education and their greatly increased subordination to professional administrators, the role of the teachers have changed. They can no longer be included among the direct and immediate carriers of bourgeois ideology as the high school and university teachers could in 1930. Rather, they should now be counted among the middle strata. (With their delegated authority to teach, they can of course never be reckoned among the working class even in the loosest sense).

The most significant change between 1930 and 1965 is the increase of the repressive apparatus, in spite of the disappearance of 12,000 rank and file professional soldiers. The police has increased by 160 per cent. Accompanying this, the governing section of the ideological apparatus has diminished in numbers.

The petite bourgeoisie

A petite bourgeois in the Marxist sense is a producer of commodities — products or services — directly for a market, who is however, neither a wage worker for a capital owner nor a self subsistence producer. This means that petite bourgeois are self employed producers in a market economy having no employees or at least so few that the employer is still primarily a commodity producer himself and not a capital owner and manager. [4]

The decline of the Swedish petite bourgeoisie as illustrated by the censuses in fact underestimates the drastic decrease that has taken place. In 1930 most of the 'helping family members' included were grown-up children, son in law or sisters and younger brothers of the owner (in most cases a farmer). In 1965 all these have virtually disappeared, and the 'helping family members' are now as a rule only the wives of the owners included according to increasingly inclusive criteria. However, in 1930, the wives of the petite bourgeois were

155

Table 8.7
Special categories attached to the bourgeoisie 1965

	Thousands
Economic apparatus	
Middle level management	15
Accountants and technical, juridical and economic consultants	8
Sum leading personnel of the economic apparatus	23
Administrative apparatus	
Leading state and municipal officials	7
Repressive apparatus	
Judiciary	2
Prosecutors and higher police officers	1
Military	18
Police	13
Sum personnel of the repressive apparatus	34
Ideological apparatus	
Heads of educational establishments	4
Directors of advertising and PR	1
Chief editors and political editors of mass media	1
Sum leading personnel of the ideological apparatus	6
Sum total	70,000
Percentage of gainfully employed	2%

Sources: Census 1965 and 1960, Wages and Salaries 1965, *Statistical Yearbook 1967, Swedish Dictionary of Occupations.*

Table 8.8
Special categories attached to the bourgeoisie 1930

	Thousands
Economic apparatus	
Middle level management	10
Administrative apparatus	
Leading state and municipal officials*	7
Repressive apparatus	
Officers and non-commissioned officers	7
Professional private soldiers	12
Police	5
Sum repressive apparatus*	24
Ideological apparatus	
High school and university teachers	6
Higher functionaries in cultural establishments	1
State church clergy	3
Chief and political editors of mass media	1
Sum leading personnel of the ideological apparatus	11
Sum total	52
Percentage of gainfully employed	2%

Sources: Census 1930, Enterprise census 1931.

*The judiciary is included in the statistics of higher officials in general.

also working and included in the figures.

Table 8.9
The petite bourgeoisie 1930 and 1965

	1930		1965	
	Thousands	Percentage of gainfully employed	Thousands	Percentage of gainfully employed
Self employed [1]	585	20	370	11
Helping family members	325	11	130	4
Sum total	910	31	500	15

Sources: Census 1930, 1965.

The development of the petite bourgeoisie has been uneven among different branches, but for the three major ones, 1950 represents an important juncture. It was during the fifties that the process of rapid decline set in. This is revealed in the following table, though it should be noted that it refers to all self employed, bourgeois as well as petite bourgeois.

Table 8.10
Self-employed in different branches
1930, 1950, 1960, 1965. Thousands

	1930	1950	1960	1965
Agriculture	392	347	228	184
Manufacturing and handicraft artisans	89	86	58	48
Trade	75	80	68	57
Construction	14	28	33	33
Transport	14	23	22	23
Services	23	37	40	39

Source: Census 1930, 1950, 1960, 1965.

Behind these figures there is another noteworthy tendency, under-lining the declining role of the petite bourgeoisie. While enterprises owned and managed by the bourgeoisie become larger and larger through the processes of concentration and centralisation, the self employed category which is dwindling most rapidly is that of those with a few employees. Between 1950 and 1965 the number of farmers with employees decreased from 105,000 to 13,000, whereas for those without employees the decline was only from 242,000 to 171,000. Similarly, those branches which show an increase or a stabilisation in the number of self employed have had a decrease in the number of employers: in construction from 12,000 to 10,000, in transport from 10,000 to 7,000 and in services from 16,000 to 15,000.

The petite bourgeoisie is not a homogeneous class. It includes both small farmers and society doctors, artisans and taxi drivers as well as more substantial farmers. In a society wholly dominated by the capitalist mode of production the petite bourgeoisie, the supporters of simple commodity production, is subjected to the basic social polarisation between the bourgeoisie and the working class. Thus, an important differentiation within the petite bourgeoisie is the proximity of its members to the two main classes of society. This distance is expressed by a number of factors characterising the different petite bourgeois occupations. One is the amount of capital (in the loose everyday sense of the term) required to establish oneself in the position, from a joiner or painter who needs only to acquire his tools, to a farmer who must buy a farm of 80-90 hectares. Those who have a couple of employees, clearly do not belong to that part of the petite bourgeoisie which is closest in proximity to the proletariat. Further if the type of work is of such a nature that an employee performing it should be counted among the middle strata, then a self employed petite bourgeois doing the same job is not among those closest to the working class. Finally, the position of an occupation in the prevailing system of ideology and authority, as a rule also expressed in large economic rewards, may place the incumbent close to the bourgeois class even though the enterprise is not particularly capital-demanding: lawyers, physicians, and dentists with practices of their own are the most important examples.

In this way, the petite bourgeoisie has been divided into three main sections: one semi-proletarian of small farmers (with less than 10 hectares) — often part time proletarians, e.g. as wood cutters or construction workers, — artisans and taxi and lorry drivers with no employees, owners of hot dog stands and similar petty 'businessmen'. Next, the main part of the petite bourgeoisie is made up of medium size farmers (up to 50 hectares), shopkeepers, and small entrepreneurs with a few employees. These are the principal and most typical representatives. Also included in this section is the intellectual petite bourgeoisie in the form of independent writers, artists, and decorators. Thirdly, there is a wealthy stratum close to the bourgeoisie, comprised of large farmers (50-100 hectares) and an intellectual group of lawyers, doctors, etc.

Table 8.11
The composition of the petite bourgeoisie 1965

	Thousands	Percentage of gainfully employed
Semi-proletarian stratum		
Agrarian	125	
Artisan	55	
Transport	16	
Commercial	3	
Service	1	
Sum	200	6
Main stratum		
Agrarian	150	
Artisan	30	
Transport	6	
Commercial	65	
Service	25	
Intellectual	5	
Sum	281	8
Wealthy (near bourgeois) stratum		
Agrarian	10	
Professional	7	
Sum	17	0.5

Sources: Census 1965, Yearbook of Agricultural Statistics 1966.

Table 8.12
The composition of the petite bourgeoisie 1930

	Thousands	Percentage of gainfully employed
Semi-proletarian stratum		
Agrarian*	122	
Artisan	64	
Transport	10	
Commercial**	4	
Sum	200	7
Main stratum		
Agrarian†	551	
Artisan	40	
Transport	5	
Commercial	62	
Service	7	
Sum††	665	23
Wealthy (near bourgeois) stratum		
Agrarian†	29	
Professional	3	
Sum	32	1

Sources: Census 1930, Agricultural census 1932.

* Mainly crofters. Fishermen with no employees also included.
**Ambulating petty tradesmen.
† The line between the medium and the large farmers has been drawn at the point where the use of employees becomes general. Around 1930 this occurred above 30 hectares (whereas in 1965 it happened only on farms above 50 hectares).
††The census has not permitted the identification of an independent intellectual stratum.

Most noteworthy of this change between 1930 and 1965 is the decline of the main — and most characteristically petite bourgeoise — stratum, from about one fourth to one twelfth of the population.

The middle strata

The middle strata constitutes no class because though they carry out necessary and useful jobs they are not the foundation of the basic socio-economic processes of any mode of production. They perform a necessary function in capitalist societies, but not, like the petite bourgeoisie, as the carriers of a subordinate mode of production (simple commodity production), and they neither produce nor appropriate surplus value. Their salaries are paid out from the total sum of surplus value produced by the working class and appropriated by the bourgeoisie. Some of them, technicians and foremen, may take part in the production of surplus value but at the same time their work is part of the command of capital over the workers. On the other hand, the functions performed by the middle strata do not require the same absolute loyalty to the ruling powers as do those of the special categories.

The growth of the middle strata with the development of capitalism was explicitly predicted by Marx (in *Theories of Surplus Value*) and it follows logically from Marxian economic theory. The Marxist theory of class might however be questioned, if the middle strata were playing a major role in the social struggles of advanced capitalist societies, a role equal to or even more important than the two principal classes (the bourgeoisie and the proletariat). Contrary to the widespread ideologies of 'middle class society' this is clearly not the case. In the present study we cannot go too deeply into this but a couple of illustrations might at least provide a perspective. In the established political party system of capitalist societies the middle strata nowhere constitute a main pillar. The usual pattern is two big parties or blocks of parties, one of them led by and anchored in the bourgeoisie — the Tories in Britain, the Christian Democrats in Italy and West Germany, the Gaullists and the 'independent republicans' in France, the block of explicitly bourgeois parties in Scandinavia — the other having its base in the working class, though nowadays often led by bourgeois politicians, like the Labour party and the West German and the Scandinavian Social Democracies. In the USA both big parties are outrightly bourgeois parties, though one of them has a major working class electorate. The same pattern recurs in the system of trade unions and collective bargaining. Though teachers' unions are significant in some countries, France for instance, the field is basically structured by, on the one hand, the working class unions and on the other the employers' organisations and the state.

The fact that they are polarised between the bourgeoisie and the working class does not mean that the middle strata are not or cannot be an important social force. Though they were over represented in Mussolini's and Hitler's parties, the middle strata did not set their imprint on the ensuing Fascist societies. However the fact that the major part of them in Italy and Germany joined together with monopoly capital and other sections of the bourgeoisie on the route of Fascism, whereas in France their majority went with the working class and the anti-Fascist Popular Front, had great importance to the different outcomes of the struggle for or against Fascism. Though, even without the middle strata, the two sides of the struggles were already present.

The middle strata have grown substantially in numbers during the past several decades, in 1965 comprising a good fourth of the population.

Table 8.13
The middle strata 1930 and 1965

	Thousands	Percentage of gainfully employed
1930	300	10
1965	980	28

Sources: Census 1930, 1965.

The middle strata can be divided into a number of main groups, with some correspondence to the main occupational groups of the working class. More or less directly connected with the productive process are technicians and foremen, and the organisers of transport and communication, telephone operators, post office cashiers, and middle level management in the field. Two groups work mainly for the realisation of surplus value, office personnel (typists, secretaries, general clerks, etc.), and a separately identifiable group of 'commercial functionaries', purchasers, salesmen, cashiers, shop managers, advertising personnel. Two other groups cater to the reproduction of the labour force, one consisting of teachers of all kinds, the other of welfare personnel: employed doctors and dentists, nurses, social workers, etc. Further the middle strata contains two main groups of a service character. One of them includes apartment

163

managers, head waiters, canteen managers and white collar personnel
in other services, the other group consists of various types of guards
and guard officers: customs officers, jailers, etc. Finally, there is a
group of intellectual functionaries: journalists, photographers,
librarians.

Table 8.14
Main occupational groups of the middle strata.
To the nearest thousand

	1930	1965
Technicians and foremen	60	230
Organisers of transport and communication	30	60
Office clerks and general administrative functionaries	50	250
Commercial functionaries	60	180
Teachers	40*	110**
Welfare personnel	20	70
Housing management and other services	10	50
Guards and guard functionaries	10	10
Intellectual functionaries	10	30

Sources: Census 1930, 1965.

* Includes 4,000 preachers. Because of the authority *vis à vis* their
  church members they are counted among the teachers rather than
  with the intellectual functionaries.
**Includes 7,000 state church clergy and preachers.

Concerning the expansion of the middle strata, at least two central
processes should be distinguished. One is their general increase in the
economy, the growing proportion white collar employees per worker,
another is the expansion of the public sector. The 1960 census gives
(which the 1965 census does not) the total number of publicly
employed (including not only middle strata but also some workers
and the special bourgeois categories but excluding those employed in
public owned corporations). They were at that time 598,000 of
whom 314,000 were in state and 284,000 in municipal employment.
The 598,000 in 1960 can be compared to 180,000 in 1924 and
390,000 in 1950. [5] During the sixties public employment has
swollen enormously. According to the labour force surveys, the

figures of which are not fully comparable to those of the censuses, there were in December 1971 out of a national total of 3,470,000 employees 1,100,000, or nearly a third, publicly employed.

Table 8.15

White collar personnel in manufacturing industry 1930-69

	1930	1940	1950	1960	1965	1969
Thousands	49	80	143	197	245	251
Per 100 workers	11	15	22	28	33	36

Sources: Swedish Official Statistics Industry 1930 . . . 1969.

Notes: The figures are corrected according to the 1965 classification of industry. These statistics are not directly comparable to census data.

In contrast to the continued growth of the public sector there has been a marked slow down of the increase of the white collar personnel in industry after 1965. The future growth of the middle strata — whatever pace that will be — is likely to take place primarily within the public sector.

Table 8.16

Groups of white collar personnel in manufacturing industry 1950-69. Thousands.

	1950	1960	1965	1969
Managers	9	12	14	14
Technical personnel	29	46	63	71
Foremen	31	39	44	41
Office personnel	74	100	125	125

Sources: SOS Industry 1950 . . . 1969. Figures corrected according to the 1965 classification.

There remains another and more important criterion for distinguishing different groups within the middle strata — suspended as it is between the two main classes of capitalist society — that is, the distance of different parts of the middle strata from either the proletariat or the bourgeoisie. However, without a great deal more investigation and analysis of the many diverse middle strata occupations and the apparatuses in which they operate, it has proven

165

to be impossible to make a meaningful tendential determination of the middle strata as a whole. What we can do though is to distinguish the part closest to the working class.

For this task there are two principal criteria. First, we must subtract, as not belonging to the part closest to the proletariat, all those which have been delegated any kind of authority, and right of command or who have any right to represent the employer. In this way managers, supervisors and foremen of all kinds are excluded, as are teachers, salesmen, guards, etc. A second criterion is the character of the work process, whether it is impersonal and collective or whether it is characterised by individual initiative and individualised performance and responsibility. By this criterion a major part of the remaining technicians must also be left out, researchers of various kinds, cashiers, and bookkeepers, social workers, intellectual functionaries, etc.

Who then remain? Laboratory assistants, industrial draughtsmen, telephone operators, post office clerks, typists and other routine office workers and most nurses. Together they constitute about 275,000 people, or more cautiously, between a quarter of a million and three hundred thousand. They occupy such a position that with the continuation of present developments they could become part of the working class in the broad and loose sense. Available statistics make a comparison with 1930 difficult, however it seems clear from the statistics concerning middle strata occupations [6] that the semi-proletarian part of the middle strata in 1930 could not have exceeded 100,000, and most likely was considerably less than that. The major part of the semi-proletarian section of the middle strata are extremely low paid women. Thus, a proletarian policy towards the middle strata must first of all be a struggle against sex discrimination.

Table 8.17
The class structure of Sweden, 1930 and 1965

	1930		1965	
	Thousands	Percentage of gainfully employed	Thousands	Percentage of gainfully employed
(Working class in the strict sense	1190	41	1330	39)
Working class in the broad sense	1590	55	1340	53
(Outer limit for the working class in the broad sense	1690	58	2140	62)
Bourgeoisie	50	2	50	1.5
Special categories attached to the bourgeoisie	50	2	70	2
Petite bourgeoisie	910	31	500	15
Middle strata	300	10	900	28
Sum*	2900	100	3440	99.5

*Rows within parenthesis not included in the sum.

166

Translator's footnote

It should perhaps be added that due to economic developments discussed earlier, the structure of the Swedish working class has altered somewhat under the specific impact of increased capital intensity in industry and expanded public employment. The size of the lumpen-proletariat most certainly has increased out of proportion with the growth of the labour force and the petite and small bourgeoisie have decreased in numbers proportional to the total bourgeoisie. In short, the trends outlined in the essay have continued — to a great extent in exacerbated form.

Notes

[1] Strictly speaking, had available statistics permitted, part of the packing workers, in all 19,000 in 1965, occupied with packing only or overwhelmingly for marketing purposes, should be deducted and counted among circulation workers.

[2] The 1969 branch classification has been adapted to that of 1965.

[3] A significant part of these workers, caring for elderly or for permanently disabled people, should in reality be counted among the service workers. However, available data has not yet permitted an estimate of their number.

[4] To the petite bourgeoisie are counted all self employed except those who belong to the bourgeoisie employers with at least five employees, landowners with more than 100 hectares arable land (50 hectares in 1930), and wholesale dealers.

[5] E. Hook, *Den Offentliga Sektorns Expansion*, Uppsala 1962, p.44.

[6] See table 8.17, 'The Class Structure of Sweden, 1930 and 1965'.

9 The Welfare Myth in Class Society

Stig Larsson and Kurt Sjöström

The myth of the welfare state is warmly cherished by both social democrats and the right wing. The welfare state is the 'Swedish' way to equality and viewed as the best method of converting capitalist society into a 'People's Home'. In reality all capitalist countries are characterised by socio-political welfare models. It is not in the least something peculiar to social democratic parties but rather also characterises the policy which is pursued by conservative, reactionary and even fascist governments. As far as is known, social policy and social services have not been the objects of any detailed Marxist analysis. Nor does the present discussion have such an intention, instead the objective is only to point out several traits in the social policy and social services, and try to evaluate these in order to stimulate debate. During the last few years, social policy and social service has been pushed towards the centre of political discussion. However, this debate has often been fragmentary and to a great extent been limited to ideology and organisation — to superstructural levels.

Social policy and social service — what is it?

The traditional bourgeois and social democratic definition of social policy is that it represents the measures taken by society to create and ensure security. The social services are a complement to the social policy which embraces among other things labour market policy, health and hospital services, family support, and the pension, sickness compensation, etc. benefits of the various branches of government insurance. Social services are usually defined as the local communities' part of the social policy, in charge of the unemployment commission, the child services commission, the alcohol commission and the social assistance commission. Economically, social policy reached an outlay of 5 billion dollars by 1969, absorbing 16 per cent of the GNP (10 per cent in 1960). Since the beginning of the sixties, social policy expenditures have trebled. From 1969 to the present, this growth rate has continued. During the same period both economic and occupational security and equality has decreased.

Every social system has had its particular social policy. The suicide precipice belongs to the economically primitive feudal society while clerical 'charity' and patriarchal guardianship prevailed in the more developed feudalism of pre-capitalist society where the Lutheran belief in asceticism and the work ethic established an ideological basis for early capital accumulation. The existing differentiated social policy measures are a necessity in today's capitalist society.

Social policy and social services characterise class society. Above all, this in itself commonplace statement implies the following:

— social policy and social services are a part of the economic system

— the welfare apparatus institutions are instruments of the capitalist state apparatus

— social policy and social services reflect the class struggle and are partially the result of gains achieved by the working class.

Economy and social policy

The early stage of capitalism was characterised by an obvious ruthless exploitation of the labour force. It was often even more evident than the exploitation of natural resources. The first social laws however, have parallels in legislation against over-exploitation of natural resources. The necessity to budget natural resources had its counterpart in the necessity of ensuring the reproduction of the work force. As in England — among the first social policy measures introduced in Sweden was the prohibition of the more gross forms of child labour and the introduction of certain regulations concerning worker safety. Against the background of the declining birth rate during the 1930s, the Myrdals' *Krisis i befolkningsfrågen* (Crisis in the Population Question) which is viewed as a classic work in social policy literature also takes up the issue of the reproduction of the labour force. Using chauvinistic arguments concerning 'the dying Swedish race', certain family policy reforms were pushed through with the intention of increasing the birth rate.

This problem of a too low birth rate has arisen once again in the last few years (*New Crisis in the Population Question?* Mundebo). But inasmuch as the need for labour power can be satisfied by importing foreign labour, it has not given rise to the same interest as earlier. It is also characteristic of the immigration policy that it has been completely subordinated to the interests of 'business'. To a great extent it is only labour market requirements which influence and determine immigration, while humanitarian rationale applies only in those instances where public opinion is strong enough to call for it (even then it does not always succeed! For example, in the case of the deportation of 49 French gypsies). Imported workers have been used preferentially in low income branches and thereby contributed to perpetuating the low income problem. They have also proven to be easier to deal with during business slumps. In a short period of time (1 October 1952-1 October 1954) during the recession of the early fifties, the number of foreigners reported to be employed dropped by approximately 10 per cent. The recession of 1957-58 saw a 30 per cent decline, or 40,000 foreign workers in one and a half years. The older and the handicapped who were thrown out of work were obliged to take employment in the municipalities' 'so called' protected work places where wage conditions are incredibly low. The trade union organisations have not shown any great interest in taking care of the interests of these displaced workers and only lately has an agreement concerning them (even though a bad one) come into effect.

In the book referred to above — *Krisis i befolkningsfrågen* — the Myrdals suggest that the aim of social policy should be to 'organise, and control national consumption'. The consequence of that control should be an increase in productivity. 'The levelling out of incomes is in fact more a bi-product.' [1] It is naturally of interest to note that the economic influence and production stimulating effect of social policy does not affect all branches of industry the same, a fact which can lead to differing views on social policy among different financial groups. It is presumably the case that those industries producing for the domestic market have a greater interest than export industries in social policy's effect on the distribution of purchasing power.

Along with Myrdal the well known Finnish social politician Pekka Kuusi has justified social policy on the basis of its economic significance. He argues that the aim of social policy is to contribute to an increase of the national income, to 'mobilise everyone in making a constant contribution in the striving for economic growth'. Kuusi claims that 'the social levelling out of incomes in a society moving towards economic growth has the constant task of mobilising the passive sector of the population . . . . The satisfied citizens, those who content themselves with little, no longer constitute the core of the population in modern society. A little place of their own, a cat, a can of coffee and a rocking chair are no longer enough for old Annie. A vital elderly person of today wants to have their own television.'

Against the background of these socio-political (and social democratic) theoreticians' perspective it is of interest to touch briefly upon the income levelling effect of social policy. In principle, income levelling can occur in three ways in the present society:

1. Income levelling between different social classes (e.g. between capitalist and workers, between the upper levels of salaried employees and workers);

2. income levelling between different population groups within the same social class (e.g. between single and married, between childless families and those with children);

3. income levelling between different periods in a human being's life (e.g. between periods of employment and unemployment, between periods of health and sickness, between periods of youth and age).

It is important to keep these three forms in mind when speaking of income levelling and the effects of social policy.

The first type is anti-capitalist and only achieved through class struggle. In general, no such income levelling has occurred in Sweden (with the exception of temporary phenomena). Capital accumulation and concentration has continued in this country and can be established by government studies. Even those who earlier tried to conceal class cleavages have been forced to concede their continued existence in spite of decades of social democratic rule. LO's (Swedish Confederation of Trade Unions) committee on family politics has established that income levelling has stagnated during the post war period. The levelling effect of the taxation system has been low — 'approximately 90 per cent of inequality prior to tax remains after taxation'. Even Kurt Samuelsson has questioned whether over all there has occurred any income levelling during this century (Kurt Samuelsson, *Från Stormakt till valfardsstat* (From Great Power to Welfare State)). The increasingly extensive experience that there has not been any income levelling between classes is the primary reason that the equality question was a central issue in the 1970 social democratic election campaign — one which contains new promises of security and welfare.

The second form of income levelling — that between different population groups within the same social class — does not lead to antagonistic oppositions. This form of income levelling can occur for example by means of differentiated taxation of unmarried persons in the form of steep progressiveness. However, this can result in antagonisms among the people!

The third form of income levelling — that between different periods in a human being's life — is found in unemployment insurance (premiums are paid in during periods of employment and taken out during unemployment periods, in this manner evening out incomes

171

during 'booms' with incomes during 'slumps'), sickness insurance and other similar insurances. The ATP (the General Supplementary Pension Scheme) — reform was originally an income levelling measure of the first type and was put into effect during a period of heightened class struggle. However it has subsequently been incorporated by the capitalists and can at present be viewed as a form of income levelling of the third type.

The present enormous social policy costs are primarily employed to achieve an income levelling between different groups of wage earners and between productive and non-productive periods. It does not require any great insight into economic matters to see that this form of 'income levelling' creates a more balanced consumer demand. It can also contribute to a dampening of the most obvious consequences of market fluctuations (by means of the unemployed receiving unemployment assistance, a delayed wage, by means of the payment of certain grants and assistance even during economic crises and thus stimulating consumption) but it of course cannot solve the crises in production which arise from the internal contradictions of the capitalist economic development. This form of 'income levelling', this type of social policy, becomes an aid to the stimulation of economic growth. Consequently such a form of income levelling is in the interest of capital. Thus its application gives rise to no political battles and there exists a prevailing unity among the political parties concerning such social policy questions.

These programmes for equality and security naturally solve neither the equality nor the security problematic. On the contrary, the process of accumulation continues with accelerated repercussions. Riches grow on the one side and poverty spreads on the other. While the number of millionaires grows by a couple of hundred per year, the number of individuals who must seek social assistance from the municipal social services increases by about 50,000 annually. In 1968, 358,000 people in Sweden received social assistance of which one-third, or over 100,000, were children. This is 'equality' after nearly forty years of social democratic government. This too is 'equality' where 5 per cent of the population owns 50 per cent of the wealth, or, where nearly one-half of the wage earners have an annual income of less than five thousand dollars (Government Low Income Study). At the same time the cost of living is rising in essential areas — not least in housing. The municipal social services have been assigned the task of giving a boost to the low wage earners. In new housing areas in the large cities more than 20 per cent of the population has been in need of social assistance (Kroksback, Malmö 19.5 per cent of the population during a ten-month period, which implies substantially

172

Table 9.1
Social assistance costs in the larger cities 1965-68,
in millions of dollars

	1965	1966	1967	1968
Stockholm	7	9	12	13
Göteborg	2.5	3.0	4	5.5
Malmö	1.5	1.8	2.9	3.0
Västerås	0.3	0.4	0.6	0.7
Uppsala	0.5	0.8	0.9	1.2
Norrköping	0.8	1.0	1.3	1.4

more during a twelve-month period). Social assistance is also used as initial settlement help to many of the immigrants recruited by the low wage branches of industry. (To avoid misunderstanding it should be pointed out that in themselves immigrants do not resort to social assistance more than Swedes. Rather it is the opposite. They receive a demonstrably lower amount per person and often lack information concerning their 'social rights'.)

The norms used for assessing social assistance payments are low — 90 dollars per month for a single person, 132 dollars per month for couples for food and other subsistence expenses, excluding rent, electricity, and the like. Calculated another way, the allowance is approximately four dollars, fifty cents per day for a married couple and three dollars for a single person (one dollar for a minor!). It requires no great imagination to realise that those who receive social assistance do not have resources for any extravagances.

In spite of this, social assistance expenditures show an almost sprint-like development and give rise to unrest in municipal budget discussions (table 9.1).

Social assistance to a great extent is financed by the municipal government budget. As is well known, municipal taxes are not progressive. Social assistance does not entail any transfer from the capitalist class to the working class. Rather it entails that the lower wage earners must pay the costs brought on by the employers — for foreign labour, for the 'rationalised' workers and others.

The capitalist state apparatus and the welfare institution

In the social services debate of the past few years the discussion has begun to deal with the social services function in the area of social control. The debate has had its conceptual basis in Edmund Dahlstroms' and other sociologists' theory of social control and social deviance (Edmund Dahlstrom, et.al., *Sociala avvikelser och social kontroll* [Social deviance and social control]). The American sociologist Amitai Etzionis' theories of forms of power (economic power, normative power and coercive power) also provided a point of departure for this debate. From these starting points a growing number of people have discovered that social services have a social control function in which the dominant value system is constituted of middle class norms. An instrument in this social control is 'the diagnostic culture' [2] which took its conceptual content not only from psychiatry but also from psychology and bourgeois social psychology and sociology (see the chapter 'Den diagnostiske Kulture [the diagnostic culture], in the Norwegian sociologist's, Yngvar Lochens' book *Idealer og realiteter i et psykiatrisk sykehus* [Ideals and realities in a phychiatric hospital]). Social service becomes an instrument to adjust people to the existing society and even to the existing system within social service institutions.

There are of course those who have taken their point of departure from the Marxist theory of the state as an instrument of the ruling class and sought to place social services in this context. The capitalist state not only has the military, the police, the courts and the prisons at its disposal (Lenin also lists the priesthood which even today in Sweden retains a function of safeguarding the status quo), the question however is whether or not social workers have in large measure taken over the functions of the priests! As long as they continue to function effectively, the capitalist state prefers to use these more differentiated, shaded (and nuance ridden) instruments. As early as 1800 Bismark was conscious of the fact that social policy could well become an effective means of minimising subjective class antagonisms (Elmer). He wished to minimise the 'danger of socialism' by giving workers a moderate degree of social security. By patching together and covering up the most glaring social deficiencies, social policy and social services have a dampening effect on the most critical issues. Social policy contributes to making objective class boundaries diffuse and unclear. Those 'solutions' achieved by social services are most often pseudo-solutions which neither alter the causes of the needs nor their economic basis. If for example a couple with two children are granted social assistance in the form of fifty dollars or so per month because the man earns only two dollars per hour, the rent of their three room apartment is one hundred and fifty dollars per month and because the wife cannot take on paid employment due to the municipality's failure to build day care centres, these few dollars of assistance solve none of the following problems.

- that the man belongs to the low wage earning group and his employer pays him too little in order to earn more profit.
- the rents in newly constructed housing units are so exhorbitant that soon no worker will be able to afford to pay them, regardless of individual family housing support and similar socio-political efforts.
- that the municipality fails to take responsibility for services in the form of child supervision.

At their best, social services solve the immediate day to day problems of providing food and shelter and also manages to present a total breakdown of the individual's situation with its attendant apathy. However it can also happen that the individual in this example is effectively passified and becomes attuned to the low standard of living necessitated by a meagre social service supplementary grant. Social services contain many mechanisms which in the long run can influence people's thinking and attitudes: petite bourgeois values of being content and satisfied with the necessities, those who are quiet and thankful are treated more courteously than those who are aggressive, make demands and are 'difficult clients', etc. Studies also show that people who have long been dependent upon social services are less politically active than others. [3]

Both the child and temperance care laws are more or less distinctively class laws. Approximately 75,000 people annually are subject to child care measures. The number affected by the temperance care laws is approximately 80,000 per year. The temperance services were the object of a government study in which its class character was clearly evident. [4] The study shows the temperance care law to be primarily directed towards the working class. Among other things, this is evident from table 9.2, taken from SOU 1967: 36.

The class character of the law is clearly reflected in the figures. It is also directly apparent from the text of the law. An indication that intervention in the form of supervision or through compulsory commitment to an institution is required when amongst other things, the individual concerned is found to 'expose anyone, who he is responsible to support, to necessity and distress or obvious neglect or otherwise gross deficiency in his duties towards such persons, or be a burden to the public, his family or others . . .'

Table 9.2
Persons (men) who were subject to the temperance
authority's measures. Socio-economic group in percentage
compared to gainfully employed men in the country

	Subject to temper-ance authority's measures	Gainfully employed men in the country (1960)
Entrepreneurs	7	20
Salaried employees	7	26
Workers	75	53
Others* (including unidentifiable occupations)	11	1

*Note that among 'others' is concealed the extreme poor in society,
  temporary workers and others who lack an occupation.

What has been said here of the temperance care law applies in the
same degree to the child care law. It is characterised by intervention
which is based upon subjective values, on arbitrary force, on an
escalation of the system of available measures and on the selective
choice of those who are to be subjected to the measures.
(Kerstin Elmhorn's studies of actual criminality among children show
that most children at a certain age in this society commit several
crimes, even of a 'serious' nature, but this as a rule does not lead to any
consequences, nor do the police even notice it. There is good reason
to believe that those who come into the custody of the child care
authorities are those who for different reasons are not able to conceal
the crime, or who do not have parents in a position to help them out
of the situation. On these issues we refer readers to the works of
Bengt Borjesson, Gunnar Bromstang, Kerstin Elmhorn, Gustav Jansson
and Knut Sveri).
   As part of the bourgeois state apparatus, social policy has the
function of mitigating, concealing and generally eliminating any
consciousness of class antagonisms. When the metal workers' union
in Trelleborg complains about foreigners coming here and receiving
social assistance, this may be seen as an indication that the state has
succeeded in its task. Had the leadership of the metal workers' union
in Trelleborg been class conscious they would have displayed
solidarity with the immigrants, particularly against the political and
racial persecution, and directed their demands at the employers that

there be an end to the import of labour power to low wage jobs.

The social service often has a more direct function in adapting people to the existing system and the established values. In the final analysis the municipal social service in co-operation with the county government boards to have the option of employing physical force (the child and temperance care laws).

Social policy, social service and class struggle

Now and then social policy has thrust forth and stood in the centre of political antagonisms. This was the case, for example, during the General Supplementary Pension reform at the end of the fifties. Those who are not of an age to be able to recall the bourgeois hate propaganda can gain some measure of the political interest shown by referring to the figures for participation in the referendum on the pension question. No less than 72.4 per cent of those holding the franchise took part in the referendum on 13 October 1957. One should keep in mind too that participation in referendums is normally lower than in general elections. The General Supplementary Pension (ATP) reform was an anti-capitalist reform. [5] However, characteristic of all reforms in a society where state power is not controlled by the working class, is the fact that the gains achieved by the reforms are easily absorbed and countered by the capitalists. [6] This is precisely what occurred with the ATP reform. The huge ATP funds which are either directly or indirectly at the disposal of the capitalists, or more correctly, the large capitalists, contribute to 'rationalising' smaller firms out of existence.

The tendency towards the reabsorption of working class gains attained in the class struggle necessitates a continued political struggle in order to maintain or expand upon that which has been won. In this context there is reason to point out that the ATP reform is overestimated in its significance and its economic value, due to the reabsorption tendency, will be decreased. By 1980 only 60 per cent of all pensioners will have the right to the ATP pension (note that among others, women not gainfully employed will be excluded). Of those who will receive ATP, only 30 per cent will receive a General Supplementary Pension in excess of one thousand dollars per year. Of the then estimated 1.5 million pensioners in the country, 1.2 million will still have a relatively low income, even taking into consideration the planned increase of the basic pension. In addition, those services upon which pensioners are dependent and which are paid on the basis of means will to an even greater degree be paid in accordance with the cost principle. Thus, precisely with reference to the ATP reform, the adoption of a modified cost payment for residence in homes for the aged is currently under discussion. The fact that social policy and social services have of late become of central interest, is directly related to the sharpening of class antagonisms which have taken on more obviously manifest expressions as the number of strikes and the total number of workers involved increases sharply. As new technology makes possible greater productive intensity, workers are subjected to increased exploitation. In latter years, the hastened changes due to structural rationalisation has subjected increasing numbers of workers to deteriorating working conditions. During the years 1960-64 an average of 80 companies, primarily within industry, gave notice of closure. The closures affected approximately 4,000 employees annually. In 1966, 236 companies gave notice and 10,421 employees were affected by company closures. According to a special study conducted by the labour market board in the spring of 1968, 150,000 people in 1967 were affected by either company closures or production slowdowns. Furthermore, approximately 1,300 food stores closed down annually. Corresponding concentration is taking place in agriculture. There has also occurred comprehensive restructuring within the company. According to a questionnaire study carried out by the Swedish Confederation of Trade Unions, it is evident that 5 per cent of the labour force annually are affected by this internal restructuring. Above all, the adverse effects fall upon the elderly, women, the handicapped, and the poorly educated.

Perspectives on the current social services debate

For many, the welfare myth has been increasingly demystified. Perhaps more so than many other occupational categories, social workers have observed the contradictions between the smug rhetoric concerning the successes and virtues of the welfare state and the hundreds of thousands of poor, who precisely because of the myth of the welfare state have experienced their own misfortune as unique and due to personal inadequacies rather than a manifestation of a social process of impoverishment. There has been an increase in the 'janitorial' demands on social services.

Much of the debate around the question of social services has dealt with surface issues, but gradually discussion has shifted from methods and organisational problems to the casual context and questions of objectives. A government study has been commissioned with the task of analysing and assessing the formal structure of social services and to a certain degree even its material content. The study has met with a solid distrust from the side of social workers and social students. Typical of this mistrust is the fact that the social workers' organisations have commissioned their own study in order to scrutinise the objectives of the social services. Similar studies have been commissioned by the National Social Welfare Board and the Swedish Labour Party at its latest congress.

In the following few pages we shall elucidate some of the questions which have been raised in these public discussions. Kurt Samuelsson has raised the issue of the need for general reforms suggesting that there are both rational/economic as well as humanitarian reasons for replacing 'microlevel' measures (social assistance, etc.) with general reforms in the nature of insurance and other macrolevel measures (labour market policy, political efforts at decentralisation, etc.). His views which in and of themselves should be adopted on the basis of their greater humanitarianism and administrative effectiveness, have nevertheless been correctly criticised because they do not affect the social structure but lead only to an extension of the present system. Harold Swedner and others have made a creditable contribution in the illumination of segregation in residential areas and schools. The fact that class differences are reflected in school attendance and living conditions have resulted in demands for the increased influence of social workers in the area of social planning. This demand which in itself is correct — does not however solve the basic problem — the questions of the influence of the populace upon social planning and the preference of 'need' as opposed to profit oriented planning. Bengt Borjesson and others have discussed social services and social control and the value system which influences the attitudes and activities of social workers. These discussions have contributed to a clarification of the role of the social worker in the service of the established society. The social heritage problematic has been illuminated by Gustav Jansson, who has shown how poverty and social problems are inherited from one generation to another and even how they have an accumulative tendency. Gunnar Inghe (together with his wife Maj) in widely circulated studies have described society's deficiencies and the social problems of single persons, the outcasts, and the social problems of the family with children and the low wage earner. The debate has taken the shape of demands for reforms within the framework of the existing society, reforms which would provide a more service oriented social service in which compulsory care would be either minimised or done away with altogether. Several have also argued that many of the problems simply cannot be solved in a capitalist society.

Minimum income, negative tax or general subsidy to citizens

The government commissioned low income study has shown that of the approximately 1.9 million fully employed people in Sweden in 1966:

- approximately 120,000 or 6 per cent earned a maximum of two thousand dollars annually
- approximately 375,000 or 20 per cent earned a maximum of three thousand dollars annually
- approximately 640,000 or 33 per cent earned a maximum of three thousand, six hundred dollars annually
- approximately 810,000 or 43 per cent earned a maximum of four thousand dollars annually.

A point seldom made in the low income discussion is the fact that in addition to those listed above there should be added approximately 1.2 million pensioners, most of whom have an extremely low annual income.

The Pensioners Insurance Committee states for example that of approximately 800,000 pensioners who submitted income declarations in 1965, approximately 600,000 had incomes below two thousand dollars (this amount includes the basic old age pension). Information was unavailable for approximately 300,000 pensioners and the committee stated that the overwhelming proportion of this group had no income at all apart from the basic old age pension. In other words they had even lower incomes than those who declared. To low income groups and pensioners should also be added those who are unemployed, those on long term illness insurance or social assistance and numerous other similar groups. A simple mathematical calculation shows that the low income earners (including their minor age children) number between 3 and 4 million people in Sweden. This, as Goran Palm has established in his book *Indoktrineringen: Sverige* (Indoctrination in Sweden), is not a question of underprivileged minorities, but rather of a pillaged majority of the Swedish population.

The low income problematic has resulted in proposals for a guaranteed minimum income. These proposals have varied from a 'minimum wage' (Left Party Communist VPK), 'negative taxation' (*Dagens Nyheter* — Sweden's largest National newspaper), 'mini-income' (Kurt Samuelsson, Bror Rexed and others) to a general subsidy to citizens (Ake Elmer). We shall not discuss here the 'minimum wage' proposal which involves an employer paid and governmént guaranteed minimum wage to employees. We shall only recall our ealier discussion concerning the 'reabsorption tendency' and also recall the Marxist theory of the state.

The notions of a minimum income (included in these are proposals for negative taxation which involves an inflation of income via the state, and the general subsidy to citizens, which implies that all citizens would receive a certain minimum subsidy) have by and large drawn from the Anglo-Saxon countries of USA and England. They are of course related to the class cleavages in these countries which are greater than is generally imagined. In spite of comprehensive information concerning the struggle against US imperialism there still exists widespread ignorance concerning class structure in USA. A survey in connection with the so called war on poverty showed that 34 million Americans lived in destitution, that is to say, they belonged to families with less than a three thousand dollar annual income, or were single persons with an annual income of less than eighteen hundred dollars. Over 8 million received social assistance of which 5 million were families with children. The number of social assistance recipients was greater than during 1936 the worst year of the depression. Conditions in England are also relatively unknown in Sweden. They have however been described in a report from the Swedish Social Attaché to England, Hornlund. According to his report, poverty is increasing and 8 million people in the country have such a low income that it is inadequate to provide a suitable living standard. According to a 1966 study, 43 per cent of all English children did not have the basic food requirements recommended by the British Medical Association (the corresponding figures for 1960 was 36 per cent). In the USA, the conservative economist Milton Freidman, advisory to Barry Goldwater, argued for a minimum income (negative taxation), and most progressive people have pleaded for some form of minimum income.

If we take as our point of departure the theory that in any event there are certain groups of capitalists (domestic market industries) who have an interest in some form of income levelling which provides a more regular and evenly distributed consumer purchasing power and which involves a levelling of incomes between various groups of wage earners as well as between different periods in people's lives (examples 2 and 3 in the section on economy and social policy) and if we also start with the proposition that from the capitalist's point of view the present efforts at income levelling have not been effective, then it is imaginable that the proposal for a minimum wage reform will most certainly be brought forth again.

With regard to the proper position to be taken on the issue of a guaranteed minimum income, from a class perspective the most important question is not the specific organisational nature of such a reform. What is of interest is whether or not the introduction of a minimum income can become an anti-capitalist reform, that is to say, can it lead to an income levelling between capitalist and workers.

It is naturally in the interest of the working class that everyone in this society is guaranteed an income which covers the most basic requirements. It is also in the interest of class solidarity that those who have higher wages work towards ensuring that those who have no income, receive one. However it is above all in the interests of the working class that the capitalists be forced to pay for the labour power they purchase, that is to say, that they be forced to raise the wages of the low income groups, and that they are obliged to pay for the prevention of, or compensation for injuries that arise from the production process (accidents, stress problems, etc.). A minimum income reform which provides everyone with a guaranteed income (and which also can replace the present complicated insurance system, sickness insurance, pension insurance, unemployment insurance) should naturally be completely financed by the employer contributions.

It then depends upon the intensity of trade union and other forms of class struggle whether the gains achieved by such a reform can be retained. An anti-capitalist minimum income reform would entail a uniting of the day to day demands of the workers' struggle with the direct interests of pensioners and other groups. (It should of course be injected here that such a reform does not finally solve the low income problem. Within a capitalist society it is unsolvable.)

The human refuse of the capitalist system of production

The capitalist system of production is geared to the accumulation of surplus value. Consideration is given to the well being of the worker only to the extent that it is necessary to maintain and reproduce the labour force or to the extent that workers through class struggle can assert their rights. This of course does not prevent individual capitalists from having a humanitarian attitude, or from pursuing a ruthless exploitation of the work force. [7] The characteristic of today's capitalist society is capitals' growing merger with the state. The concentration of capital is accentuated. This development is reflected even in the concentration of the population in certain regions in the country, primarily Stockholm, Göteborg and Malmö

182

regions. People are wrenched out of traditional and ingrained places of residence and packed into high rise flop houses while the country-side has been depopulated. Part of the problem which this process leads to may be seen in the area of social work. Alcohol and narcotic abuse, mental damage and other handicaps which the social services work with are often especially related to the large city areas. The committee on narcotic abuse services estimated the number of people misusing narcotics to be approximately 10,000, 8,000 of which were in the large city areas. Of the 80,000 cases of drunkenness nearly one half were in the large city areas.

Technological developments make possible an increased exploitation of the labour force with consequent severe mental and physical exhaustion. At the same time there has developed a heightened frequency of occupational accidents. 130,000 employees annually are injured on the job, approximately 500 die and 2,500 became permanent invalids. Thus during a ten year period, capitalism produces 1.3 million accidents, 5,000 deaths and 25,000 permanent invalids. Of all occupations, mining has the highest frequency of on the job injuries. Corresponding to the increased work pace there has been an increased number of cases of mental or psychological illness. In 1967, 1,702 people committed suicide (1,254 of which were men). It is also significant that Sweden has a higher rate of death due to heart attack than most other European countries.

Capitalist class society sets its mark on family and living conditions. In the cities the population is stratified on the basis of economic and social criteria. At the same time old slums and large family houses are disappearing, entire city sections with the same characteristic features are growing as the old slums and large family houses are replaced by large family city quarters. The working class sections have inferior commercial and cultural services. Schools are segregated — certain schools have 30 per cent immigrant children, others have only children from the working class and still others have only children belonging to middle class homes. [8]

The number of divorces is increasing. The ratio between the number of new marriages and divorces is currently 5:1. Experienced social workers can confirm the relationship between divorce frequency and housing shortages, low incomes and other problems which are a consequence of the social structure. In most large cities nearly 5 per cent of the population are on housing queues, having no housing of their own. (Malmö 1968, approximately 10,000). [Translator's note: the quantitative housing shortage has by and large been over-come in the 70s, but the qualitative problems, i.e. segregation, poor milieu, etc. remain and are probably even aggravated.] While the birth rate is declining, of those born an increasing number are born to single mothers (approximately 20,000 annually). The single mother very often lives in difficult conditions partly manifest by an infant mortality rate nearly twice as high as that of children born to co-habiting parents. Many are forced to seek social assistance in order to manage economically. The guardianship system still exists for the single mother and whether they wish it or not, the child care authorities appoints a 'child care officer' whose task it is to establish paternity and take care of support questions — even to the extent of being responsible for certain counselling functions.

The search for profits and consequent stress in the work place results in an increasing number of workers being excluded from the production process — individuals who must be sluiced over to the municipalities' so called 'protected workshops' where the wages are poor. Workers in these factories are involved in production tasks for private companies. Older workers are currently the most hard pressed on the job. During economic downswings even 45-50 year old workers have difficulty finding employment. Various studies have shown that between 15 and 20 per cent of the adult population have handicaps of different types (see Granath, Helander, Oldhagen). If one adds to that those who are mentally handicapped the figures increase substantially. The cause of these handicaps is not only the clearly higher frequency of accidents on the job but also the damage and injury resulting from long term stress, noise and air pollution endured in the work place.

Social policy, social service and reformism

The adverse consequences of the production system on the population has led to social-liberal conceptions of social intervention. There is a desire to improve the situation of the poor by means of a better social policy and better social services. There is no reason to suspect the good intentions of most of these 'social reformers'. However, their efforts lack analysis. They forget to ask themselves: who gains by reforms? Who do they hope to benefit from reforms? From a life in a sheltered environment, these reformists are often frightened of exposing antagonisms and class conflicts. It is against this background that a series of left social democrat reforms have come forth. In the socio-political debate it is possible to discern the clearly conservative and reactionary views which simply formulate demands designed for the protection of the status quo. These are reflected in the demand for expanded police resources, stiffer sentences for petty drug abuses

184

and expanded legal recourse to compulsory measures concerning psychiatric care. There exists another more liberal stream of thought which wants to adapt people to the existing society through the use of modern psychological, social psychological and pedagogical techniques and principles. The third line of thought which has supporters over a wide political spectrum ranging from left liberals to left social democrats, wants to adapt the society to the individual, however their frame of reference is limited to the general framework of existing society. Among other places the dilemma confronting these reformists is revealed in the social democratics so called 'Programme for Equality'. We quote:

> In spite of the fact that we are quite aware of the connection between social discrepancies and economic and cultural poverty, we lack an acceptable explanatory theory upon which to base social services — in a society which in and of itself changes rapidly. We have certain laws which are built upon an hypothesis of the 'different discrepancies'. Upon this basis, the methods for dealing with the issues have produced demonstrably poor results in those social services dealing with both alcohol and criminal cases. A new explanatory model should have as its point of departure the assumption that those who deviate are, fundamentally, the same as we. This hypothesis is already strongly supported by facts.
>
> From such an ideology, new laws can be legislated and new methods of treatment can be developed, in which one begins with the proposition that we are all more or less weak. And we, conscious of that, must not push aside the weakest, who are weak primarily as a result of the performance and competitive mentality which continues to dominate most areas of society. This is the case despite those breakthroughs which the social democratic policy has in many respects achieved. We have the capacity to have a generous attitude towards those who have not succeeded in our complicated society. A social service must be built-up which begins from the proposition that its primary and most pressing task is to provide services to those individuals who for one or another reason have ended up outside the framework approved by the career society.

The reformists lack what they refer to as an 'explanatory theory' but they are prepared to show generosity towards human waste of the capitalist production system by means of social services. In other words, the social service will continue to serve as capitalism's charwoman.

In PK's (Left Party Communist) programme — there is a section concerning minimum social standards. Even though it contains a number of correct statements, there are also ambiguities. We quote one of these:

> Important demands are:
>
> — a debureaucratised and humanised social service organisation which does not cease with emergency assistance but rather, and above all, focuses upon methodical rehabilitation. Present social, child, and alcohol services should be integrated and tied in more closely to the general health services.

Exactly what is 'methodical rehabilitation' — is it readaption to the industrial milieu which turned previously whole people into invalids, gave them heart attacks, ulcers and silicosis? What is meant by suggesting that the social services should be more closely tied to the general health and hospitalisation services? Does this not mean that one uses these health services' 'diagnostic culture' to conceal the social causes of people's problems? What sort of possibilities do general health services have to influence the fact that 90 per cent of all youth in their early teens commit an average of ten criminal infractions? (see Kerstin Elmhorn).

Those demands for social service reform put forward by the left social democrats involve among other things, a deaccentuation of the 'guardianship' attitude of the social services, a reduction of compulsory social measures, a broadening of general economic support measures, increased social service and information concerning social rights and increased influence of social services in social planning. There is no reason whatever to oppose such demands under certain definite conditions, namely:

> — that these short range reforms be set in the context of a socialist strategy which aims at a revolutionary restructuring of society
>
> — that they are formulated as anti-capitalist reforms
>
> — that the general reforms for a minimum economic standard should not only entail a redistribution between different periods in individual's lives or between different groups within the same social class but above all an income levelling between capitalists and workers, and
>
> — that mechanisms be built into the reforms to safeguard them

against the 'reabsorption process'.

A different social service?

In the foregoing discussion we have attempted to illuminate social policy and social services as a link in the capitalist economic system. We are conscious that our discussion needs to be deepened, as does the analysis of the social services as a part of the bourgeois state apparatus. It has not been possible to either theoretically or practically further illuminate the discussions and rationale concerning social policy, class struggle and the reabsorption tendencies. These deficiencies are primarily due to our inadequate knowledge. We wish to emphasise this and point out that the primary intent of the present article is to stimulate Marxist discussion concerning these questions. Nevertheless we shall also attempt to draw certain conclusions.

During latter years there has arisen a vast number of organisations whose objectives are to change the service institutions in our country, including the social services. Among these organisations are KRUM, which is involved in the penal system, RMH which deals with the mental illness service, RFHL which has taken upon itself the problem of the misuse of pharmaceutical preparations, and also A Different Social Service (or KAMP [struggle] for a different social service) which has as its objective the restructuring of the social services (or social welfare system). There is also Anti-Handikapp and a large number of other organisations which are engaged in more direct and immediate issues. Together these organisations differentiate themselves from earlier traditional organisation types in that they are strongly critical of the service system and use new methods in their work. In any event, they are not corporative organisations (it should also be added that there are also some associated organisations which refuse to accept state and municipal grants, avoid employing functionaries and take other steps to prevent a corporative development). We believe that all of these organisations have great significance. We also believe that in certain conditions, they could contribute to the humanising of the penal systems, mental care institutions and the social services. We also view these organisations objectively as a part of the class struggle (nevertheless most of these organisations naturally do not subjectively view themselves in this manner). At the same time however, on the basis of our theory of the state, we believe that those 'functions' which institutions within the penal system, mental care services and the social services, fulfil in the service of 'social control' (to borrow a term from bourgeois

187

sociology), will most certainly not disappear. They will either remain but in more concealed forms (instead of compulsory measures — pedagogical, social psychological and psychological treatment methods) or be transferred to other state organisations. At the present stage, state power is exercised primarily through economic and normative instruments. Naked force remains in the background as preparedness (and is shown only in emergency situations towards demonstrating youth and all activists).

What has been said here applies to those social workers who wish to see a fundamentally altered form of social service. Social services can change in its form, become more service oriented, compulsory measures can be minimised or transferred to other state organisations. Through active opinion the social service can provide for the interests of those worst off in society in an improved manner. It can also be improved as a place of employment.

In his work the social worker can take the initiative in changing society, if by social change one means more day care centres, cleaning up slum areas, and better residential milieu. However, the social services of course cannot become an instrument for changing the basic social relations which necessitate social assistance — namely the capitalist system of production.

The 'occupational' role of social workers can be altered so that the work becomes more directed towards milieu prevention measures. But it is utopian and absurd to think that within the framework of existing social institutions, social workers could become a 'revolutionary cadre'. An increasing number of them are observing the class antagonisms in society and their underlying causes, as well as the steadily increasing need for social assistance. The social changes which these social workers want to bring about must occur outside the framework of the social services. It can only occur through their involvement in political work.

Translator's footnote

In the past few years state expenditures for social welfare programmes and variants thereof have risen sharply under the impact of a worsened economic situation. Indeed financing of these growing expenditures had been perhaps the central problem facing the new coalition government. There has been no significant expansion of social assistance programmes as the financial scope for such innovations is severely limited. With rising unemployment, increased occupational injury, job related mental and physical disorders, inflation and declining real wages, the budgets of existing programmes have been taxed to their limits and beyond.

Notes

[1] Myrdal, a.a., p.173 ff.

[2] 'The diagnostic culture' is reflected in the terminology used in medicine and psychiatry — a terminology not foreign to social service workers. Diagnostic terms and clichés are used to classify people's difficulties and troubles, in terms of personal inadequacies, isolating them from their social context. They are 'psychopaths', 'sociopaths', 'subcapacity', 'immature', 'apathetic', etc. This establishes a defence against attacking the underlying social problems while at the same time transferring or heightening the 'patients' or 'clients' sense of personal responsibility for the difficulties experienced and their 'personality created' inability to manage them.

[3] See Lena Altvall's study: *Östergård/Österhus, En Slumstudie i Malmö* (a slum study in Malmö). It should of course be emphasised that this low degree of political activity among the poor may be the result of numerous factors. It is conceivable for example, that generously increased economic assistance could help break down this passivity. Social assistance, for example, currently allows no expenditures for cultural activities. The fact that electors from the working class participate to a lesser degree than their bourgeois counterparts in general elections may be due to their experience of the inadequacy of parliamentary activities in solving problems.

[4] SOU 1967:36, *Nykterhetsvardens läge* (the condition of temperance services).

[5] Regarding ATP reform as an anti-capitalist reform, see our definition of different forms of income levelling. The characterisation 'anti-capitalist' reform we use in the restricted sense — that it would lead to an increase in the price of the labour force at the expense of profits. We see the struggle for the ATP reform as an economic struggle. It was never a part of a socialist ideology and was naturally not directed against the prevailing social system.

[6] Because the capitalists have economic and political power due to the fact that they control the state apparatus, there exists a tendency for those advances won by the working class to be returned, reduced or exploited to the capitalists' advantage.

[7] See Sara Lidman's *Gruva* (the mine).

[8] Those who may be interested in studying housing segregation in the large cities more closely might look at part of Göran Lindberg's

189

Socio-ecological Study of 20 Housing Areas in Malmö, Lena Altvall's study *Östergård/Österhus*, B. Pettersson/K. Sjöström, *Fattiga barnfamilier i Malmö* (Poor Families with Children in Malmö), Kristina Belfrage, *Jugoslaver i Malmö* (Yugoslavs in Malmö) and Harald Swedner and others, *Study on School Segregation*).

This article originally appeared in Swedish in the Independent Socialist political journal *Zenit* in the early seventies.

10 The Swedish Labour Market Policy

Gunnar Persson and Lennart Berntson

Foreign politicians and authors who are prone to present Sweden as an ideal model of a calm and well administered society often focus their interest upon the labour market policy. Conservative, liberal and social democratic reformist politicians from abroad all manifest the same interests, which may seem paradoxical considering that all advanced capitalist states have a more or less developed labour market policy.

This interest can be explained in part by the unprecedented expansion achieved by the Swedish labour market policy and in part because it has developed along new lines in Sweden. The expansion — AMS' (Labour Market Board) total expenditures have risen from 34 million dollars in 1956 to 450 million dollars in the 1968-69 budget year — should among other things be viewed against the background of the long periods of relative scarcity of labour power characteristic of post war Sweden, and the consequent intensified demand for more effective utilisation of the existing labour force. This has in turn resulted in demands for new methods and approaches in the labour market policy, or more correctly stated: new methods for channelling the working class to meet the requirements of the uneven development of Swedish capitalism.

Once the social democratic rhetoric presenting the labour market policy as a guarantee for freedom of occupational choice has been shorn away, what remains is a work force adaption policy built upon capitalist priorities and rationality.

The social and political roots of the labour market policy

Labour market policy in the modern sense can be traced back to the first post war economic boom period. The fact that the first developed labour market doctrine and practice emerged precisely in a

191

period of economic boom is important to note. However, more about that later. Up until the early thirties Sweden's 'unemployment policy' was for the most part geared towards supplying the basic necessities and preventing overly widespread public discontent with the high unemployment rates. As such it was similar in both purpose and character to other social policies.

The then current economic theories offered no scientifically credible explanation of the causes of the recurrent economic crises nor could it offer any effective advice on their remedy. Economists generally viewed unemployment as self-inflicted of course, and that the only means of eliminating it was for individual workers to accept lower wages thus encouraging capitalists to once again buy their labour. The unemployment policy was oriented towards arranging relief work (at lower than the average market wages) for the unemployed.

For Marxist economists these recurrent economic crises were not so problematic. Marx had grasped the critique of the theoretical foundations upon which the political economists based their assumption that unemployment derived from the overly high wages of the workers, even though it was J.M. Keynes who went down in history as the 'discoverer' of unemployment. (In itself an admirable achievement for a bourgeois economist at that time). [1] And social democracy in its turn derived its conception of the rise and mediation of economic crises from those explanations which bore the mark of Keynes as he was refined by Wigorss and Myrdal, etc.

For Keynes, the central problem of the economic situation of his time was the insufficiency of 'effective demand'. The old relief work could be supplied with an economic rationale by making several simple modifications. At the practical political level, this economic reorientation entailed that employment was stimulated through state expenditures, that wages for the average worker were adjusted upward to the level paid for unskilled labour, and that there was a rapid rise in the cost of the unemployment policy. During the period from 1914-34, the total cost of the unemployment policy rose 100 million dollars, 40 million of which were expended in the years 1933-34 alone. [2]

The post war period: the trade union movement and the wage policy

The new labour market policy which emerged during the latter half of the forties should be viewed in part against the background of the favourable post war economic conjuncture with its tendency toward

192

'overfull' employment, and in part against the background of the regulation of the labour market which to a great extent began during the special conditions prevailing in the military alert period of the second world war. At the outbreak of the war the Unemployment Commission was replaced by the state's Labour Market Commission. As was the case in many other European countries, the war fostered the welding together of the leading strata in the state, the economy and organisations, the strengthening of co-operation, and the development of social solidarity — that is, a solidarity with the prevailing social and economic order — which came to play an important role for future economic policy. In addition, numerous administrative routines developed by the war time commissions were later adapted to the requirements of the post war period.

During the war period and for several years afterwards there were only small changes in workers real wages. When the situation of the working class improved as a result of the acute labour shortage employers and 'labour leaders' in SAP and LO demanded in the name of social solidarity and economic stability that the working class should display 'moderation' and not exploit its temporary position of strength to win large wage increases. Their continual warning was that wages must not rise faster than productivity, in other words, the prevailing distribution between labour and capital must be preserved. LO (the Swedish Confederation of Trade Unions) economist Gösta Rehn however was somewhat more clever. He understood that for an organisation whose main task was the struggle for improved wages, too much timidity and moderation in that struggle might damage the internal stability of the trade unions. Thus trade unions should in fact pursue a fairly aggressive wage policy and the state could assume responsibility for economic stability using increased taxation to indirectly reduce the wage gains achieved by the workers through union struggles. In this context, Rehn had the dubious honour of being ten years ahead of his time in proposing sales taxes. [3]

Another LO economist, Rudolf Meidner, was also of the opinion that at least in the current situation the labour movement could not assume the responsibility for maintaining economic stability because it would entail too much strain on the movement. However his perspective was somewhat different:

> The origins of these strains do not simply lie here. To appeal
> to responsibility for the long term interest of the whole
> society as well as the working class — for economic stability —
> in opposition to the groups own obvious short-range interest
> of immediate wage increases, presumes an education of the

rank and file union members which not even such well-developed trade union movements as the English and Swedish are able to achieve within reasonable time. [4]

Labour as market disturbance

The other important problem which engaged LO economists and which is concerned less with wage policy and more with labour market policy, is how labour power could be best employed from the viewpoint of the 'national economy'. The problem was actualised by the labour shortages in certain expansive sectors of business and an inadequate, spontaneous movement of labour into these branches. The upward shifting of the age pyramid toward the higher ages, favourable conjunctures for the entire economy and several other factors resulted in the sluggish mobility of the labour force. By the term 'sluggish mobility' is meant that the labour force would not quickly and willingly allow themselves to be steered from one branch or occupation to another by the differences in wage levels. According to liberal economic theory the labour force should have shifted automatically — an assumption of questionable truth. According to pace setting social democratic economists such as Rehn the labour force ought to do this. For Rehn as for other liberal economists, market economy (that is — free competition — capitalism) is not simply a theoretical explanation of how the various production factors should best be distributed for different purposes, but rather it was the ideal. This means that to the greatest extent possible, a self-regulating market should determine the direction and placement of capital and labour power. From the perspective of the national economy this would result in the best possible combination of capital and labour because — in the final analysis — the restriction of production would be decided by the consumers. The notion of consumer sovereignty, cultivated for the purpose of self defence by the apologists of capitalism is an idea as incorrect as it is cherished. Economists as diverse as Marx and Schumpeter have demonstrated the primacy of production over consumption, simply expressed: it is not changes in consumption or demand which explains the dynamic of capitalism and technological changes.

Rehn draws a sharp distinction between economics and politics. In a volume written in honour of Tage Erlander he expresses it in the following manner: 'A fundamental obstacle in directing the economy is the politicisation of decisions which should be of an exclusive economic — market nature . . . . ' [5]

In Rehn's distorted perspective, which is in fact characteristic of the basic line in Swedish labour market policy, socialist politics become synonymous with the recreation of the liberal order through social measures (see the article cited in note [5]).

As a description of a previous or present capitalistic or 'mixed economy' system, the liberal model is simply unrealistic. As an objective for economic policy, it leads to the re-enforcement of capitalism. Rehn and other leading social democratic economists now know that Swedish capitalism does not operate like their ideal market economy, there exists a series of 'market disturbances' which threaten the equilibrium of the system. A worker who will not move even though he lacks steady employment or can receive better wages in another region is a market disturbance. [6]

It is in this context that an important aspect of the labour market policy enters the picture. When the labour force will not readily allow itself to be steered and channelled between different branches of industry and geographical areas by differences in the price employers are willing to pay, then the labour force is not functioning in accordance with the liberal theory (or in accordance with the wishes and objectives of capitalist in the dynamic sectors of the economy) and other methods must be employed to ensure that labour functions along the general lines prescribed by the theory.

From theory to practice

At least in the initial stages of modern labour market policy, it was thought that the sluggish mobility of the labour force was due to a lack of information concerning the situation in the labour market. Important aspects of the labour market policy have been developed pursuing this notion: the dissemination of information by and through state operated employment offices, the publication, *Placement Journal — The Labour Market* and various forms of occupational and employment counselling. Not only do such services reduce both the contact and employment service costs of companies by shifting it onto the state, but it also means that employers can cut down on their traditional — and during boom periods, ineffective and costly — 'information system' (namely price competition for available labour power which parenthetically speaking, favours those selling their labour power). The dissemination of information and to an especially high degree occupational and unemployment counselling, are selective and determined by the prevailing labour market situation. In issue after issue the publication *The Labour Market* unceasingly hammers home its 'adaption' ideology.

Occupational counselling which is systematically applied to each new batch of labourers is geared towards steering and channelling employment expectations and ideals among this upcoming labour force, to streamline while at the same time giving the illusion of free and independent choice of work.

There soon developed certain doubts regarding the effectiveness of simply disseminating information concerning employment opportunities as well as the efficiency of the traditional employment agency system. It became clear that it would be necessary to utilise measures of a more or less openly arbitrary nature in order to 'adapt' the labour force. Certainly, proposals for the use of administrative coercion were avoided — at least at the level of official rhetoric, on the other hand however the government took positive measures to strengthen the market and economic coercive measures which are integral to the capitalist economy. Hans Hagnell of the Metal Workers Union suggested for example that wage differentials between various branches of industry should be increased in order to effect the transference of labour power between different sectors that is considered desirable from the point of view of the 'national economy'.

The view exaggerated wage differentials would then be modified once the desired shifts in the work force had been achieved. [7]

That labour market policy would strengthen the market forces, or stated more correctly, facilitate their influence by the occupational and geographic adaptation of the labour force, has become a central premise in the Swedish labour market doctrine. The immediate result has been the establishment of the entire system of 'mobility stimulating' measures ranging from relocation and resettlement grants to assistance for the purchase of individual homes. (While these measures were anticipated by Rehn, they only came to have determining significance during the 1960s).

From this perspective labour market policy is but a reflection of capitalism's spontaneous and uneven development. However there is good reason to view it as having strengthened tendencies towards the depopulation of certain parts of the country (not only in the north) which has resulted in the concentration of industry and population in a very few unhealthy centres — a concentration which is only justifiable from a strictly company economic perspective. In this we come to another of the many inaccurate and unscientific notions inherent in Swedish labour market theory, namely that there exists no conflict or contradiction between what is profitable from the point of view of company economy and what is rational from a social economic perspective, or better expressed: that there is no conflict of interests between employers and wage earners.

When Rehn and the other social democratic economists speak about what is best from the viewpoint of 'national economy' it is merely a *aposteriori* construction of those tendencies which have already emerged in the economy. Those companies which 'best' require labour power are quite simply those which were most profitable and expansive from the viewpoint of private economy. Whether they produce balloons or christmas tree decorations has nothing to do with the matter.

During the sixties it has been precisely those measures directed at 'branch' mobility (retraining) and geographic mobility (retraining and resettlement assistance, home purchase assistance) which grew in significance compared with other labour market policy methods. From having been completely insignificant during the fifties it has grown during the sixties to account for approximately 10 per cent of the Labour Market Board's budget. If one discounts the largest expenditure in the Labour Market Board's budget, namely relief work, these measures together with expenditures for the employment of the handicapped are the dominant means employed by the labour market policy.

Characteristically, the 1960 labour market study addresses itself chiefly to finding new means of promoting geographical mobility. It is said to be a 'prerequisite for a well functioning labour market', but it quite simply involves the price which Swedish workers must pay because there is no goal conscious economic planning and industrial distribution in Sweden. [8]

Labour market policy as compulsion

At least one sociologist has already received his PhD by figuring out how to talk people who do not want to move, into moving neverthe-less. Researcher, Per Kempe, writes: 'Deliberations with the client [Labour Market Board and the 1960 Labour Market Committee] revealed that studies should be conducted of people who actually showed themselves to be reluctant to move even with the aid of the mobility easing policy and whose unemployment could not be attributed to simple chance.'

Note that the language used in Kempe's perspective is typical also of that of the Labour Market Board. The objective of this particular study, which was to find new methods to 'encourage' the labour force to move, has a dash of that raw matter of factness which is attempted to be kept concealed by the social democratic rhetoric in which the labour market policy is couched. In the Government proposal 1966:52 it is stated for example, that the labour market policy shall promote full, productive and freely chosen employment in the individual's as well as society's interest. [9]

Let us make perfectly clear at the outset that in a class society, the concept 'society's interest' is both metaphysical and meaningless. The concrete situation in which the individual worker finds himself is one in which he must constantly defend himself against the demands of employers. With regard to the Labour Market Board, it is absolutely clear that it does not take the side of the wage earners against the employers.

In actual fact, the bulk of the Labour Market Board budget supports objectives which have not even the remotest connection to the 'free choice of work'. During the entire sixties more than half, sometimes up to 60-70 per cent of the budget went to public relief work. This type of activity is partly oriented to shifts in economic conjunctures but is also utilised as a type of defensive policy against the increasingly catastrophic depopulation which threatens certain regions. [10]

Table 10.1 clarifies the significance of other important support measures in the labour market policy. The quantitatively most important is also the traditional, namely the dissemination of information regarding employment opportunities. (Economically however, this activity does not require any greater resources than do those programmes designed to stimulate labour mobility). In this capacity the employment exchange functions as a sort of central clearing house. There are primarily two categories of job seekers who can make use of the information regarding their entry into the labour market, specifically the unemployed and those newly graduated from schools and universities. An important and relatively new aspect of labour market policy is the retraining activities (which falls under the general rubric of labour market education) which in addition to shifting the cost of such education and training from the companies to the taxpayers, is also utilised as a smokescreen to conceal the inability to solve the problem of unemployment. [11] Labour market education has on more than one instance been employed in a first attempt to erode the reluctance to move which characterises those individuals who suffer from the remarkable 'illness' which Labour Market Board bureaucrats choose to call 'reluctance to move' (the feeling of strong ties to one's traditional village or region).

In the first instance however, the retraining programme is a response to the demands of modern industry for trained and educated personnel. An expanding programme which table 10.1 does not reveal is Labour Care which is aimed at providing training and employment for the mentally and physically handicapped under conditions less pressing and hectic than those which are normal in a conventional work place. To a certain degree this labour power is recruited from groups who were not earlier active in production or who were engaged in more or less meaningless therapy employment. In the future however, Labour Care will to an increasing degree take charge of those growing groups of individuals who have been mentally and/or physically exhausted or handicapped as a result of the current conditions of industrial employment. Between 1951 and 1966, the number of 'Labour Care Measures' (roughly calculated as the number of persons who have become subject to Labour Care), has increased five fold to approximately 50,000 per year. At the same time it has become increasingly difficult to place 'Labour Care cases' on the open market. 'Protected work places' which were practically unknown at the beginning of the fifties, now account for the bulk of such employment placements. A government study states: 'The primary cause of the stagnation in the placement of "Labour Care cases" in the open market seems to be their increased numbers and seriousness. A further reason is probably the general decline in demand for labour during the last few years.' [12]

Table 10.1
The use of certain labour market policy assistance measures
during the years 1955-67

Means of assistance	Number of persons				
	1955	1960	1965	1966	1967
'Vacancy and applicant information'					
Labour applicants	684,087	716,098	820,431	864,481	799,318
Vacant places	1,263,884	1,167,156	1,180,028	1,104,134	946,307
Positions filled	1,049,829	942,469	920,315	876,896	774,973
'Labour Market Training' (average measurement)		6,580	15,922	18,846	23,549
'Financial Grants for Moving' (relocation aid)		6,950	21,144	18,078	18,677
'Employment Creating Measures' Relief work, (average measurement)	1,010	6,102	9,824	9,189	13,712
Archive work and Aid to Musicians, (average measurement)	800	1,482	2,718	3,068	3,617

Source: SOU 1968:60, p.109

Labour market policy during high economic conjuncture

The working class naturally has greater possibilities to protect their immediate interests during high economic conjunctures. It is then that employees have increased opportunities for changing places of employment (without the necessity of changing occupation) and in this manner choose those places of employment which offer the best combination of wages and working conditions. Inasmuch as high economic conjunctures can be presumed to benefit even generally declining companies or branches of industry, worker security in these areas too is improved. This in turn effects a slowdown of labour force mobility away from these sectors and into the more expansive branches experiencing acute labour shortages. In such situations labour market policy is aimed at restricting wage earners temporary, even though limited freedom of choice, within wage branches, i.e. freedom to choose and change places of employment and the possibility to gain wage benefits over and above union agreements, at the same time that mobility from low to high wage branches is stimulated.

Work place mobility within high wage branches is hindered through the efforts of both the Labour Market Board and the employers. The Labour Market Board monopolises the detailed information regarding the labour market and offers no help whatsoever to any worker who wishes to change his place of employment within — for example, the metal industry. It is well known that there exists an agreement within, among others, the Engineering Association to refrain from advertising in the newspapers for collectively employed personnel. Furthermore there is a sort of employment cartel among many large companies which is based on the agreement that one neither employs nor competes for each other's labour force. Such an agreement exists for example between LKAB and the Uddeholm's owned TGA.

Not of least interest is the fact that one of the social democratics leading economists, Rudolf Meidner, concludes one of his most important works [13] with detailed concrete proposals concerning how one may best restrain this type of worker mobility which he terms, 'maladjustment mobility'. Why should workers and salaried employees be well adapted to employers?

Concluding views

We have sought to show that the doctrine and politics of the labour market grew out of monopoly capitalism's need for a mobile and easily adaptable labour force. The immediate background has been partly the exceptionally rapid concentration of capital (so called structural alterations) and partly the relative scarcity of labour power during long periods in post war Sweden.

The social democratic labour market ideology presents the labour market policy as being directed at satisfying the need of private individuals for service to facilitate so called freedom of choice of employment. These assessments are supported also by some economists from a so called welfare theory and utopian viewpoint.

In certain cases of course, the labour market policy does satisfy the individual's occupational ambitions; it can assist those concerned to gain a better paid job and reduce the duration of unemployment, etc. However the conclusion cannot be drawn from this that the social function of the labour market policy is directed at the satisfaction of the needs of private individuals. On the other hand it can be pointed out that individual occupation expectations and capitalism's demand for an easily adaptable work force can sometimes coincide.

However this is not the dominant side of the labour market policy, nor is it along these lines that one should seek its origin and background. An illustration of this can be found if one reads for example the Labour Market Board magazine *Arbetsmarknaden*. The journal's leading articles revolve around the problem of how the labour force should be shifted, retrained and more extensively educated so as to satisfy 'demand' (read, companies). It is at all times a question of how workers should be adapted to the company requirements, never is it seen as a problem of how to transfer companies and capital to where labour power is already available. From this perspective certain groups in the labour force become difficult to adapt: those who are handicapped, workers who are too old or exhausted, workers who refuse to move from their home areas (so called 'ortsbundenhet' — to be psychologically bound to one place), workers with minimal education, housewives who wish to take jobs, etc. These are the groups which the labour market policy is focusing upon.

The fact that the labour market policy can in certain individual cases offer assistance, should not be allowed to conceal its function *vis à vis* the working class in its totality. Contrary to what is claimed by the spokesmen and sympathisers of the so called 'workers-government', the labour market policy has not been a reform which has strengthened the position of the working class in Swedish society. Rather its effects have been just the opposite. Through the labour market policy the working class is subjected not only to capitalism erratic fluctuations and changing needs, but this basic relationship has also been strengthened as the demands of the bourgeoisie are achieved with increasing effectiveness in the form of administrative compulsion, pressure, and persuasion, underpinned by the threat of unemployment, etc. The labour market policy is in the first instance an instrument used by the bourgeois state to support and make more effective the position of large finance — domestically in relation to the working class, internationally in relation to monopoly capital of other countries.

Translator's footnote

As is the case with social service programmes, government expenditures on labour market policies have increased dramatically under the impact of the current economic situation. Programmes for job training and retraining, early pensions, worker-care and relocation are placed under unprecedented financial strain. Thus there has been no significant innovations in labour market policy during the tenure of the new coalition government.

The area in which innovations have continued, has been in the realm of job reform and industrial democracy. Indeed, in terms of labour market innovations in the last few years, most have been in this relatively inexpensive and politically advantageous realm of work organisation, and job reform.

Notes

[1] Keynes' and Marx's theory of economic crisis are not identical. While Marxists pursue an analysis of the method of functioning and non-functioning of capitalist economy, Keynes discusses, in psychological terms, the increasing 'propensity to save' which would create insufficient demand.
[2] SOU 1968:62, p.27.
[3] Tiden, NR.3, 1948, p.135 ff.
[4] Tiden, NR.9, 1948, p.469.
[5] 'Arbetsmarknadspolitik som samhallside' in *Fifteen Years with Tage Erlander*, Stockholm 1961, p.80.
[6] Wallenberg and other monopoly capitalists operate also as the instigators of market disturbances (any honourable liberal would readily concede this), but it is hardly that the social democrat government would think to force them back into line with an orderly market in the same brutal way which they handled, for example, the labour

force in Northern Sweden.

[7] Wage policies and full employment, Fackforeningsrorelsen, Mr.43, 1949.

[8] In this context there is reason to warn against 'village romanticism' which is embraced by a section of intellectuals from large cities. Geographic and occupational mobility can be both desirable and necessary. However in a society where capitalists have been expropriated, it is then possible through general planning to attempt to move capital to the workers instead of the opposite. This is not so remarkable when one recalls that the migration of labour power from Northern Sweden is in general related to industrial investments — though they were investments in Göteburg, Stockholm and Malmö areas.

[9] It is interesting to note that to the degree that conflict is perceived, a liberal conflict model is employed in which the contending parts are the individual vs. society, and not a scientific theoretical approach, which analyses class conflict.

[10] This aspect of the labour market policy which is usually called 'employment creating measures' is to a great degree part of the general economic policy, so we shall not concern ourselves with it further.

[11] With the expansion of retraining programmes the state powers could consciously lower the rate of employment. See Villy Berstrom: *Economic Policy in Sweden and its Effects*, Uppsala 1969, p.39 and note 4.

[12] SOU 1968:61, p.146.

[13] Rudolf Meidner, *The Swedish Labour Market with Full Employment*, Stockholm 1954.

This article originally appeared in Swedish in the Independent Socialist political journal *Zenit* in the early seventies.

11 Work Milieu — Part I

Olle Jepsson and Gunnar Ågren

During the beginning of this century mining in South Africa expanded tremendously. This occurred primarily through the introduction of new technical methods. These altered mining techniques however resulted in 25 per cent of all miners, primarily Africans, being affected by silicosis. The death rate was extremely high. The mine owners who suffered economic losses because they also 'owned' the labour force, very quickly began to study the causes of silicosis. It was found that the most important cause was the stone dust in the mines caused by new boring techniques. In relatively short order they designed methods for minimising the spread of stone dust with the result that by the 1920s the silicosis frequency had dropped to 3.5 per cent.

In Sweden today, a silicosis rate of 6 per cent is expected for workers involved in 'silicosis threatened jobs' (miners, steelworkers, quarry workers, etc.). The relationship between stone dust and silicosis is of course as well known in Sweden as in South Africa and yet no effective preventive measures are taken against the illness. While it is relatively easy to measure stone dust, no systematic measurement is carried out. No effective measures are taken to decrease the dust content in the air. Primary interest is concentrated on X-ray examinations so that those who already have lung damage can either be given other work or put on the sick list (that is, shift the problem of support onto the society). Inasmuch as silicosis is progressive, these measures do not prevent many from dying of the illness.

In a nutshell this example reflects a large number of work milieu problems. What is it that differentiates employers in Sweden and South Africa? It is hardly that the latter are more humane or less profit oriented. The important difference lies in the fact that South Africa has many similarities to a slave society. Mine owners own their workers in about the same way that farmers own cattle. In the same way that farmers suffer economic losses if the cows are struck by a fatal illness, the mine owners suffer economic losses if their labour force dies off too quickly.

Sweden on the other hand is a rather cultivated capitalist society. 'Freedom of work' is defended, that is to say, the employers' right to freely pick and choose from the labour supply. It has a labour market policy through which the capitalist state commits large resources to ensuring the supply of properly educated, trained, and situated labour force to employers. Thus, silicosis stricken workers can be readily replaced by healthy ones. Employers do of course have an interest in the prevention of occupational illnesses if they too rapidly deprive them of difficult to replace trained labour power. In general however silicosis is not such an illness, it follows a relatively high age when work ability normally declines. Consequently the employer hardly has any strong motive for preventing silicosis unless he is forced to by union action or political measures.

There is a crystal clear relationship between the economic system and the work milieu. Nevertheless this relationship tends to be mystified and one instead hears most often reference made to 'technological development', as a sort of abstract all encompassing cause of the deteriorating work milieu. Such an argument is nonsense, for to the contrary, technological development provides improved opportunities to avoid occupational illnesses if one is permitted to utilise them.

Overly comprehensive measures to protect workers from sicknesses are often portrayed as a threat to our economic standards and development. This too is absurd, as in numerous socialist countries there is more rapid economic development than in Sweden. In spite of this, legislation has been passed which sets a very low limit for numerous dangerous substances which can be found in work places. In the Soviet Union, the silicosis frequency is between 1 and 2 per cent with the lowest rate existing in the most highly productive mines and factories.

Consequently work milieu problems must be viewed in the context of the capitalist relations of production and their development. The two most important developmental tendencies affecting work milieu are structural rationalisations and increased exploitation. Structural rationalisations are related to the tendency towards capital concentration and monopolisation. The most important effects are that numerous companies are closed down, operations within remaining companies are shut down making production more one sided, and numerous companies become 'satellites' to, and therefore dependent upon larger companies. The effects for society are huge population shifts. Business is impoverished and becomes more one sided in the depopulated areas, where the low wage situation is often exploited to carry out the routinised production of components for the products of other industries. In large urban areas milieu destruction and social problems increase in the form of high rents, and high rates of alcoholism, mental illness and suicide.

According to information from the Central Bureau of Statistics, approximately 150,000 people are affected each year by company closures and cutbacks in operations. In a three year period, about one-fifth of the members of the LO (National Confederation of Trade Unions) are affected by reassignments within companies. To this should be added those so called 'free will' job changes which are usually estimated to annually reach about 50 per cent of the industrial labour force. In 1958 the method of presenting statistics was altered so that it is at present difficult to gain an especially detailed picture of this mobility. So much is clear however, that free agency in the 'free will' change of jobs is most often illusory.

Population relocation in stages

Employment changes most often occur in a definite direction. Moves are usually from smaller to larger units. Workers are forced to change from nearby work places to jobs which lie a long way from their place of residence. These changes also tend to be from work tasks of a relatively independent and manual character to routinised assembly line tasks and monotonous attendance jobs. People move from their own individual dwellings to high rise ghettos where social contacts are often absent.

Population relocation is selective in the sense that in the event of a company shut down, the youngest and healthiest are most often successfully transferred to new positions. The older workers and those with poorer health end up instead either under 'labour care' or condemned to 'early pension'. Structural conversion thus functions as a screen whereby the best labour force (from a capitalist employer's viewpoint) remains while the worst part is continually sorted out.

In 1968 the Labour Market Board carried out a study which showed that of all those affected by lay offs during that year, 64 per cent had found new employment, 16 per cent had left the labour market permanently due either to long term sick leave or early pension, and 20 per cent were registered as unemployed. For the older and female employees the figures were considerably above the average.

The second major tendency in working conditions in capitalist society relates to increased exploitation. This increased exploitation is a necessity for employers. The production process within a branch changes constantly with the result that it continually costs more money to set up new plants. One hundred and twenty-five thousand dollars investment per employee is an average figure in the most technologically advanced industrial sectors. In order to pay the interest on these increased investments and maintain an unchanged distribution on the expended capital it is necessary that every worker produces more suplus value.

In this context the most important methods for increasing surplus value is an increase in the intensity of labour and a lengthening of labour time. (One other important method, which falls outside the scope of this study is a decline of real wages). In practice, the change over to shift work has the same effect by entailing the exploitation of more workers per volume of capital investment.

The lengthening of labour time appears to be counter to the legislation and contracts which have dealt with the shortening of work hours. However, the government commissioned 'Low Income Study' shows that many people are obliged to work hours far above the legally established limits in order to maintain themselves. In many places actual work time is increased by measuring it with punch clocks and eliminating wasted time and work pauses. This development is more important than one might think inasmuch as these brief pauses significantly minimise continual stress, decreased the risk of hearing damage and provided opportunity to air poisonous gases out of the lungs of employees.

Increased work intensity can be achieved in a variety of ways. One important method is to break down simply and design labour tasks so that they can be repeated at a rapid pace. Methods and time/motion studies are primarily employed to design work locations and movement patterns in such a manner that no energy is lost to the employer. Thus, to an increasing degree the work place is determined by the production process.

Piece work

The most important means of intensifying the work pace is various forms of piece work. Straight accord entails the entire wage being determined by performance of the individual employee. Mixed piece work involves having part of the total wage paid on the basis of a fixed hourly rate. Group piece work entails a work group sharing the surplus earnings. In this manner, employee supervision is replaced by group pressure upon the lowest or least productive workers.

Piece work can either be paid in proportion to specifically evaluated work tasks or be based upon various labour measurement systems. Foremost among these is the MTM system which involves dividing each labour task up into small individual moments. Thus putting in a screw can be broken down into the following moments: 1) pick up the screw driver 2) move it to the screw 3) turn the screw driver 4) take hand back, etc. For such a system to function, every movement must be carried out in a predetermined manner. On the basis of a time study, each movement is attributed an ideal time which then provides the basis for calculations of piece work payment.

Initially it was only possible to employ time study based piece work in assembly line production where movement patterns were repeated in rapid sequence. Presently however, systems which are based upon MTM can be used even in mining and ship building.

In the short run MTM based piece work systems may appear to be to the advantage of the workers, which partially explains the ease with which they were introduced. For younger workers and during shorter work periods it is often possible to perform faster than the ideal time for various work moments, with the consequence that earnings increase. However, such a pace soon has the additional consequence that new time studies are carried out and the piece work payment table is recalculated. In this manner there is a spiral effect in which the work pace is continually increasing. Such a rapid tempo most often affects older workers where physiological changes in the nervous system and muscles decrease the possibility of maintaining the rapid pace. This explains why it is necessary for ASEA to replace assembly line workers once they reach thirty-five and at Volvo people over forty are disuaded from taking employment on the assembly line. It is also an important reason as to why, according to recent studies, 50 per cent of industrial workers over the age of fifty are considered only 'conditionally' fit for work.

The MTM system is built upon the so called Taylor school of labour psychology. According to it, all work should be divided into carefully predetermined work moments and workers should receive instruction on how the work operations should be carried out leaving as little room as possible for independent thought. It also suggests that wages based on piece work should be the rule rather than the exception and that payment be made as close as possible to the period worked. Thus, weekly wages are considered preferable to monthly wages.

It has now been shown however that the Taylor system is not adequate to break down the solidarity among the workers. In many work places there has developed a practice of working below maximum capacity; settling for about 75 per cent of the possible wage attainable. Consequently they have spontaneously chosen somewhat more suit-able working conditions and solidarity with their older comrades instead of allowing themselves to be exploited one hundred per cent by employers.

The possibilities of the psychology of work

To a great extent, the psychology of work deals with the development of methods for breaking down spontaneous solidarity among workers. Terms such as company democracy, involvement and participation all suggest an effort to have the worker experience a feeling of alliance with the company without in fact having any influence over it. In the so called mental health campaign carried out by Folksam LO and SAP (the Swedish Labour Party) the plea is made among other things for shop foremen to also function as group therapists for the employees. By letting employees talk about their family relations and personal problems it is hoped to minimise their tendency to take such aggressive actions as wildcat strikes.

A comparatively new development of the same basic idea is the 'self-determining' group. For reasons which are quite incomprehensible some view the formation of these groups as a method of giving employees real power over their places of work. It should be mentioned that the primary reason experimentation was begun with such 'self-determing' groups according to the method's leading theoretician — Norwegian Einar Thorsrud — was that the cost of employee supervision had become too great. An overly large supervisory apparatus also entailed greater difficulty in making changes in the company. Instead, an attempt is made to persuade employees to supervise themselves. In this manner employees can be permitted to even take care of the foreman's job. Overall it entails an increase in labour intensity and the possibility of decreasing personnel strength. Employees remain as powerless as ever concerning production planning and overall working conditions.

It is sometimes suggested that piece work is antiquated. There is even a certain — though very weak tendency to change over to hourly wages. This is related to the fact that many work tasks are so effectively determined by machines that there exist no real opportunities to vary the work pace. At times it is more important for employers to encourage a steady work tempo rather than uneven peak performances.

One very common method of increasing the labour intensity is to have ever fewer employees doing a certain task. A work team which was previously comprised of six persons is now made up of perhaps four. The two 'rationalised' employees have been 'replaced' by various technical aids but in reality this 'minimising' of the term size generally entails a greater pressure on those remaining.

About 15 per cent of the members of the LO do shift work. Significantly, there are no reliable statistics but only figures which have been obtained by indirect methods (the fact that shift workers generally work shorter hours however is clearly noted in the statistics). Shift work is on the increase and is even spreading to office work. Shift workers are demonstrably poorly off. On the average they sleep one hour less per day than their daytime working colleagues. The worsened possibilities for regular meal times have the consequence that such workers more often have upset stomachs and ulcers. They become socially isolated and are not able to take as active a part in political or union organisations as others. And finally, they are more frequently subject to psychological difficulties.

Effects of work milieu

The connection between work milieu and injury and illness among the employees is concealed in a number of ways.

Statistics concerning occupational illness and injury are clearly misleading. In the first place they are not published until three years after the illness or injury occurs and are consequently out of date. Furthermore, a number of important occupational illnesses — back troubles, ulcers and mental problems for example — are excluded from the statistics. The verification demands are such that many injuries and illnesses are not reported. Although it is possible to ascertain that between 50 per cent and 75 per cent of all industrial workers have hearing damage, each year only about ten noise injuries are registered.

The cause of injuries is most often sought in the so called 'human factor'. A large proportion of research concerning occupational injuries is a desperate search for 'accident prone' workers. Clearly, there is a human factor in an accident. However if the objective is to prevent accidents, this is not of particular importance. 'Carelessness' and 'unwatchfulness' are generally the logical consequences of an overly rapid work pace, poor safety devices, poor training, high noise levels, etc. In the last analysis it is a question of the interests of profit and of employee health being in absolute opposition. A common type of injury is having a finger cut off in a press. It is possible to construct 'idiot safe' presses but they cost more money than normal. In the last analysis it is a question of what is most important; profits or workers' fingers.

The focus of the medical practice is generally such that the cause of illnesses and injuries are concealed. Many papers have been written on different methods of operating on ulcers. On the other hand there is for the most part an absence of studies concerning the relationship between ulcers and various types of working conditions. The point of departure for psychiatric explanations of the problem is an individualistic frame of reference. Depending upon the school he belongs to, the psychiatrist looks for biochemical disorder, tragic childhood experiences, etc. Investigating the work situation is most often seen as either uninteresting or unscientific. Most often the treatment recommended amounts to a mere concealment of the symptoms. With the help of 35 million tranquillising and sleeping pills each year, the anxiety level of the Swedish working class is kept down. It can be expected in the future that various forms of conversation therapy will find increased use in the effort to alleviate antagonisms at work. A conception of illness with such an inbuilt individualistic explanation of human behaviour is an effective means of breaking down the solidarity between those who remain in the productive process and those who have been cast out.

There are three major types of damage done to workers:

1   Mental and physical exhaustion

2   'Accidents'

3   Injury arising directly from external factors such as noise, dust, poisonous gases, solvents, etc.

The role of the Swedish National Confederation of Trade Unions (LO)

In 1928 the collective bargaining law as well as legislation establishing and laws establishing labour courts were passed. They were passed contrary to a solid worker opinion. It is in fact a class law designed for the interests of employers. Paragraph four forbids the use of strikes during a contract period. On the other hand, under the rights of private ownership capitalists can introduce whatever changes they wish, including those which will deteriorate the work milieu. The decisions of the labour court give clear evidence of how the law functions in the interests of employers. Workers who refuse to carry out health hazardous jobs can be fired and punished if they shut down operations. The collective bargaining law was worked out with the active participation of leading social democratic politicians and it was not long before the leadership of the LO accepted it whole heartedly. This was the beginning of an increasing policy of developed class co-operation. The 'Saltjöbads' agreement, as it is called, between LO and SAF (the Swedish Employers Confederation) was signed in 1938. In 1942 the organisations reached a settlement concerning safety committees and established a joint worker safety board. The agreement on company safety committees was reached in 1946 and in 1948 they arrived at settlement regarding labour studies. The present agreement on company health services was arrived at in 1967.

The agreement involving labour studies is illuminating concerning the character of this co-operation:

> Efforts at increasing effectivity within every company must be continual in order that the company will be able to maintain an even pace with technological developments. It is a common interest that all the employees co-operate so the company can be effective in competition. As every other member of society, the employees benefit from rationalisation, which leads to increased production and to that extent thereby creates the basis for a general raising of the standard of living. An important element in this rationalisation are measures aimed at reducing the use of unnecessary materials and labour in production. Labour studies, properly conducted, are a rational means to achieve that objective.

Precisely what this co-operation has meant in practice for workers, is at present well known. MTM for example was introduced in the Metal Workers Union agreement during the beginning of the fifties by a social democratic union leadership against widespread worker opinion. This rank and file opposition was effectively countered by fanning and exploiting the then prevalent anti-communist sentiments and by means of an under the table agreement for a one time wage increase if the MTM system was adopted. Workers have since been obliged to resort to 'wildcat strikes' and lacked support from 'their' organisations whenever they have tried to protest the increasing pace and intensity of work.

As late as 1969, the secretary of the LO, Olle Gunnarsson made a statement which elucidates the co-operation ideology:

> The relationship between employers and wage earners is characterised by the fact that in certain areas there exists a clear opposition of interests, for example, in the question of wages and terms of employment. In other areas the parties can have certain common objectives. As examples, good industrial safety, a good working milieu, occupational training, work studies, and production technology co-operation can be mentioned. Herein have we concluded a number of co-operation agreements. Naturally, even in these areas of co-operation, one can find certain controversial questions. This can give rise to different views and this is

212

quite normal — regarding the correct means of attaining the objectives. But it is also clear that in certain areas both parties have an interest in co-operatively trying to achieve the best possible results.

Behind the efforts of the LO leadership at co-operation with employers lies an altered view of the tasks and objectives of the trade union movement. Back of this again lies the need of capitalists to merge workers organisations with the power apparatus of the monopoly capitalistic state. This objective is concealed with phrases and rhetoric concerning the LO's responsibility for society development and the competitiveness of Swedish industry. The report of the so called fifteen man committee was adopted at the 1941 LO congress. In this report the committee, and subsequently the LO, declared that it accepted both state intervention in the labour market and rationalisation. Regulations were adopted at the same time which limited local strike rights. This was carried out under the protection of an unparalleled anti-communist frenzy. In 1961 the report on 'co-operative business policy' was issued which gave complete support to structural rationalisations and presented the so called solidarity wage policy as a means to accelerate this.

The function of the state apparatus-helper,
problem concealer and sorter

> The goal of the labour market policy will be to achieve such flexibility that the labour market will be adjusted as rapidly as possible to changes in conditions of production. Not the least during a boom period, when there may exist local or branch delimited employment difficulties, these labour market measures have a great significance. In such situations society must try to see to it that the demand for labour is satisfied by transferring labour from areas and branches with poorer employment possibilities to those which have a strong demand for labour power. (SOU 61:42)

> In the future the labour market policy, to a greater degree that ever before, will be used as an instrument to ensure labour force support within the high productivity branches of economy. (AMS 1967 [the Labour Market Board])

During the 1960s about 90,000 people were moved from Norrland (Northern Sweden) at a cost of fifty-thousand dollars per person. In the period from 1965 to 1970 approximately 8,000 employment opportunities were created by localisation support. Many of these positions were either of a short term nature or would have arisen without state financial support. According to a proposal in the regional plan it is calculated that one million people will be moved to greater Stockholm during the forthcoming thirty years.

The essential function of the labour market policy is to move labour power from small towns and villages to large cities on the conditions set down by capital. In the case of new employment opportunities being created in outlying areas this often implies the creation of satellite industries by means of which large concerns can take advantage of cheap labour for carrying out routinised production. The municipal 'protected workshops' which in general carry out undiversified assembly line work on a piece work basis have a similar function. In the work world there is a continual process of screening and sorting out people. The result of this sorting out is not generally manifest in the form of open unemployment but instead takes the form of being written off sick, early pension and 'protected' employment.

On an average around 400,000 people per day are put on the sick list, that is: 10 per cent of the total work force. In round numbers the figure has doubled during the last ten year period. The increasing frequency of being written off sick follows very closely the heightening degree of labour intensity. Top bureaucrats have a very low sick leave frequency while those in departments having assembly line production usually have around 20 per cent of employees on the sick list. Being written off sick often leads to passivisation and social isolation. Each year approximately 350 million sleeping tablets and tranquillising pills are prescribed which effectively contribute to the creation of apathy and listlessness. The most central causes of long term sick leaves are illnesses caused by exhaustion and stress, for example back problems, stomach aches and nervous problems.

In general long term illness results in an early pension. Around 200,000 people are now on early pension and the number increases each year. Several years ago it was decided that a person could be given early pension without a doctor's certificate. A contributing factor to this decision was probably the inability of the care apparatus to fulfil the demands for the sorting out workers. The tendency to resort to early pension without first attempting worker treatment measures has also increased. An early pension certainly provides basic economic security but at the same time it entails the final condemnation of the individual to life long unemployment. Approximately 100,000 people are engaged in retraining programmes. Clearly retraining can sometimes be of use but the effect is often to lull both the person being reschooled as well as the labour exchange officer into the illusion that something is being done when in fact nothing effective is.

Every year approximately 100,000 people are referred to labour care institutions. Only 10,000 of these return to the labour market. In spite of the enormous build up of labour care services, the number who return to work has not increased since the fifties. The remainder are either early pensioned or given 'protected' employment. There are at present around 30,000 places in relief work, archive work and protected workshops. There are plans to increase that number to 100,000. Therein, the state is well along the way to creating a special 'B' labour market for the 'defective' part of the population. According to a state commissioned study tabled in 1965 one can expect this to embrace from 500,000-900,000 people.

When official spokesmen for the Labour Market Board (AMS) want to explain this development they use such terms as 'illness' and 'handicap'. This expression is ideal if one wishes to conceal the problem. The conception conveys the illusion that what is involved are people who for the first time with the help of the resources of the welfare society can be assisted to some form of employment and economic security. In fact, most of the 'handicapped' suffer from exhaustion illnesses which are a direct consequence of their previous employment. Writing people off sick also prompts them to experience themselves as sick and consequently seek the cause of their illness in themselves. Of course the correct conception is to see that what is involved is rather mass unemployment.

This article originally appeared in Swedish in the Independent Socialist political journal *Zenit* in the early seventies.

12 Work Milieu — Part II

Olle Jepsson and Gunnar Ågren

Sweden has a capitalist market economy. In the market the company operates according to the laws of the market and it of course strives to increase its profits and capital while minimising its costs. The latter includes material costs such as machines, buildings, transportation, etc. but also expenditures for employees, whether it be for wages or health or hospital care.

These rules of course apply whether the company is privately or state owned. This is what Strang (a leading social democrat politician) is referring to when he says that 'LKAB [1] will be run according to business principles.' The rules are not derived from the philosophical or moral speculations of company directors, but from the market in which they operate.

Although we are studying the functioning of company health services, it is necessary to take these laws of the market into consideration inasmuch as they make it essential to treat workers in the same manner as any other production factor:

> Personnel is a production factor and like all production factors it is an investment. Through good personnel planning it can be made a profitable investment. (FAKT for LKAB management employees in Kiruna)

The company health service is part of that planning apparatus. The objective is given in the quotation above. What consequences does this lead to?

The first and most obvious is that workers should not demand the hiring of more company doctors and engineers of the same type employed until now. That is the demand of LO (the Swedish Confederation of Trade Unions), SAF (the Swedish Employers Confederation) and SAP (the Swedish Labour Party). Instead the demand must naturally be to change the entire system so that health care services serve the interests of the workers rather than those of capital. This also leads us to see the basic conflict between the demands of workers and of capital.

It is clear that the worker wants a just wage for a job which does not exhaust his body and is edifying and rewarding for him as a human being. He wants to control his work and its products, not be controlled.

The employer wants to keep the worker's wage as low as possible and get him to give maximum production, by among other things, steering production according to that wish. He wants to decide what and how he shall produce in order to maximise profitability.

The traditional methods utilised by employers in this struggle are:

— to technologically rationalise operations and decrease the number of workers

— to get the maximum from every worker by increasing the work load. Here, employee health services are of assistance.

The framework of company health services

The LO and SAF try to claim that company health services are of common interest to both workers and employers, this is the reason for their mutual consultation.

To increase bio-technological research should be a common interest for both employers and employees — employee protection pays. (Bolinder, of LO)

It is crystal clear however that for the employers' part, this interest persists only as long as company health services increase profitability:

It is the company however, which must bear the investment and operating costs. Thus the condition upon which the individual and society can continue to benefit from this enterprise is that it shows itself to be profitable or in any event not unprofitable. (Dr Ponten, Domvarvet [2])

The government commissioned study of company health care will also '. . . emphasise the production promotion intent of company health services.'

Basic facts

Company health services are grounded in 1967 agreement concerning 'voluntary co-operation' between LO and SAF. In principle it entails that workers are placed at the mercy of the employers' good will. Both LO and SAF have repeatedly rejected workers' demands for

217

statutory company health services with the rationale that 'in the case in question, the voluntary approach binds the parties morally to a greater degree.'

Company health care is carried out under the direction of the employer: the doctor as well as the safety engineer (if the case requires it) are employed by him. The employer receives economic compensation from the state for these expenditures. LO and SAF claim, as does the government study of company health care (SOU 1968:44), that this does not mean the doctor is in a conflicting position to his patient. In view of the workers' strike demands during the last few years, their attitude is clearly the contrary. The international labour organisation (ILO) is also clear concerning the risks involved and in their 1959 recommendation on company health services they stated, among other things, that:

> Doctors within company health services should in both the context of their duties and their moral perspective take an independent position in relation to employers and employees alike. For the purpose of securing this independence, the employment conditions of industrial doctors, especially with reference to dismissal and initial appointment, be regulated by national legislation or by agreements between the parties or organisations involved.

Functioning in accordance with conditions laid down by the employer provides the only possibility of gaining influence in the company. Consequently, says Palme, those who doubt that this approach is proper are seen as opponents of company health services in general.

Company health services are to function as a management operation within the company. This means that it must be co-ordinated with other management operations and like them be subordinate to the search for highest possible profits as well as the supervision and control of the employees.

What are the further characteristics of company health services?

> — *Company health services are a mediating*
> *link between capital and the state*

It is natural that LO, SAP and SAF should categorically reject all demands that workers be the directors of such a health service. Its function is not to serve the interests of the working class. It is the employer's instrument for handling the worker as a commodity, to wear down and have repaired in the state financed hospital care, to transfer on an AMS (Labour Market Board) train, to exploit and exhaust and finally cast aside onto society's worker care, protected workshops, retraining institutions, early pension systems, and physical or mental illness institutions.

The government study (SOU 1968:44) regarding company health services does not attempt to conceal or 'beautify' that function. Still less does it wish to see a company health service which sides with the workers and offers resistance to the monopolisation process of capital and the ruthless exploitation of people. The study only describes what transpires as if it were an unavoidable natural phenomenon:

> The need for efforts in the work places along these lines (company health services — our notation) grows in pace with the rapid development and variability of work life. Scientific advancements, especially in technology, have made it possible to introduce to an increasingly comprehensive degree, more rationalised forms of production. These changes in the productive apparatus in turn often entail drastic changes in the work tasks and work milieu of the individual worker. Earlier occupational experience can quickly become irrelevant, necessitating comprehensive retraining and new orientation. A further consequence of this development is that the need for individual efforts in various work situations is subject to huge dislocations, whereby employees must be prepared to accept new work tasks and adapt themselves to altered situations and work demands. Particularly drastic repercussions follow structural changes. Displaced personnel must often be retrained and placed in another type of work, and at times be transferred to another town and a new social milieu.

Subsequently the company doctor is designated as the key man in the work place. Here he can see how the workers cope with capital's new demands and direct to state care those who are sorted out:

> Society's efforts in the area of worker care are insufficient and will often be ineffective without the aid of experts working in the company and intimately acquainted with the conditions in the individual work places.

*— Company health services employed in capital's
struggle against declining rates of profit*

The employer is forced to lengthen the employees work time. For this
to occur within the 8 hour day, time must be utilised to the maximum.
MTM and biotechnology methods facilitate the detailed study and
organisation of the work process so as to eliminate wasted time.
Further, biotechnology provides employers with a means of attaining
maximum physical work by utilising medical knowledge in the
organisation of production. It is a misconception to view
biotechnology as a method primarily employed to ease the strain on
the worker's body. Professor Lundgren of the Labour Medical
Institute, thinks that it involves

> . . . discovering the precise limit over which the physical
> ability to work begins to be effected, and thus from the
> point of view of production, where the tolerance limit lies,
> based on more incipient symptoms.

He also tells of having been assigned the task of constructing a wheel-
barrow which minimised the load on the worker's back, and presenting
the results he says,

> That there is now a two wheeled barrow which allows at
> least a 40 per cent increase in worker performance with
> the same load or — stated another way — a decrease in the
> work load with the same performance.

*— Company health services dampen the
dissatisfaction and the social unrest with
capital and its adjustment processes*

During the initial medical examination for employment, doctors
select those workers who can best cope with a rapid production pace.
Through the use of certain interview methods, outlined in the state's
'anti-mental health campaign' he can also protect the employer from
disloyal workers or individuals interested in organisations or influence.
He at all times has the task of watching over the employees and can
quickly pick out those 'neurotic individuals' who spread discontent
among their fellow workers. Dr Heijbel speaks of the importance of
regular examinations of the workers where the doctor can assess the
'degree of adaption' in order to 'detect early any adaption disorders'
and deal with them before they can lead to 'work insufficiency'. All
the while the doctor carries out his espionage, his transferring and

sorting out is under the guise and protection of his supposed neutrality as a doctor. Those workers cast aside are of course sick — not worn out and exhausted by an inhumane work pace — sorted out and exchanged for new and healthy workers. In this manner the pro-capital relationship is concealed and political reaction delayed.

— *The health care becomes a guise for selection,*
  sorting out and the creation of a reserve army
  of workers

Mindus for example recommends that if possible, during examinations of prospective new employees 'more applicants than are intended to be employed be examined and ranked in respect to their qualifications'. The clear intent here is the creation of a reserve army of 'B-workers' (an objective which the so called capacity profiles work towards) which provide a counter pressure to increasing wage demands and calls for improved working conditions. Dr Heijbel speaks openly of this army: '. . . it would of course be ideal to be able to consistently have at one's disposal personnel who could be transferred according to the requirements of production.' But he is forced to declare that '. . . the scarcity of labour power obliges the company to utilise those resources which are available'.

It is also easy to see that this ranking provides the personnel office with a black list of lay offs during business slow downs. Bolinder of the LO says in a retrospective comment that '. . . 20 per cent of the labour force had appreciable medical handicaps. This should partly be seen as the result of the post war boom at the end of the forties and the consequent relatively undiscriminating hiring of employment seekers. It was not until 1955 that companies set up their own health services with more goal oriented health examinations in connection with new employment'.

The literature in the field of labour medicine continually discusses this sorting out process. For example, Dr Lokander states that at '. . . 40-50 years of age an individual's work pace begins to decline markedly, so it hardly pays to hire 40 year old women for assembly line work at ASEA'.

It is obvious that the consequent policy of creating a reserve army of workers and the sorting out processes can only be carried out under the cover of the social democratic state apparatus which takes care of those cast out of the labour force, by means of pensions and workers care. Thus, the social unrest which would naturally emerge in reaction to this process, is hindered.

— Company health services have a
mystifying function

A system which lays major emphasis upon passive doctors involved in treating illnesses and injuries already contracted rather than preventative techniques, is an obscuration from the outset. Specifically, most occupational illnesses can quite easily be prevented but extremely seldom cured. Silicosis and deafness caused by noise are only two such examples. In the same manner it is often stated that there is a great need for research in the area of labour medicine. This too conceals the fact that the overwhelming majority of occupational illnesses are already well known and technically completely preventable. The discussion often has the purpose of delaying the introduction of these sometimes expensive technical methods.

The limits which are established can also serve to confuse the issue. The worker gets the impression that there is a fixed level, for example, of dust content in the air which there is no risk of developing silicosis. In fact the intent of such 'limits' is not to protect all, but rather a non-existent 'normal' worker. If for example one has a pronouncedly crooked back, he is still in the risk zone. These limits are either estimations or based upon animal experimentation. One need only point out that as a rule the Soviet Union sets its limits ten times lower than USA and Sweden. Only recently it has been found that carbon monoxide and nitrogen gases probably cause damage at levels of concentration far lower than previously thought.

The limit set does not represent an absolutely certain safety boundary for all, but is rather a weighing on the basis of medical experience, of what is a safe level for the 'normal' worker and of the costs involved in decreasing the concentration of the particular substance. This weighing of the dangers and costs reflects the political balance between the employer's desire to drive costs down and the worker's interest in protecting his health. The 'safety limits' can thus be shifted in one or another direction through political struggle. When a 'scientific' character is given to the established 'limits', it is implied that the whole issue is something for the experts to evaluate and determine. In this way the workers are deterred from taking the struggle into their own hands.

What is occupational illness?

Company health services offer a concept of illness which facilitates

222

the repressive purposes of the employer. By saying that the worker has fallen ill, that he is struck by an occupational illness, suggests that this sickness is of the same type as other illnesses. It is something which individuals are always subject to, no one is to blame, and the doctor can cure it.

Occupational illnesses however are not of this type. In the first place they are well known, their causes are understood and they can be prevented (but most often they cannot be cured). They are the quite natural consequence of work which is so designed that the workers' bodies are damaged in performing it. This unfortunate by product is included in the employer's economic calculations.

Thus it is not an individual misfortune such as gall stones or appendicitis. The entire working class is subjected to the capitalist production process in which health is merely one more 'production factor'. Occupational illnesses can be prevented by political struggle concerning the ownership of the means of production and the organisation of work so it does not damage health. Consequently, occupational illness is not an individual, but a working class concern.

Psychiatric terminology serves the same repressive purpose. Dr Mandus speaks of the fact that

> . . . personnel often have a fear of ill health and are naturally inclined to perceive a relationship between their work and all types of illnesses. Experience has shown that a liberally applied health control in such cases has a positive psychological effect and dampens apprehensions.

The result is that Mindus find that

> . . . one or two neurotic people, on the basis of their own uneasiness, frequently spread a substantial fear of possible occupational health risks among their fellow workers.

The proper corrective measure is to 'transfer the neurotics'.

Thus, it is of course the individual who is ill and should be treated.

— *Through passivity the company health service is subordinated to the company's profit interests and productivity demands*

One of the key concepts in the 1967 agreement between SAF and LO is 'company adapted company health service'. In part, the ILO recommendation defines the objectives of company health services, in the following manner: 'To contribute to the employees' mental and physical adaption, especially by means of adapting the work to the

223

employees'. This statement seems harmless enough, yet it occasioned the Commission on company health services (with no objection from the LO representative) to make the following comment:

> We wish however to clarify the statement by pointing out the relationship between labour adaption and labour effectivity and emphasise the production promoting aim of company health services. The objective should be to promote health and working ability together with contributing to work satisfaction, safety and effectivity.

Further on the passive role of company health services is illustrated by means of the following rationale:

> In the ever more common highly mechanised assembly production, it is generally demanded for reasons of production technology that every employee carries out a predetermined and fixed work function. Inasmuch as work is also dictated by machines and the technical process in general, it offers very little scope to adapt the quantitative work effort according to individual resources. These conditions make it still more urgent, through bio-technical measures, to regulate the adaption in other respects between individual and work.

Read now very closely the following piece from an article by a leading Swedish industrial doctor:

> Unlike society's medical care institutions, industry must be concerned with profit: that is to be profitable to be of benefit to the employees as well as the company and society. Each and every department within the company must in its own way contribute to profitability.
>
> Society's health and hospital care institutions are paid for by all, are intended for everyone and should be used by everyone, whether they are associated with an industrial company or not. If a company organises their own department for health and hospital services, which I shall hereafter refer to as industrial doctor care, it is with the intent of providing services somewhat over and above those supplied by society, specifically an adequate concentration of health and hospital services designed for the companies' special tasks and requirements. It is expected that such an investment will contribute to profitability. The company consists of people and machines. From the point of view of company economy our activity should lead to increasing effectivity of

the labour production factor in the same way that good and specially oriented care of a machine shop, aims at increasing the effectivity of that production factor.

The increase of personnel efficiency results from using various methods, both individual and collective, to strive for the improvement and maintenance of good health for every individual in the company's employ. If this activity is profitable for the company, so is it also — perhaps even more so — for the employee. No one has greater need of good health and working ability than the worker himself.

Herein lies also a secondary social effect of great significance. It is nevertheless the company which is responsible for the investment and operating costs. The prerequisite for the individual and society to benefit from this activity is that it proves itself profitable for the company, in any case, not unprofitable. (J. Ponten, *Socialmedicinsk Tidskrift*, 1962:10, pp 420-6)

Consider now for a moment in whose interest company health care services operate.

The Development Council dealing with questions of co-operation is an organisation consisting of representatives from LO, SAF and TCO (Swedish Central Organisation of Salaried Employees). This advisory group has recently presented a course in personnel administration for heads of company boards. The course posits the fictitious company Plansam, which find itself in a perplexing situation. Productivity is dropping, people are quitting and sick leaves are increasing. In other words worker satisfaction is declining. The introduction of controls and attendance rewards is considered but is seen not to be a good solution. What is involved here is to see to it that the employees are happier in their work — reforms are instituted — a company health service is established.

Company health services as a means of getting employees to work better — herein lies the key to 'company adapted company health services'.

The role of the doctor

— *Within company health services stress is placed upon 'defensive' doctors, not on active prevention technology and safety engineers*

We have earlier stated that industrial illnesses are well known, in

225

principle incurable but preventable. Why then invest in doctors? One of those primarily responsible for the study of the Labour Medicine Institute and company health services presents the objective in this manner:

> In Sweden, those measures taken by a company to watch over labour, operations and milieu for the purpose of not only, alleviating injury but also optimising teamwork in a direction beneficial to production, have received the name 'company health services'. Early in their history, company health services began as a rear guard operation. It has increasingly taken on a more preventative nature and in a 1967 agreement between LO and SAF it had its primary emphasis placed in the area of technological and medical prevention. For obvious reasons the technological aspect is more economically prominent than the medical, due to the fact that the technical aspect plays a role in the priority setting and planning of those measures seen to be necessary for maintaining production and calculating future demand . . . . Those demands now specified in various regulations are calculated on the basis of current not future conditions. Numerous companies calculate in the same manner. They do not have the resources to make future oriented investments in uncertain milieu problems, but to a *certain degree* are able to see their way to take into consideration predictable short term requirements. In this, the company health service has a great responsibility and is of great value as prognosis instrument.

Gerhardsson presents the following company health service costs:

Year	Medical share dollars per employee	Technical share dollars per employee	Total million dollars per year
1970	6	19	75
1975	12	25	112
1980	19	30	150

Gerhardsson's figures should be compared with the costs to society of work injuries sustained. If there was adequate technological prevention, the costs for treating such injuries would be comparable to the fire insurance premiums of Swedish companies. Once again, however, it is easier for capital to let society and the workers pay the costs.

*— Doctors involve themselves in treatment
of illness rather than in preventative
health care*

Medical care services are also viewed as a means of supervising and minimising employees' sick leaves. So Volvo for example, has tried to persuade the government social insurance office in Gothenburg (where its huge assembly plant is located) to only approve employee sickness certification carried out by the company's own doctors.

A further cause of this passive medical care is probably the inadequacy of doctor's training in preventative health care. This involves doctors who have previously functioned essentially as general practitioners. In this capacity they are able to give employees the feeling of care and security even though there has been no change in the work milieu nor measures taken to eliminate or reduce health risks. The X-ray examination replaces the struggle against air pollution, hearing measurements is put before efforts at creating a noise free milieu. Tranquillisers are distributed like medicine against a work pace that is too rapid.

This is precisely the function of the 'military doctors'. In war, attempts are made to increase the fighting morale of soldiers establishing the doctor as close to the front as possible. If the soldier is shot, he will receive quick care. The doctor however doesn't concern himself with the shooting itself. The same is true with company doctors. He does not become involved in the issue of a health hazardous work milieu, rather he conveys moral support while standing in the background in the event something should happen.

*— Company health service has a control
function over employees which endangers
the confidentiality between doctor and
patient*

The ILO recommendations concerning company health services propose that such services should have no controlling function in the issue of employee absenteeism due to illness. The reason is because such activity could call into question the neutrality of company health services; it would become supervisory. In reality, Swedish company health services have both direct and indirect supervisory functions. Currently at LKAB, the mining company's own computer registration handles all employee sickness certification and registration instead of the government's regional social insurance office in Kiruna. In particular, short term absence from work is viewed as an indices of 'poor work adaption' on the part of the worker. It was this information which was used by Bertil Gardell in his study of 'mental health' among industrial workers. Company doctors obviously see their task as holding down absenteeism due to illness and consequently check closely illness certification as well as request case records from other hospitals.

Regardless of the traditional notion of the doctor's oath of confidentiality, it seems self evident that the company doctor shares with management whatever he can find out about his patient. If necessary, the information is computed in the form of a capacity profile which describes the patient's mental and physical capabilities, his suitability for advancement, etc. All this is presented as a 'profile', in the same manner one outlines the performance of other machines.

— Because of their personal characteristics
company doctors are considered to be
above all conflict of interests

Rooted in the covenants of doctors' ethics, the myth of objectivity in medicine is much cherished. Regardless of who is his superior, the doctor is supposedly only concerned with the interests of his patients. In this manner, when unsatisfactory conditions do arise, the burden is placed upon the individual doctor rather than the entire system. In the debate following the Kockum's report, LO secretary Gunnarsson proposed that doctors violating this confidentiality should be reported to the National Social Welfare Board. The notion that the problem might instead be due to the fact that the doctor is employed by the company to act in its service does not even exist in LO's world view. Thus, they merely call for more doctors rather than for changes in the system. The ILO on the other hand, has a crystal clear view that doctors are influenced by their superiors, in this case the companies.

— Questions of health are not seen as
issues for union struggle

The ideology of co-operation that company health services and worker safety is an area where mutual understanding prevails between employees and workers. Only very late did the LO employ its own medical expert who in reality co-operated intimately with SAF's doctors. Compared with the very large number of economists who take part in the planning of wage and political questions, LO has employed very few officials in the area of worker safety and occupational hygiene.

The union organisations have no expert support to offer workers who wish to press forward health issues at the grass roots level. Thus, in the realm of scientific knowledge of the issues, employers consistently gain the upper hand. After all these years the LO has only opinion studies to offer such as the series, 'Job Risks', concerning the on the job risks which workers either suspect or experience, but it is unable to support their fears with facts which may be used in a political struggle. Quite by chance, completely over-looked dangers such as Radon gases in Zinc mines or hundreds of unreported silicosis sufferers are continually being discovered. One suspects an iceberg just below the surface which the LO does not dare to discover and engage in political struggle over.

The obligation towards industrial peace entrenched in the labour agreement leaves workers with no legal right to pursue the struggle to protect their health by using the strike weapon. To strike in order to get rid of health hazards in a work milieu is illegal. Formally, the Work Inspection and Health Service Board have broad powers to halt production if it is dangerous. However, in practice this possibility is never utilised nor do they have the necessary time or the experts at their disposal. Neither are workers able to utilise society's courts or the police to rid themselves of hazardous work milieu. The work place is the private domain of the employer. He does with it as he wishes even at the cost of workers' health and life — if he does not remember his 'moral responsibility'.

> — *In spite of more than thirty years'*
> *'co-operation', health services are*
> *very poorly developed*

In Sweden today there are approximately 3.8 million people employed at 85,000 work places. Only 15 per cent of these are covered by any type of company health service, primarily those employed in larger industries. Only 1.5 per cent are reached by the government central health office and only several per thousand by technological work milieu service. An example of this catastrophic situation is seen in the fact that only 33 of 68 mines prescribe obligatory silicosis analyses. Approximately 25 cases of silicosis per year develop in the iron foundries, yet for all practical purposes there is no obligatory silicosis inspection. The risk of developing silicosis is still 6:1000, that is to say four times greater than of being killed in a traffic mishap. Within the steel foundries and stone industry, the risk is a further four times greater.

At present there are approximately 22,000 poorly trained safety ombudsmen, 500 poorly and 70 qualified trained safety engineers, 6 qualified industrial hygienists, 200 industrial doctors, 345 industrial nurses and 120 job inspectors. To the degree that small work places are supervised at all, it is carried out by authorities of the government central health office.

'To cover the need' a government study calls for 1300 doctors, an equal number of engineers and other technicians together with 1950 nurses. The only target date suggested is 1980 but with the present educational capacity it will take ninety years to train that number of doctors and engineers. At present there is absolutely nothing to indicate that these plans risk anything approximating fulfilment.

Even if this objective were accomplished it would mean only that each doctor could devote one hour each per week per 100 employees for both prevention and treatment activities, nurses 1.5 hours, safety technicians 2 and safety engineers 3. All of these personnel however, will engage in the same defensive objectives as present and be employed under existing conditions.

> — *Company health service is only seemingly a*
> *medical since, in practice it is the employer's*
> *science of manpower*

The worker is lulled into the notion that he is dealing with a traditional doctor, that is to say, a person interested in the worker as a human being. This is not the case. The employer is interested only in purchasing the worker's labour power. Company doctors are the agents of employers and assigned the task of examining, treating and extracting the maximum from the worker's labour power.

One need only read a course book in modern biotechnology to understand that the worker's conception of himself as a human being does not coincide with the doctor's conception of him as labour power and machine:

> As a guideline in this case it may be stated, that heavy active
> work can be calculated as work which requires an oxygen
> usage of 1.5 litres per minute, calculated for a work period
> of 50 minutes per hour and 10 minutes pause per hour.
> This corresponds to an energy usage of 3,000 calories per
> 8 hour work day.

Axel Ahlmark states unambiguously in whose interest company health services operate:

Somewhat schematically one may say that if the goal of the earlier work illness prophylaxis can be said to have been to decrease the frequency of sickness, so must today's labour research strive towards increasing the productive life of the population.

What can be done?

According to a study carried out in the Metal Workers Union, health risks and debasing working conditions are one of the most common causes of so called wildcat strikes. The struggle for improved working conditions is often met by a greater resistance from employers than is the direct wage struggle. When Volvo workers went out on strike in 1969 they had two major demands: improvement of hourly wages and a slower speed on the assembly line. The wage demand was met almost immediately but not the demand for a lower assembly line speed. Similar experiences were witnessed regarding those demands put forward during the miners' strike.

The struggle for a humane work milieu represents a higher form of struggle than the direct wage struggle. In a more obvious manner it touches on the employer's autocratic control over the work place, and if carried out correctly calls into question the rights of private property. It is logical therefore, that the struggle must not only be carried out against employers, but also against the LO leadership and trade union bureaucrats.

This type of struggle will encounter an opposition which in the first instance concentrates its efforts on breaking it down into various forms of class co-operation, mental health campaigns and company health services, under the direction of employers. The next stage will be the mobilisation of the open apparatus of violence in the form of dismissal or relocation of the 'disruptive elements'. It is therefore important to prepare and develop the struggle in the correct manner.

The first step then is to carry out *studies* in the local work places. A study can be carried out by an individual or a small group and should encompass:

1. General data concerning the company. Structure of ownership? Profit per employee? Production trend? Is the company dependent upon other larger industries? Does the company receive any government support?

2. Do there exist any concrete health risks and in what way do they affect the employees? Study especially:

231

a) Noise. Have any measurements been carried out? How many employees have hearing damage?

b) Vibrations. Especially in regard to transport, work tools and machines. Is there any vibration damage? These are often manifest in vascular spasms and a decline in touch perception.

c) Gases: especially exhaust gases from combustion engines. What type of air circulation and conditioning exists? Have any measurements been carried out?

d) Dust. Especially stone dust. This may be found in glass, steel, stone industry and mining operations. Asbestos is found in a number of material forms, above all those materials used for insulation. It is especially common within transport and construction work.

e) Paints and solvents. Are there any content declarations? Are any vapours emitted? Are there any cases of eczema or skin damage? Nausea? Tiredness?

f) Temperature fluctuations. Are there any draughts or great changes between warm and cold? Muscle aches? Trouble with joints?

g) Physical work load. Are there any heavy lifts or uncomfortable work positions required? Are employees obliged to work in awkward positions in order to manage piece work demands? Back problems? Pains in the joints?

3 What changes have taken place at the work place. Has there been any rationalisation of positions? Any increase in the work pace? In what manner does piece work function to influence the work pace? Have any new chemical-technical products been introduced? Does anyone know what they contain or what the damaging effects on workers are?

4 Injuries. Study those accidents which have occurred. Have any injuries occurred which have not been reported? What is the most common type of injury? Has there been any increase? To what degree has an increased work pace contributed to the frequency and nature of accidents? How are new employees instructed, especially those who have language difficulties? How are accidents investigated — are the causes usually attributed to the work milieu or to the 'human factor'?

5   Development of illness frequency. What are the most
     common types of illness? Has there been any increase in
     writing-off employees sick? How are the older workers
     affected? Is there much exhaustion illness, such as stomach
     problems, back pains, insomnia, headaches and nervous
     problems? At what age are workers usually completely
     exhausted, i.e. incapable of further work? Has that age
     level declined?

6   Is there a company health service? How does it function?
     Are examinations carried out on all new employees? How
     are these used? Are there any attempts to decrease the
     frequency of illness caused worker absenteeism by forcing
     the employees to go to the company doctor? What type of
     coercion is used? Does he prescribe much tranquillising
     medicine?

7   Does there exist any co-operation between union
     organisations and management concerning work milieu
     questions? Have study circles been organised? Find out
     about these and study their content. Are they aimed at
     influencing change in the working conditions or do they
     involve making the employees 'well adapted' to existing
     conditions?

8   What is the position of the safety ombudsman? Does he
     have any possibility of intervening in apprehended health
     risks? Is he subjected to pressure from above? Has any
     attempt been made to call for work inspection or other
     supervisory authorities?

Studies are only the first step in the task. The next step involves
spreading information and knowledge among fellow workers. In the
discussions then carried out on this basis, the task is to formulate
demands which as many as possible are willing to struggle unitedly
for. Often the demands will be concerned with concrete conditions
such as demanding that specific safety laws be adhered to before it is
possible to carry out a certain undertaking; that the work pace must
be slowed; that older workers be assigned to suitable work tasks; the
right to information and to have meetings during working hours.

If careful studies have been carried out, it is often possible to put
heavy pressure behind the demand and it is further possible to
broaden the struggle in the form of strikes or stoppage of certain work
tasks. When the level of knowledge and consciousness rise it is possible
to raise the struggle to a higher level, for example, through solidarity

action with groups in other work places or by direct action in the form of taking away from the employer the right to make all decisions concerning the work place, especially with regard to dismissal, new employment, and transfers. During the struggle it should be possible to set up permanent committees which continue to study working conditions and initiate appropriate action. In addition to these committees, it is often possible to call in outside help.

Notes

[1] A large state run mining operation.
[2] A ship building company.

This article originally appeared in Swedish in the Independent Socialist political journal *Zenit* in the early seventies.